Class IV. In certain verbs ending in **-iar** and **-uar**, the **i** and **u** acquire the graphic accent on the forms of the present indicative, subjunctive, and imperative in which the stress is on the stem of the verb: **envío, envías,** etc.; **continúa, continúas, continúa,** etc.

Class V. Verbs ending in **-uir** (except **-guir**) insert **-y-** before any vowel of the endings except **i**.

IRREGULAR VERBS

Infinitive	Pres. Ind.	Pres. Subj.	Imperfect	Preterite	Imperf. Subj. I	Imperf. Subj. II	Future	Conditional	Pres. Part.	Past Part.	Imperative
(fingir) to pretend	finjo finges fingís fingen	finja finjas finjamos finjáis finjan					etc.	etc.	fingiendo	fingido	finge fingid
distinguir to distinguish	distingo distingues distingue distinguimos distinguís distinguen	distinga distingas distinga distinguimos distinguáis distingan	distinguía etc.	distinguí etc.	distinguiera etc.	distinguiese etc.	distinguiré etc.	distinguiría etc.	distinguiendo	distinguido	distingue distinguid
huir to flee	huyo huyes huye huimos huís huyen	huya huyas huya huyamos huyáis huyan	huía etc.	huí huiste huyó huimos huisteis huyeron	huyera huyeras huyera huyéramos huyerais huyeran	huyese huyeses huyese huyésemos huyeseis huyesen	huiré etc.	huiría etc.	huyendo	huido	huye huid
andar to walk, go	ando etc.	ande etc.	andaba etc.	anduve anduviste anduvo anduvimos anduvisteis anduvieron	anduviera anduvieras anduviera anduviéramos anduvierais anduvieran	anduviese anduvieses anduviese anduviésemos anduvieseis anduviesen	andaré etc.	andaría etc.	andando	andado	anda andad
caber to be contained	quepo cabes cabe cabemos cabéis caben	quepa quepas quepa quepamos quepáis quepan	cabía etc.	cupe cupiste cupo cupimos cupisteis cupieron	cupiera cupieras cupiera cupiéramos cupierais cupieran	cupiese cupieses cupiese cupiésemos cupieseis cupiesen	cabré cabrás cabrá cabremos cabréis cabrán	cabría cabrías cabría cabríamos cabríais cabrían	cabiendo	cabido	
caer to fall	caigo caes cae caemos caéis caen	caiga caigas caiga caigamos caigáis caigan	caía etc.	caí caíste cayó caímos caísteis cayeron	cayera cayeras cayera cayéramos cayerais cayeran	cayese cayeses cayese cayésemos cayeseis cayesen	caeré etc.	caería etc.	cayendo	caído	
conducir to conduct, lead, drive	conduzco conduces conduce conducimos conducís conducen	conduzca conduzcas conduzca conduzcamos conduzcáis conduzcan	conducía etc.	conduje condujiste condujo condujimos condujisteis condujeron	condujera condujeras condujera condujéramos condujerais condujeran	condujese condujeses condujese condujésemos condujeseis condujesen	conduciré etc.	conduciría etc.	conduciendo	conducido	

A NEW
SHORTER
SPANISH
REVIEW
GRAMMAR

THE SCRIBNER SPANISH SERIES

GENERAL EDITOR: JUAN R.-CASTELLANO

Duke University

A NEW
SHORTER
SPANISH REVIEW
GRAMMAR

BY

JUAN RODRÍGUEZ-CASTELLANO
Duke University

AND

CHARLES BARRETT BROWN
Vanderbilt University

CHARLES SCRIBNER'S SONS, *New York*

**PICTURE
ACKNOWLEDGMENTS**

The Hispanic Society of America: title-page decoration
from a plate made in Perpignan, France

Iberia Airlines: pages 37, 125, 135

Spanish Tourist Office: pages 27, 47, 54, 65, 72, 82, 102, 112, 144

The Weyhe Gallery: illustration for *Don Quixote* by
Antonio Frasconi, page 93

To
Barbara Brown Fields

PREFACE

THE AIM of this book is to provide for the second year of college Spanish a thorough review of the essentials of Spanish grammar, including the standard vocabulary and idioms appropriate to that level of instruction. Based on well-known word, idiom, and syntax counts, as were our previous successful texts, the present text is offered in the conviction that the results of frequency investigations furnish an indispensable minimum of materials for mastery during the first two years of foreign language study, either in a terminal course or as the foundation for further study. In the treatment of grammar, stress has invariably been placed on the divergent aspects of Spanish and English usage. The language throughout is idiomatic and natural.

The Spanish text, a connected, original story, illustrates many of the fundamental points of grammar and contains the most common idioms. To facilitate recognition, these have been placed in bold-face type and the others in Section B bear an asterisk. In Section B the idioms will be found in the order that they appear in the text.

The types of drill exercises are varied to appeal to individual tastes. To stimulate the student to think in Spanish and to suggest classroom conversation, *Cuestionarios* based on the Spanish text and on material which will encourage the beginner to speak *extempore* on his own experiences have been placed for convenience after the Appendix.

While Preliminary Lessons I and II can be reviewed in one recitation each, it is suggested that two recitations be devoted to each of the subsequent fifteen Chapters; sections *A–C* can be treated in the first recitation and *D–F* in the second. The book can therefore be completed with ease in one semester.

We wish to acknowledge our indebtedness to all grammars that we ourselves have read or used; to our colleagues who have made valuable suggestions leading to effective presentation of grammar; and to the following objective studies:

M. A. Buchanan, *A Graded Spanish Word Book*; H. Keniston, *Spanish Idiom List, Spanish Syntax List,* and *A Standard List of Spanish Words and Idioms,* and E. L. Thorndike, *A Teacher's Word Book.*

J.R.-C.
C.B.B.

CONTENTS

PRELIMINARY LESSONS

CHAPTER

A NEW
SHORTER
SPANISH
REVIEW
GRAMMAR

PRELIMINARY LESSON ONE

A. GENERAL REVIEW OF THE VERB

1. Formation and Tenses of Regular Verbs

Spanish has three conjugations; the second and third, however, differ in only *four* forms: the infinitive, the first and second persons plural of the present indicative, and the plural imperative.[1]

The endings of all forms of verbs, except those of the future and conditional tenses of the indicative, are added to the stem, which is obtained by dropping the **-ar, -er,** or **-ir** of the infinitive.

FIRST CONJUGATION (*hablar*)	SECOND CONJUGATION (*comer*)	THIRD CONJUGATION (*vivir*)
	INFINITIVE MOOD	
cant **ar** *to sing*	beb **er** *to drink*	viv **ir** *to live*
	PRESENT PARTICIPLE	
cant **ando** *singing*	beb **iendo** *drinking*	viv **iendo** *living*
	PAST PARTICIPLE	
cant **ado** *sung*	beb **ido** *drunk*	viv **ido** *lived*
	INDICATIVE MOOD	
	PRESENT	
I sing, do sing, am singing, etc.	I drink, do drink, am drinking, etc.	I live, do live, am living, etc.

CHARACTERISTIC VOWEL OF ENDINGS:

a		e		e, i	
cant **o**	cant **amos**	beb **o**	beb **emos**	viv **o**	viv **imos**
cant **as**	cant **áis**	beb **es**	beb **éis**	viv **es**	viv **ís**
cant **a**	cant **an**	beb **e**	beb **en**	viv **e**	viv **en**

Observe the graphic accent on the second person plural.

---

[1] beber bebemos, bebéis bebed   vivir vivimos, vivís vivid

3

IMPERFECT *(if happened more than once)*

I was singing, used to sing, sang, etc.		*I was drinking, used to drink, drank, etc.*		*I was living, used to live, lived, etc.*	
cant **aba**	cant **ábamos**	beb **ía**	beb **íamos**	viv **ía**	viv **íamos**
cant **abas**	cant **abais**	beb **ías**	beb **íais**	viv **ías**	viv **íais**
cant **aba**	cant **aban**	beb **ía**	beb **ían**	viv **ía**	viv **ían**

**FORMATION
AND TENSES
OF
REGULAR
VERBS**

The first and third persons singular are always identical in all verbs.
The graphic accent is required on the first person plural of the first conjugation (**-ábamos**) and on every person in the second and third conjugations (**-í-**).
All verbs are regular in the imperfect tense except **ir—iba; ser—era; ver—veía.**
(to be)

FUTURE

I shall sing, etc.		*I shall drink, etc.*		*I shall live, etc.*	
cantar **é**	cantar **emos**	beber **é**	beber **emos**	vivir **é**	vivir **emos**
cantar **ás**	cantar **éis**	beber **ás**	beber **éis**	vivir **ás**	vivir **éis**
cantar **á**	cantar **án**	beber **á**	beber **án**	vivir **á**	vivir **án**

All forms except the first person plural bear the graphic accent.
The endings are those of the present tense of **haber**: he, has, ha, hemos, habéis, han.

CONDITIONAL

I should sing, etc.		*I should drink, etc.*		*I should live, etc.*	
cantar **ía**	cantar **íamos**	beber **ía**	beber **íamos**	vivir **ía**	vivir **íamos**
cantar **ías**	cantar **íais**	beber **ías**	beber **íais**	vivir **ías**	vivir **íais**
cantar **ía**	cantar **ían**	beber **ía**	beber **ían**	vivir **ía**	vivir **ían**

The endings are those of the imperfect tense of **haber**: había, habías, había, habíamos, habíais, habían; the graphic accent appears throughout on **-í-.**

PRETERIT *(finished, happened once)*

I sang, did sing, etc.		*I drank, did drink, etc.*		*I lived, did live, etc.*	
cant **é**	cant **amos**	beb **í**	beb **imos**	viv **í**	viv **imos**
cant **aste**	cant **asteis**	beb **iste**	beb **isteis**	viv **iste**	viv **isteis**
cant **ó**	cant **aron**	beb **ió**	beb **ieron**	viv **ió**	viv **ieron**

The graphic accent is required on the first and third persons singular of all regular verbs. In the first and third conjugations the first person plural of the present and of the preterit tenses are identical in all regular verbs.

4

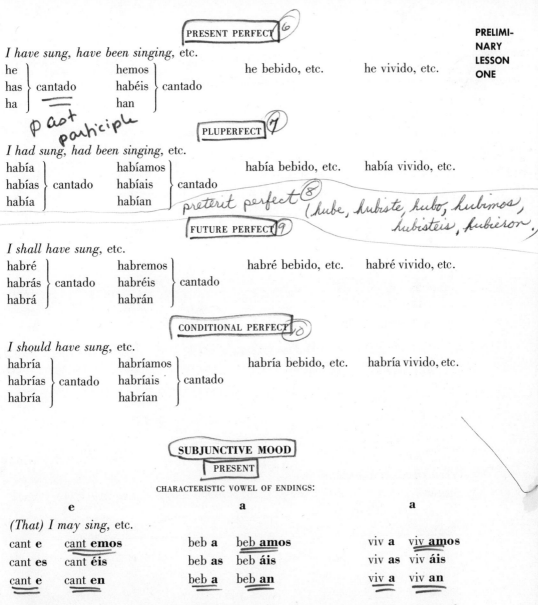

PRESENT PERFECT ⑥

I have sung, have been singing, etc.

he		hemos	
has	cantado	habéis	cantado
ha		han	

past participle

he bebido, etc.   he vivido, etc.

PLUPERFECT ⑦

I had sung, had been singing, etc.

había		habíamos	
habías	cantado	habíais	cantado
había		habían	

preterit perfect ⑧ (hube, hubiste, hubo, hubimos, hubisteis, hubieron.)

había bebido, etc.   había vivido, etc.

FUTURE PERFECT ⑨

I shall have sung, etc.

habré		habremos	
habrás	cantado	habréis	cantado
habrá		habrán	

habré bebido, etc.   habré vivido, etc.

CONDITIONAL PERFECT ⑩

I should have sung, etc.

habría		habríamos	
habrías	cantado	habríais	cantado
habría		habrían	

habría bebido, etc.   habría vivido, etc.

SUBJUNCTIVE MOOD

PRESENT

CHARACTERISTIC VOWEL OF ENDINGS:

e   a   a

(That) I may sing, etc.

cant **e**	cant **emos**	beb **a**	beb **amos**	viv **a**	viv **amos**
cant **es**	cant **éis**	beb **as**	beb **áis**	viv **as**	viv **áis**
cant **e**	cant **en**	beb **a**	beb **an**	viv **a**	viv **an**

The third person of this tense is frequently used to express a direct command: **¡Cante Vd.!** *Sing!* **¡Beban Vds. esto!** *Drink this!* Similarly, **Cantemos.** *Let's sing.*

Note the interchange of the characteristic vowels: **e** is now the characteristic vowel of the first conjugation and **a** that of the second and third conjugations. The graphic accent appears on the second person plural.

5

IMPERFECT

This tense has two sets of endings: **-ra** and **-se**. It is formed for *all* verbs by dropping the **-ron** of the third person plural preterit and adding either the **-ra** or **-se** forms:

Preterit third person plural:		Imperfect subjunctive, first person:	
canta **ron**		canta **ra,** etc.	canta **se,** etc.
bebie **ron**		bebie **ra,** etc.	bebie **se,** etc.

(That) I might sing, would sing, etc.

cant **ara**	cant **áramos**	beb **iera**	beb **iéramos**	viv **iera,** etc.
cant **aras**	cant **arais**	beb **ieras**	beb **ierais**	
cant **ara**	cant **aran**	beb **iera**	beb **ieran**	

cant **ase**	cant **ásemos**	beb **iese**	beb **iésemos**	viv **iese,** etc.
cant **ases**	cant **aseis**	beb **ieses**	beb **ieseis**	
cant **ase**	cant **asen**	beb **iese**	beb **iesen**	

The graphic accent is required on the first person plural of each conjugation.

present PERFECT

(That) I may have sung, etc.

haya		hayamos		haya bebido, etc.	haya vivido, etc.
hayas	} cantado	hayáis	} cantado		
haya		hayan			

PLUPERFECT (Past Perfect)

(That) I might have sung, etc.

hubiera		hubiéramos		hubiera bebido, etc.	hubiera vivido, etc.
hubieras	} cantado	hubierais	} cantado		
hubiera		hubieran			

hubiese		hubiésemos		hubiese bebido, etc.	hubiese vivido, etc.
hubieses	} cantado	hubieseis	} cantado		
hubiese		hubiesen			

IMPERATIVE MOOD

PRESENT

This mood consists of only one tense, the present, and of only two forms, the second person singular and plural.

6   cant **a** (tú) *sing*   beb **e** (tú) *drink*   viv **e** (tú) *live*

Note that this singular form and the third person singular form of the present indicative are identical; thus, **canta** (tú) *sing;* (él) **canta** *he sings.* This identity of forms exists in all regular verbs and in several irregular ones.

The plural of all verbs in the imperative is regular; it is formed by dropping the **-r** of the infinitive ending and adding **-d:**

cant **ad** (vosotros) *sing*   beb **ed** (vosotros) *drink*   viv **id** (vosotros) *drink*

B. COMMON REGULAR VERBS

acabar   *to end, finish*
amar   *to love*
asegurar   *to assure, assert*
bajar   *to go down, come down*
callar   *to be silent, keep still*
cansar   *to tire out*
comprar   *to buy*
contestar (a)   *to answer*
dejar   *to leave; let*
desear   *to wish, desire*
echar   *to throw (out); pour*
entrar (en)   *to go in, come in*
escuchar   *to listen (to)*
esperar   *to hope; wait (for)*
ganar   *to win; earn* (a living)
hablar   *to speak, talk*
comer   *to eat; dine*
comprender   *to understand*
correr   *to run, hurry*
deber   *to owe; ought, should, must*
permitir   *to allow, permit*
recibir   *to receive; take*

guardar   *to guard; keep*
hallar   *to find*
llamar   *to call; knock* (at a door)
llevar   *to carry, take; wear*
llorar   *to cry, weep*
mandar   *to order; send*
matar   *to kill*
mirar   *to look, look at* (buscar - to look for)
necesitar   *to need*
olvidar   *to forget*
pasar   *to pass; happen; spend* (time)
preguntar   *to ask* (a question)
quedar   *to remain; be left*
quitar   *to take away, take off*
tomar   *to take; drink*
trabajar   *to work*
meter   *to put in, put inside*
responder   *to reply; correspond*
suceder   *to happen; turn out*
temer   *to fear, be afraid*
subir   *to go up, come up; climb*
sufrir   *to suffer; endure*

caer - to fall

C. ORAL OR WRITTEN EXERCISES

1. *Translate:*

   (a) *the words in parentheses:*

   1. (*I bought*) una flor.   Compré
   2. (*We are going-down*) la escalera con cuidado.   Bajamos   (carefully)

7

A NEW
SHORTER
SPANISH
REVIEW
GRAMMAR

ORAL OR
WRITTEN
EXERCISES

Contestarán
3. (*They will answer*) a la carta. (letter)

baila (boy)
4. ¡(*Keep-still*), chico!

Entraba (livingroom)
5. (*He was entering*) en la sala.

acababa (work)
6. La señorita (*had finished*) el trabajo fuera de la clase.

comió
7. El muchacho (*ate*) muchos dulces.

Usted Comprende
8. (*You understand*) las cosas principales al instante.

Corrían against wind
9. (*They were running*) contra el viento.

Deberemos
10. (*We shall owe*) dos dólares al criado.

permitimos left
11. Le (*we permitted*) pasar a la izquierda.

many headaches
12. (*Did you suffer*) muchos dolores de cabeza?
Sufrió usted

(b) *leave*
let it
1. Lo dejé.

He waited
5. Esperó.
We were wishing
2. Deseábamos.

We should win
6. Ganaríamos.

may he/may
9. (*Que*) él responda.

We are throwing
3. Echamos.

7. Metía.

they may be frightened
10. (*Que*) temiesen

We have heard
4. Nos han escuchado.

they ran
8. Corrieron.

we will climb
11. Subiremos.

they had suffered
12. Había sufrido.

2. *In the following sentences substitute the proper form of the verb for the infinitive in parentheses and translate:*

hablé
1. Ayer yo (*hablar*) con él abajo.

llamamos
2. Nosotros (*used to*) (*llamar*) a nuestros amigos por teléfono.

hallaron pencil floor
3. Anoche ellos (*hallar*) el lápiz en el suelo.

Tomorrow *llevará* picture
4. Mañana Vd. se (*llevar*) el cuadro.

mande magazines
5. Deseo que él me (*mandar*) (*pres. subj.*) tres revistas.

miró watch 2 times afternoon
6. Ayer ella (*mirar*) el reloj dos veces por la tarde.

necesitaríamos 5 more dollars
7. Nosotros (*necesitar*) (*conditional*) cinco dólares más.

olvide fill glass
8. Por favor, no (*olvidar*) llenar el vaso.

whathappened *pasaba* last
9. ¿Qué (*pasar*) la semana pasada?

had asked *preguntado* real name
10. Yo le había (*preguntar*) su verdadero nombre.

willremain *quedarán* next month
11. Ellos (*quedar*) en casa cuatro días el mes que viene.

quitó dress or chair
12. Ella (*quitar*) el vestido de la silla.

(used to eat) *tomaba* every morning young
13. Ella (*tomar*) (*imperf.*) chocolate todas las mañanas cuando era joven.

We didn't want *trabajaran* too much
14. No deseábamos que ellos (*trabajar*) (*imperf. subj.*) demasiado.

3. *Translate:*

El No toma agua con sus comidas.
1. He does not drink (take) water with his meals.

*Les *~~too~~* Preguntamos a nuestros amigos que luego había *~~se~~* pasado.*
2. We asked (a)[1] our friends what had happened next.

---

[1] Parentheses are used to present explanatory or additional material to be *included* in the Spanish translation; brackets indicate material that is to be *omitted* in the Spanish translation.

La familia compraba ~~las~~ cosas en la ~~ciudad~~ ciudad.
3. The family used to buy things in the city.
Cada ~~uno~~ debe ganar más dinero.
4. Each one ought to earn more money.
Temo que ~~no~~ entren
5. I am afraid (I fear) that they will not come in (*pres. subj.*).
Mientras ~~él~~ trabajaba en el campo yo ~~leía~~ leía.
6. While he was working in the field, I was reading.
El muchacho pasará casi todo el verano ~~en el~~ el campo.
7. The boy will spend almost all the summer in the country.
Ellas recibieron las noticias ~~del~~ del accidente el sábado.
8. They received the news about the accident (the) Saturday.
Cuando escuchaban, comprendían
9. When they listened, they understood.
No ~~esperen~~ el tren esta tarde.
10. Do not wait for the train this afternoon.
Pocos olvidarán a ~~sus~~ profesores.
11. Few will forget (**a**) their teachers.
No ~~querían~~ tomar el café además de ~~la~~ la leche.
12. They did not want to drink coffee in addition to milk.
Su padre ~~le enviaba~~ le enviaba dinero todo ~~mes~~ cuando vivía en España.
13. His father used to send him money every month when he lived in Spain.
Cantamos toda la noche.
14. We sang all (the) night.

If happened once, use the preterit.
If more than once, use the imperfect.

PRELIMINARY LESSON TWO

A. VERB REVIEW

2. Conjugation of ser, estar, and haber

INFINITIVE

ser *to be*	**estar** *to be*	**haber** *to have*

PRESENT PARTICIPLE

siendo *being*	**estando** *being*	**habiendo** *having*

PAST PARTICIPLE

sido *been*	**estado** *been*	**habido** *had*

INDICATIVE MOOD

1 PRESENT

I am, etc.		*I am*, etc.		*I have*, etc.	
soy	somos	estoy	estamos	he	hemos
eres	sois	estás	estáis	has	habéis
es	son	está	están	ha	han
				hay[1]	

2 IMPERFECT

I was, used to be, etc.		*I was, used to be*, etc.		*I had*, etc.	
era	éramos	estaba	estábamos	había	habíamos
eras	erais	estabas	estabais	habías	habíais
era	eran	estaba	estaban	había	habían

4 FUTURE

I shall be, etc.		*I shall be*, etc.		*I shall have*, etc.	
seré	seremos	estaré	estaremos	habré	habremos
serás	seréis	estarás	estaréis	habrás	habréis
será	serán	estará	estarán	habrá	habrán

---

[1] This is a special form in the third person singular of this tense, meaning *there is, there are*. The third person singular of the other tenses of this verb may be similarly translated: *there was, there were; there will be; there has been*, etc. Followed by **que** plus an infinitive, these forms translate *it is necessary, it was necessary; one must*, etc. See §11.2-3.

5 CONDITIONAL

I should be, etc.		*I should be, etc.*		*I should have, etc.*	
sería	seríamos	estaría	estaríamos	habría	habríamos
serías	seríais	estarías	estaríais	habrías	habríais
sería	serían	estaría	estarían	habría	habrían

3 PRETERIT

I was, etc.		*I was, etc.*		*I had, etc.*	
fuí	fuimos	estuve	estuvimos	hube	hubimos
fuiste	fuisteis	estuviste	estuvisteis	hubiste	hubisteis
fué	fueron	estuvo	estuvieron	hubo	hubieron

6 PERFECT

I have been, etc.   *I have been, etc.*

he sido, etc.   he estado, etc.   ha habido[1]

7 PLUPERFECT

I had been, etc.   *I had been, etc.*

había sido, etc.   había estado, etc.   había habido[1]

8 preterit perfect
hube hubiste hubo hubimos hubisteis hubieron

9 FUTURE PERFECT

I shall have been, etc.   *I shall have been, etc.*

habré sido, etc.   habré estado, etc.   habrá habido[1]

10 CONDITIONAL PERFECT

I should have been, etc.   *I should have been, etc.*

habría sido, etc.   habría estado, etc.   habría habido[1]

SUBJUNCTIVE MOOD

11 PRESENT

That I may be, etc.		*That I may be, etc.*		*That I may have, etc.*	
sea	seamos	esté	estemos	haya	hayamos
seas	seáis	estés	estéis	hayas	hayáis
sea	sean	esté	estén	haya	hayan

[1] Third person, impersonal; see note on preceding page.

11

A NEW
SHORTER
SPANISH
REVIEW
GRAMMAR

VERB
REVIEW

12+13 **IMPERFECT**

I might be, etc.		*I might be*, etc.		*I might have*, etc.	
fuera	fuéramos	estuviera	estuviéramos	hubiera	hubiéramos
fueras	fuerais	estuvieras	estuvierais	hubieras	hubierais
fuera	fueran	estuviera	estuvieran	hubiera	hubieran
fuese	fuésemos	estuviese	estuviésemos	hubiese	hubiésemos
fueses	fueseis	estuvieses	estuvieseis	hubieses	hubieseis
fuese	fuesen	estuviese	estuviesen	hubiese	hubiesen

14 present **PERFECT**

I may have been, etc.	*I may have been*, etc.	
haya sido, etc.	haya estado, etc.	haya habido[1]

15+16 **PLUPERFECT** (*past perfect*)

I might have been, etc.	*I might have been*, etc.	
hubiera ⎫ ⎬ sido, etc. hubiese ⎭	hubiera ⎫ ⎬ estado, etc. hubiese ⎭	hubiera ⎫ ⎬ habido[1] hubiese ⎭

IMPERATIVE MOOD

PRESENT

sé (tú) *be*	estáte (tú) *be*
sed (vosotros) *be*	estad (vosotros) *be*

B. ORAL OR WRITTEN EXERCISES

1. *Conjugate:*
   (ser) 1. Somos[2] (*conditional, preterit, present and imperfect subjunctive*).
   2. Es (*imperfect, future, preterit, pluperfect*).
   3. Estoy (*imperfect, preterit, imperfect subjunctive*).
   4. Hemos (*future, preterit, present subjunctive*).
   5. Han (*imperfect, conditional, imperfect subjunctive*).
   6. Aguardamos (*imperfect, preterit, present perfect*).
   7. Corresponde (*future, preterit, pluperfect*).
   8. Consideran (*conditional, preterit, present subjunctive*).
   9. Cumplimos (*future, present perfect, imperfect subjunctive*).
   10. *Give the present participle, past participle, imperative singular of* ser,
   estar, haber, ocurrir, acostumbrar, conceder.

---

[1] Impersonal; see notes on preceding pages.

12 [2] This means: give the form in the same person and number in the tense suggested.

2. *Identify and translate:* *I am* *he was*

1. Soy *I am*
2. Esté *he was*
3. Habrá *he will have*
4. Éramos *We used to be*
5. Estaban *they used to be*
6. Fué *he was*
7. Hemos *We have*
8. Estuve *I was*
9. Ha habido *I had*
10. Somos *We are*
11. Estuviera *He will be*
12. Fueran *they were*
13. Sea *that I may be*
14. Habría *You/he should have*
15. Estén *that they may be* *past subjunctive*
16. Hayamos *that we may have*
17. Fueron *they were*
18. Estuvimos – *preterit*
19. Hubo – *preterit* *I had*
20. Fuí – *preterit* *I was*

3. *Translate:* **(ser)**
1. I used to be. *Era*
2. He will be. *Será*
3. They were (*pret.*). *Fueron*
4. We have been. *Hemos sido*
5. He may be. *Sea*
6. I might be. *Fuera or fuese*
7. Being. *Siendo*
8. She was (*pret.*). *Fué*
9. I am. *Soy*
10. **(estar)** I am. *Estoy*
11. You were (*pret.*) *Fuiste*
12. They used to be. *Eran*
13. We should be. *Estaríamos*
14. I may be. *Esté*
15. You might be. *Estuviera*
16. They had been. *Habían estado*
17. We shall be. *Estaremos*
18. They were (*pret.*). *Estuvieron*
19. **(haber)** There is. *Hay*
20. There was (*pret.*). *Hubo*
21. He will have accompanied. *Habrá acompañado*
22. There has been. *Ha habido*
23. There used to be. *Había*
24. There will be. *Habrá*
25. There may be. *Haya*
26. They might have. *Hubieran (or) Hubiesen*
27. There would be. *Habrían Habieran*
28. I have approached. *He acercado*

4. *Translate, using a form of the infinitive in parentheses:*
1. (*amar*) They love their country. *Aman su país.*
2. (*asegurar*) I assure you (**le**) that it is true. *Le aseguro que es verdad.*
3. (*cambiar*) He changed (**de**) clothes. *Cambió de ropa.*
4. (*enseñar*) He will teach three hours tomorrow. *Enseñará tres horas mañana.*
5. (*faltar*) She failed [to appear] at (**a**) the class yesterday. *Faltó a la clase ayer.*
6. (*gustar*) If you like (if it pleases you), we shall read it. *Si le gusta a usted, lo leeremos.*
7. (*importar*) It does not matter to me. *No importa.*
8. (*disponer*) She (**lo**) arranges everything carefully (with care). *Ella lo dispone todo con cuidado.*
9. (*romper*) The maid broke the plate. *La criada rompió el plato.*
10. (*subir*) They will come-up at once. *Subirán en seguida.*
11. (*bajar*) The brother-and-sister came-down slowly. *Los hermanos bajaron despacio.*
12. (*llorar*) The children used to cry every day. *Los niños lloraban todos los días.*
13. (*vivir*) We lived in the east. *Vivimos en el este.*
14. (*comer*) They eat dinner late in the south. *Comían... comen en el sur.*
15. (*dejar*) He left his watch upstairs in his room. *Dejó su reloj en su cuarto.*

upstairs – arriba

Abrían la puerta cuando llegamos.

16. (*abrir*) They were opening the door when we arrived.
17. (*cerrar*) He locked the window and went-to-bed.
18. (*levantar*) She raised her hand to (**para**) answer.
19. (*necesitar*) We need more time to (**para**) study.
20. (*perdonar*) Pardon me, will you pay the bill?

5. *Translate:*

1. He presented me to his sister.
2. She will try to (**de**) take the flowers from the table.
3. All (everyone) will come with us.
4. He used to read only at (**por la**) night.
5. She always explains the lesson well.
6. Don't waste too much time playing.
7. We reached the city before (the) dinner.
8. We remember all the regions that we visited.
9. Do they sell hats in this store?
10. I desire you to reply (*pres. subj.*) to us next week.
11. It seems best [to] remain here until (the) Sunday.
12. They are sad because they can not dance.
13. After speaking (*infinitive*) with Pedro, they left.
14. He woke us and began to (**a**) talk.
15. Our uncle-and-aunt always treated us well.
16. According to the professor, we should study more.
17. On account of the cold, he wore his (**está de**) overcoat.
18. When he has [a] headache, he is in a (**está de**) bad humor.
19. I should learn more if I studied (*imperf. subj.*) more.
20. Are there classes tomorrow?

for Sept. 27 – exercises
5 sentences for Mon. Sept. 30.
test

CHAPTER ONE

A. GRAMMAR AND IDIOM PRACTICE

Pedro Burk era un estudiante de tercer año en la universidad. Era un muchacho serio, inteligente y aplicado; obtenía muy buenas notas en todas las asignaturas y ocupaba puestos de responsabilidad en el gobierno de las asociaciones estudiantiles. También jugaba al* golf y formaba parte del equipo que representaba a su universidad.   5

Estaba muy interesado en el estudio del español y había leído más que sus compañeros. **Sin embargo** el pobre Pedro pronunciaba muy mal y apenas podía decir dos palabras en español. Cuando el profesor hacía preguntas* en esta lengua, él nunca levantaba la mano para contestar. Un día, después de la clase, se acercó al profesor para preguntarle si creía que los norteamericanos 10 podían aprender lenguas extranjeras.

— ¡Ya lo creo! — contestó el profesor. — **Por supuesto.** Esa idea de que los norteamericanos son incapaces de aprender otras lenguas es una tontería. La prueba es que **hay** muchos que las hablan.

— Es posible — dijo Pedro. — Pero probablemente esas personas han 15 visitado otros países o han tenido oportunidad de hablar la lengua con naturales de esos países. ¿No cree Vd. que muchos, como yo, tenemos algún defecto en los órganos vocales?

— **De nuevo** le digo, señor Burk, que ésa es una tontería. Lo que Vd. necesita es irse por unas semanas a un país de habla española. Entonces 20 perdería el miedo de hablar en público. Si no tiene otros planes, ¿por qué no se va a España o a Méjico el verano próximo? Perdería Vd. ese complejo de inferioridad y volvería hablando la lengua. **Una vez** allí debe hablar con **todo el mundo,** de lo contrario* no vale la pena* salir del país.

— Muchas gracias, señor profesor. Escribiré a mis padres. Ellos me han 25 dicho que me pagarán un viaje **al** terminar mis estudios, pero como el año que viene* **tendré que** entrar en* el ejército o en la marina comprenderán

que éste es el único *only* verano en que puedo hacer un viaje* al extranjero.
Vamos a ver, si escribo hoy, jueves, y ellos reciben mi carta el sábado, el
lunes próximo tendré su contestación. Si mi padre está en casa,* estoy seguro *sure*
de que me contestarán lo antes posible.* Hasta la semana que viene, don José
5 — dijo Pedro al salir.

B. IDIOMS AND PHRASES

hacer

jugaba a(l golf) *he played* (golf)
sin embargo *nevertheless, however*
hacía preguntas *he asked questions*
¡ya lo creo! *I should say so!*
por supuesto *of course*
hay (muchos) *there are* (many)
de nuevo *again*
una vez *once*
todo el mundo *everybody*
de lo contrario *otherwise*
vale la pena (salir) *it is worth while*
(to leave)

al (terminar) *on* (finishing), *when* (I finish)
(**el año**) **que viene** *next* (year)
tendré que (entrar) *I'll have to* (enter)
hacer un viaje *to take a trip*
vamos a (ver) *let's* (see)
en casa *at home, home*
lo antes posible *as soon as possible*

C. GRAMMAR REVIEW

3. Forms of the Articles.

	MASCULINE		FEMININE		NEUTER
	Singular	*Plural*	*Singular*	*Plural*	*Singular*
Definite	**el** the	**los** the	**la, el** the	**las** the	**lo** the
Indefinite	**un** a	**unos** some	**una, un** a	**unas** some	

el acto *the* act
el momento *the* moment

los animales *the* animals
los colores *the* colors

un general *a* general
un minuto *a* minute

la familia *the* family
la mano *the* hand; paw

las causas *the* causes
las personas *the* persons

una fortuna *a* fortune
una idea *an* idea

16

MAR CANTÁBRICO

FRANCIA

O C É A N O

Santiago

Oviedo

Pamplona

Burgos

Valladolid

Zaragoza

Barcelona

Medina
del Campo

Segovia

La Granja

Ávila

Madrid

Escorial

E   S   P   A   Ñ   A

RÍO TAJO

Toledo

Valencia

ISLAS BALEARES

Palma

P O R T U G A L

Lisboa

E

Córdoba

Sevilla GUADALQUIVIR

RÍO

Gibraltar

Granada

Almería

MAR MEDITERRÁNEO

A T L Á N T I C O

Tánger

Á   F   R   I   C   A

VIAJES DE PEDRO POR ESPAÑA

Millas

Kilómetros

0	50	100		200
0	100	200	300	

palacios

**A NEW
SHORTER
SPANISH
REVIEW
GRAMMAR**

**GRAMMAR
REVIEW**

El, not **la,** is used immediately before a feminine singular noun which begins with a stressed **a** or **ha.**

el agua *the* water   **el** alma *the* soul   **el** hacha *the* axe   **el** hambre *the* hunger

But:

la acción *the* action   **la** alcoba *the* bedroom   **la** mala agua *the* bad water
la habitación *the* room   **la** hacienda *the* estate   **las** aguas *the* waters

Similarly, **un,** not **una,** ~~usually~~ *sometimes* appears before a feminine singular noun which begins with a stressed **a** or **ha.**

un ala *a* wing; brim   **un** arma *a* weapon   **un** arpa *a* harp

But:

una abuela *a* grandmother   **una** avenida *an* avenue

Unos, -as has the meaning of *some, a few, a pair of.*

unas plantas *a few* plants   **unos** guantes *a pair of* gloves

The neuter article **lo** *the* is not used with nouns. It appears before the masculine singular form of adjectives and past participles to translate *thing, part, what is,* etc.

lo importante *the* important *thing*   **lo** escrito *what is* written
lo interesante *the* interesting *part*   **lo** dicho *what is* said

4. Contractions.

a + el = al to the, at the   **de + el = del** of the, from the
al caballero *to the* gentleman   **del** mar *of the* sea

5. Use of *al* with the Infinitive.

Al followed by an infinitive translates *on, upon, while, when one,* etc.

al declarar *on* declaring   **al** nombrar *when* I named

The only form of the verb used after a prep. is the infinitive!

6. Repetition of the Articles.

The definite and indefinite articles are repeated in Spanish before each noun they modify, even though they may be omitted in English.

el café y **el** azúcar   the coffee and sugar
una pluma y **un** lápiz   a pen and pencil

7. Uses of the Definite Article.

The definite article appears more frequently in Spanish than in English. It is required in Spanish:

(1) (*a*) With abstract nouns.

El amor lo vence todo.   Love conquers all (everything).
La vida es breve.   Life is short.

    (*b*) With nouns used in a collective or general sense, that is, when "in general," "all," or "every," etc. is understood with them.

El hombre es mortal. Man is mortal.   **El** dinero habla. Money talks.
El oro es útil. Gold is useful.   Me gusta **el** café. I like coffee.
Las flores son bonitas.   Flowers are pretty.

        When "some," or "any" rather than "all" is understood, the article is not used.

¿Tiene Vd. fósforos?   Have you *any* matches?

(2) Before all titles (but not **don, doña, San** or **Santa**) *(Master)* *(Saint)* except in direct address.

El señor Salinas era poeta.   Mr. Salinas was a poet.
El capitán Aguirre está herido.   Captain Aguirre is wounded.
Don Carlos lee el diario.   Don Carlos reads the newspaper.
San Luis fué rey.   St. Louis was a king.
Muy buenas tardes, señora de Gil.   Good afternoon, Mrs. Gil.

Hello señorita,
where is the señorita.

(3) With names of parts of the body and articles of personal wear or something closely associated with the subject, instead of the possessive adjective as in English, when no confusion would result.

Levanto **la** mano.   I raise *my* hand.
Tengo **el** reloj en **el** bolsillo.   I have *my* watch in *my* pocket.

The use of an indirect object pronoun avoids confusion.

Le quito el sombrero.	I take *his* (from him the) hat.
Me quito el abrigo.	I take off *my* (to me the) overcoat.

The singular of the noun is used in Spanish, contrary to English usage, when each member of a group possesses one each of an object.

Abrimos **la boca.** — We open *our mouths.*

But:

Cerramos **los ojos.** — We close (both) *our eyes.*

(4) With infinitives used as nouns.

El dormir es necesario.	Sleep (to sleep) is necessary.
El hablar es lo difícil.	Speaking is the hard part.

(5) In expressing time of day. **La** or **las** accompanies the numeral, agreeing with **hora** or **horas** understood.

Es **la** una. It is one o'clock.   Son **las** dos y media. It is 2:30.

(6) With proper names of persons when modified. *except in direct address*

El pobre Pablo no llegó a tiempo.   Poor Paul didn't arrive in time.

(7) With names of streets, avenues, squares, meals, and games,

Conocemos bien **la** Calle Mayor.	We know Calle Mayor well.
Viven en **la** Plaza Colón.	They live on Columbus Square.
Jugamos **al** fútbol.	We play football.
antes **del** desayuno	before breakfast

Sunday – el domingo — *dinner – la comida*

(8) With all expressions of time when modified, and with the names of the days of the week and of the seasons, except after **ser.**

la semana próxima next week	**el** mes pasado last month
Llegará **el** lunes.	He will arrive (next) Monday.
No tenemos clases **los** sábados.	We don't have classes Saturdays.
el verano y **el** otoño	summer and autumn

spring – la primavera

But:

Hoy es miércoles, ayer fué   Today is Wednesday, yesterday was
    martes y mañana será jueves.   Tuesday, and tomorrow will be Thursday.

    Note the distinction:

el domingo next (or last) Sunday   **los** viernes Fridays, every Friday
              pasado

(9) In certain set prepositional and adverbial phrases:

a la escuela *to school;* **en la escuela** *in school;* **de la escuela** *from school;*
a (de, en) la iglesia *to (from, in) church;* **a (de, en) la cama** *to (from, in) bed.*

Va a **la** escuela.   He goes to school.   Está en **la** iglesia.   He is in church.
Sale de **la** iglesia.   He leaves church.   Fuma en **la** cama.   He smokes in bed.
    from

(10) Before certain geographical names (countries, cities, states) when un-
    modified, and before the names of *all* countries when modified.

la Argentina   **la** China   **el** Perú   **la** Florida
el Canadá   **el** Ecuador   **la** Habana   **la** España antigua

(11) With the names of languages except immediately after **hablar** (and some-
    times **aprender, escribir, estudiar,** and **saber**) and after the preposi-
    tions **de** and **en.**

El italiano es difícil.   Italian is difficult.
Hablan francés.   They speak French.
Aquí se habla español.   Spanish is spoken here.
Escriben en portugués.   They write in Portuguese.
un profesor de alemán   a German teacher

But:

Hablan bien **el** ruso.   They speak Russian well.
Aprendieron de prisa **el** árabe.   They learned Arabic fast.

D. VERB REVIEW

Ir[1] *to go* (with present participles) *to be;* **irse** *to go away;* **salir** *to go out,* *learn*
come out, depart.   *these*

Voy a jugar al tenis.   *I'm going to play tennis.*
Van fumando.   *They are smoking.*

––––––––
[1] See Chart for forms of irregular and spelling-changing verbs.   **21**

¡Vamos! *Come on!*

 ¡Vamos a ver! *Let's see!*

Me voy esta noche.　　　　　　　*I'm going away* tonight.

Salgo de la escuela a las tres.　　*I leave* school at three o'clock.

Salió bien (mal) del examen.　　*He passed (failed)* the examination.

E. GRAMMAR EXERCISES

1. *Translate:*

1. He goes. *él va*
2. I go. *yo voy*
3. Going. *yendo*
4. We were going. *nosotros íbamos*
5. Go! *vaya usted*
6. He went. *él fue*
7. We went. *nosotros fuimos*
8. (That) we might go. *que fuéramos nosotros*
9. I go out. *yo salgo*
10. They will go out. *saldrán ellos*
11. Come out! *salga usted*

2. *Replace the dashes* (a) *by the definite article and* (b) *by the indefinite article:*

1. el / un arma *army*
2. el / un hambre *hunger*
3. la / una altura *altitude, height*
4. el / un ama *housekeeper*
5. la / una hacienda
6. la / una abuela *grandmother*
7. el / un ave pequeña
8. el / un hacha *axe*
9. la / una habitación
10. el / un alma *soul, heart*

3. *Supply the definite article where necessary:*

1. Jugamos a *la* pelota.
2. *El* señor López es profesor.
3. Levantan *la* mano derecha. *(right)*
4. *ø* señor López, ¿es Vd. *ø* profesor?
5. *La* vida es breve. *(short)*
6. Me duele *la* cabeza.
7. *El* ruso es difícil.
8. Leo en *ø* italiano.
9. Lo busca en *ø* bolsillo. *pocket*
10. Después de *ø* almuerzo van a *la* cama.
11. *La* pobre Conchita salió mal del examen.
12. Vamos a aprender *el* francés.
13. Son *las* cuatro en punto de la tarde.
14. Sus sobrinos viven en *la* Calle Mayor.
15. Visitamos *la* Habana.
16. Aquí se habla *ø* inglés.

22

17. Volvieron del Perú el *(Tuesday)* martes pasado.
18. El oeste *west* y el *east* este son puntos cardinales.
19. Compramos leche para la comida.
20. Es una clase de inglés.
21. El oro es de mucho valor.
22. El cumplir una promesa es un deber.
23. No tenemos clases los domingos.
24. Leemos lo importante del libro.
25. Las flores son bonitas.
26. A los hombres no les gusta ir de compras.
27. Ayer fué miércoles.
28. Saldremos el lunes.
29. Tomo chocolate para el desayuno.
30. Escribimos bien el portugués.
31. El viernes próximo sufriremos un examen.
32. Van a la escuela pero no a la iglesia.
33. Los niños deben obedecer a sus padres.
34. El saber es poder.

4. *Translate:* *write these out.*

(a)
1. Pedro reads only what is important in the newspapers.
Pedro no lee mas que lo importante en los periódicos
2. It is one o'clock in **(de)** the afternoon; not two o'clock.
Es la una de la tarde; no las dos.
3. Nearly always when he leaves church he goes to Bravo St.
Casi siempre cuando él sale de la iglesia va a la calle Bravo.
4. That's why life here is not interesting except on week ends.
Por eso la vida aquí no es interesante excepto de fin de semana.
5. In winter we do not play **(al)** tennis very often.
En el invierno no jugamos al tenis a menudo.
6. Next summer she will not return to school.
El verano que viene no volverá a la escuela.
7. Last year he did not have to sing on Sundays.
El año pasado no tuvo que cantar los domingos.
8. Captain Rojas and Miss Rojas will arrive Monday after lunch.
El Capitán Rojas y la Señorita Rojas llegarán el lunes después de almuerzo.
9. Italian is a beautiful language.
El italiano es una lengua hermosa.
10. They speak French in Canada and Louisiana.
Se habla francés en Canadá y en Luisiana. *or (Hablan)*

(b)
1. Pedro is very [much] interested in Spanish.
Pedro se interesó mucho en el español
2. Poor Pedro speaks and pronounces Spanish very badly.
El pobre Pedro habla y pronuncia muy mal el español.
3. He and the others in class never raised their hands in order to answer questions.
El y los de la clase nunca levantaron la mano para contestar a las preguntas.
4. You need to go to a foreign country for **(por)** a few weeks.
Usted necesita ir a un país extranjero por unas pocas semanas.
5. North Americans also can **(pueden)** learn foreign languages.
También los norteamericanos pueden aprender lenguas extranjeras.

23

6. You can (**puede**) go to Argentina, Peru, or Spain.
7. On arriving there, you will begin to (**a**) speak immediately.
8. Moreover, travel teaches a great deal.
9. The professor and student dined together.
10. Pedro bought a pair of shoes for (**para**) the trip.

F. EXERCISE ON IDIOMS AND PHRASES

Translate the words underlined:

1. However no podía contestar cuando el profesor asked questions.
2. Iré a verle as soon as possible.
3. Si Vd. no desea estudiar, it's not worth while comprar los libros.
4. El padre de Pedro had to take a trip y no estaba at home.
5. Next year volveré a la universidad.
6. Let's see, ¿ha recibido Vd. la carta?
7. Once en España, Vd. debe hablar con everybody.
8. Of course, you'll have to perder el complejo de inferioridad.
9. Again le digo que there are muchos americanos capaces de aprender otras lenguas.
10. Pedro también used to play tenis bastante bien.

el asunto — the matter

CHAPTER TWO

TRANSLATE This Page!!! for Wed. Oct. 2

A. GRAMMAR AND IDIOM PRACTICE

Una semana después Pedro volvió a* hablar con el profesor. Cuando entró en su oficina parecía **otro** hombre. Hasta saludó en español. Don José le invitó a* sentarse.

— Bueno, ¿qué hay?*; **¿algo de** nuevo? — le preguntó. — Parece Vd. muy contento. ¿Han contestado sus padres? El corazón me dice que su contestación ha sido favorable. 5

— **Tiene Vd. razón** — contestó Pedro. — Tuve carta de mis padres y están dispuestos a pagarme un viaje a Europa. He tenido mucha suerte*, **¿verdad?**

— Bueno, bueno, vamos a hablar más del asunto. ¿Tiene Vd. clase la próxima 10 hora?

— No, señor, no tengo más clases hoy. ¿Tiene Vd. tiempo para contestar a mis preguntas?

— Estoy a su disposición — dijo el profesor. — Pero bien, ¿**piensa** * Vd. ir a* pasearse por Europa o a estudiar? Hasta ahora* no ha dicho nada de sus 15 planes.

— Pienso hacer las dos cosas: estudiar primero y viajar después, o viceversa. Tendré tiempo para todo y . . . dinero — añadió Pedro muy satisfecho. — **Por eso me gustaría** saber si hay Cursos de Verano para extranjeros en España y cuándo se celebran. 20

— Muy bien. Veo que sus padres son personas sensatas y desean que Vd. se aproveche de* esta oportunidad para ver mundo. En su lugar, yo estudiaría primero y me divertiría después. Sí, en España hay Cursos de Verano en varios sitios.

El profesor entonces sacó de un cajón de la mesa varios folletos. Después 25 de* un rato dijo: — Aquí veo que en Segovia tienen una Escuela de Verano desde el 15 de junio hasta últimos de* julio. **¿Qué le parece?** Segovia tiene la ventaja de no estar lejos de* Madrid y de tener un clima más agradable que **25**

that of *Besides,*
el de la capital. Además, como es una ciudad pequeña Vd. puede conocer a
mucha gente y tener más oportunidades para hablar la lengua. Sin embargo *I must warn you*
he de* advertirle que es una ciudad vieja, muy histórica y muy artística, pero *without* *charm*
sin los atractivos de las grandes poblaciones.
marked on *places that also had*
5 Don José marcó en un mapa de España otros lugares donde también había
Cursos de Verano: Santander, Madrid, Jaca, Palma de Mallorca, Valencia, etc. *did not want* *He stood up*
Pero Pedro no quiso saber más. Se levantó y dijo:
I can
— Muchas gracias, don José. Creo que en una ciudad pequeña puedo *to travel*
aprender más. Iré a Segovia, y después de aprender a* hablar español viajaré *to*
10 por otras partes de España y por Europa.
thru

B. IDIOMS AND PHRASES

returned

volvió a (hablar)   (he spoke) *(again)*

otro (hombre)   *another* (man)

(le) **invitó a** (sentarse)   *he invited* (him) *to* (sit down)

¿qué hay?   *what is the matter? what's up? what is the news?*

algo de (nuevo)   *something* (new)

tiene Vd. razón   *you are right*

he tenido mucha suerte   *I have been very lucky*

¿verdad?   *haven't I?*

¿piensa Vd. (ir)?   *do you intend* (to go)?

ir a (pasearse)   *to go to* (travel for pleasure)

hasta ahora   *so far*

por eso   *that's why, for that reason*

me gustaría (saber)   *I would like* (to know)

aprovecharse de (esta oportunidad)   *to take advantage of* (this opportunity)

después de   *after*

últimos de (julio)   *the end of* (July)

¿qué le parece?   *what do you think?*

lejos de   *far from*

he de (advertirle)   *I must* (warn you)

aprender a (hablar)   *to learn to* (speak)

C. GRAMMAR REVIEW

8. Omission of the Articles.

a or an
(1) The indefinite article is *omitted* in Spanish before an unmodified predicate
noun denoting a social class or group (profession, nationality, religion, etc.).

Su amigo es médico.   His friend is *a* doctor.

Mi padre es inglés.   My father is *an* Englishman.

SPAIN

But:

Es **un** médico famoso.	He is a *famous* doctor.
Es **un** soldado valiente.	He is a *brave* soldier.
Era **un** santo.	He was a (*real*) saint.

(2) Neither article appears with nouns in apposition, except in emphatic use.

Larra, autor del siglo XIX	Larra, *a* (*the*) XIXth-century writer
Lima, capital del Perú	Lima, *the* capital of Peru

Superlative

But:

El Misisipí, **el** río más largo de los Estados Unidos	The Mississippi, *the* longest river in the United States

(3) The definite article is *omitted* before a numeral in the title of a ruler.

Pedro III Peter *the* Third	Pío Nono (IX) Pius *the* Ninth

(4) The indefinite article is *omitted* especially after negations.

No tengo clase hoy.	I don't have *a* class today.
Salí sin gabán.	I went out without *an* overcoat.

(5) The indefinite article is *omitted* with

ciento (cien) *a* (*one*) hundred	**cien** mujeres *a* hundred women
cierto *a* certain	**cierto** asunto *a* certain matter
medio half *a*, *a* half	**media** hora half *an* hour
otro *an*other	**otro** camino *an*other road
qué what *a*	**¡qué** cara! what *a* face!
tal such *a*	**tal** dolor such *a* pain

ordinal #'s are not used above the #10

mil – a thousand ?
? se mejante – such a ?

9. Gender of Nouns.

(1) Names of male persons, days, months, and parts of speech used as nouns are masculine. Nouns ending in **-o** and several of Greek origin ending in **-ma, -pa,** and **-ta** are masculine (exceptions: **la mano,** hand, **la radio,** radio).

el cura *priest*	**(el)** mayo *May*	**el** idioma *language*
el papá *papa, father*	**el** saber *knowledge*	**el** mapa *map*
el martes *Tuesday*	**el** por qué *reason*	**el** cometa *comet*

(2) Names of female persons are feminine; nouns ending in **-a, -d, -ie, -ión,** and **-umbre** are feminine (exceptions: **el día,** *day,* and those of Greek origin mentioned above).

la mujer *woman*	**la** ausencia *absence*	**la** serie *series*
la actriz *actress*	**la** gracia *grace*	**la** opinión *opinion*
la virgen *virgin*	**la** merced *mercy; favor*	**la** expresión *expression*
la miseria *misery*	**la** felicidad *happiness*	**la** costumbre *custom*
la persona *person*	**la** bondad *kindness*	**la** legumbre *vegetable*

only masculine "ión": { *el avión – airplane* *el ostión, – oyster* *el sarampión– measles* }

(3) Many nouns vary in meaning according to their gender.

el capital *capital* (money	**la** capital *capital* (city)
el corte *cut*	**la** corte *court*
el cura *priest*	**la** cura *cure*
el frente *front*	**la** frente *forehead*
el orden *order* (arrangement)	**la** orden *order* (command)

(4) The gender of many nouns must be learned through observation.

el ángel *angel*	**el** cristal *glass*	**la** paz *peace*
el árbol *tree*	**la** fe *faith*	**la** sal *salt*
la corriente *current*	**la** gente *people*	**la** víctima *victim*

10. Plural of Nouns.

(1) Nouns (*a*) ending in a vowel (accented or unaccented) add **-s** to form the plural; (*b*) ending in a consonant or **-y** add **-es** to form the plural.

(*a*) el labio, los **labios** *lip(s)*
    el papá, los **papás** *papa(s)*

la falta, las **faltas** *error(s)*
la mamá, las **mamás** *mama(s)*

(*b*) el papel, los **papeles** *paper(s)*

la ley, las **leyes** *law(s)*

A few nouns ending in a stressed vowel add **-es: el rubí, los rubíes.**

z in front of e or i always changes to c.

(2) (*a*) Those ending in **-z** change **z** to **c;**
   (*b*) those having a final stressed syllable ending in **-n** or **-s** lose the graphic accent; and
   (*c*) those having a final unstressed syllable ending in **-n** receive the graphic accent in the plural.

A NEW
SHORTER
SPANISH
REVIEW
GRAMMAR

GRAMMAR
REVIEW

(a) la luz, las **luces**   *light(s)*   la voz, las **voces**   *voice(s)*

(b) el corazón, los **corazones**   *heart, hearts*
    el inglés, los **ingleses**   *Englishman, English*

(c) el joven, los **jóvenes**   *young man (men)*
    la orden, las **órdenes**   *command(s)*

(3) Nouns ending in unstressed **-es** or **-is** do not change in the plural.

el viernes, **los viernes**   *Friday(s)*   la tesis, **las tesis**   *thesis, theses*

11. Uses of *Haber*.

(1) **Haber** means *to have*[1] when used to form the compound tenses.

don't ever separate

¿**Ha** leído Vd. el periódico?   Have you read the paper?
Habíamos acabado la carta.   We had finished the letter.

(2) **Haber** is used as an impersonal verb, that is, only in the third person singular. It then translates *there is, there are; there was, there were; there will be, there has been;* etc. In the present indicative it has a special form **hay.**

¿**Hay** algo de nuevo?   *Is there* anything new?
Había muchas personas allí.   *There were* many people there.
Habrá mucha animación.   *There will be* a great deal of gaiety.
Ha habido mucha lluvia este año.   *There has been* much rain this year.
Puede **haber** mucho lodo.   *There can be* much mud.

(3) **Haber** is also used impersonally followed by **que** and an infinitive to express necessity (*one must, it is necessary*).

tengo que – I must

Hay que escuchar con más atención.   *One must* listen more attentively.
Había que esperar el autobús.   *It was necessary* to wait for the bus.
Habrá que enviarlo.   *It will be necessary* to send it.

No hay que is best rendered by *one must not, one should not.*

No hay que reírse de él.   *One should not* laugh at him.

---

[1] To indicate possession, **tener** *to have*, must be used.

Tienen poco dinero.   They **have** little money.

(4) **Haber** followed by the preposition **de** with an infinitive denotes futurity, promise, or mild obligation[1] (*to be to, shall, will, to be supposed to, should, ought, must*).

Ella **ha de** cantar esta noche.	*She is to (will) sing tonight.*
Habían de ir y no fueron.	*They were to go and did not.*
Hemos de prepararlo a tiempo.	*We should (must) prepare it in time.*

Less frequent uses of **haber** are:

(5) As an impersonal verb, with visible atmospheric phenomena, to render the English verb *to be*.

Hay sol. *It is* sunny.	**Había** luna. The moon *was shining.*
Habrá polvo. *It will be* dusty.	**Ha habido** niebla. *It has been* misty.

(6) As an impersonal verb, meaning *to be the matter.*

¿Qué **hay?** What *is the matter?* (What *is the news?*)

D. VERB REVIEW

Tener[2] *to have = possess;* **tener que** plus infinitive *to have to, must* (strong obligation); **saber**[3] *to know; know how; find out; taste.* conocer – be acquainted with

Tengo calor. *I am* warm.	**Tiene** miedo. *He is* afraid.
Tengo la culpa. *It is* my fault.	**Tiene** prisa. *He is* in a hurry.
Tengo frío. *I am* cold.	**Tiene** razón. *He is* right.
Tengo ganas de descansar.	*I feel like* resting.
Tengo mucha hambre.	*I am* very hungry.
Tiene mucha sed.	*He is* very thirsty.

---

[1] Mild necessity and moral obligation are expressed by **deber.**

Debo (debiera) saludarle.	*I must (should)* greet him.
Vd. **debe (debiera)** venir a verme.	*You must (should)* come to see me.

[2] Conjugated like **tener: contener** *to contain;* **detener** *to stop;* **mantener** *to maintain;* **obtener** *to obtain;* **sostener** *to hold.*

[3] **Saber** means *to know* a thing or fact, *to have exact information;* with an infinitive it means *to know how.*
Conocer means *to know* in the sense of *to be acquainted with, be familiar with,* a person or thing; *to recognize.* **31**

A NEW
SHORTER
SPANISH
REVIEW
GRAMMAR

VERB
REVIEW

Tiene mucho[1] sueño.	*He is* very sleepy.
¿Qué **tiene** Vd.?	What *is the matter with* you?
No **tengo** nada.	Nothing *is the matter with* me.
Tenemos que perdonarle.	*We must* pardon him.
Tiene poco **que** hacer.	He *has* little *to* do.
¿Cuántos años **tiene** Vd.?	How old *are* you?
Tengo diecisiete años.	*I am* seventeen.
Tuve una tarjeta de su primo.	*I received* a card from his cousin.
Tiene escrita la carta.	*He has* the letter *(all) written.*
Tiene las manos blancas.	Her hands *are* white.
Sabe mucha medicina.	*He knows* much about medicine.
Sé tocar el piano.	*I know how to* play the piano.
Sabe a tabaco.	*It tastes of* tobacco.
No lo **sabía.**	*I didn't know* (it).
Lo **supe** ayer.	*I found* (it) *out* yesterday.

E. GRAMMAR EXERCISES

1. *Translate:*

1. I have.
2. We will have.
3. They have.
4. He had (= received).
5. Be patient (Have patience).

6. I know it.
7. They will know it.
8. (That) she may know it.
9. He found it out.

2. *Give the gender of:*

1. jueves *el*
2. pared *la*
3. mano *la*
4. planeta *el*
5. poder *el*

6. día *el*
7. especie *la*
8. monarca *el*
9. octubre *el*
10. virtud *la*

11. relación *la*
12. calidad *la*
13. muchedumbre *la*

3. *Use the proper form of* **haber** *with or without* **de** *or* **que** *as required:*

1. (*There are*) caminos en buen estado.
2. (*One must*) descansar de vez en cuando.
3. (*There has been*) mucha nieve este año.
4. Ella (*is to*) cantar esta noche.

─────────

32 [1] These idioms are used only with personal subjects; with them *very* is translated by **mucho, -a.**

Hay que

5. (*It is necessary to*) escuchar con atención.
6. (*There will be*) clases mañana por la mañana. *Habrá*
7. (*I had*) tomado dos vasos de leche. *Había*
8. No (*there is*) mal que cien años dure. *Hay*
9. (*One should not*) burlarse de los profesores. *No hay que*
10. (*We have*) entregado el papel. *Hemos*
11. (*They had*) concedido el premio. *Habían*
12. (*He was to*) evitar el peligro. *Había de*

4. *Translate* for Wed. Oct. 2

(a)
1. He is a lawyer and his father is an excellent writer. *Él es   su padre   excelente.*
2. He does not even have a car, nevertheless he wants to know how to drive. *El   coche, sin embargo   (conocer)*
3. Such a young man will not be happy without one. *joven   Sin uno.*
4. It will be necessary to wait a few years before buying (*inf.*) one. *comprar uno.*
5. What a pleasure to be without a headache! *cabeza.*
6. A certain friend (*f.*) presented him to another pretty girl. *muchacha bonita.*
7. He spent half an hour talking about the matter.
8. Almost a hundred persons are to be there. *Casi   están   allí.*
9. His companion will not go because he has a toothache.
10. They visited England during the reign of George the Sixth. *visitaron*

(b)
1. The professor is an American. *el profesor es americano.*
2. He is a very famous teacher. *Él es un profesor muy famoso.*
3. He has visited Madrid, the capital of Spain, several times. *El ha visitado   veces.*
4. Today Pedro greeted (**a**) the professor in Spanish. *Hoy Pedro   en español.*
5. In a small city you will be able to (**podrá**) meet (**a**) more people. *En una ciudad pequeña   más gente.*
6. You are to write to your parents as soon as possible. *Usted es   cuanto antes.*
7. One should not leave things until the last minute. *No hay que   minuto.*
8. There is not time always for (**para**) everything. *No hay tiempo siempre para*
9. Pedro left the office, but another student remained half an hour more. *a hora más.*
10. He went out of the room without a hat. *Sin sombrero.*

F. EXERCISE ON IDIOMS AND PHRASES

Translate the words underlined:

1. Aquel día Pedro parecía another hombre. *otro*
2. What's the news? ¿Tiene Vd. something nuevo que contarme? *¿Que hay?   algo de*

33

3. I am very lucky, Mis padres me darán dinero y I intend ir a España. *[Tengo mucho suerte.] [pienso]*

4. I shall take advantage of esta oportunidad para learn to hablar español. *[Aprovecharé] [aprender a]*

5. ¿What do you think [of] mi idea? Vd. no ha dicho nada so far. *[¿Qué le parece] [hasta ahora.]*

6. El plan es excelente, pero I would like to saber cuándo Vd. intend hacer el viaje. *[me gustaría] [piensa]*

7. Hacia the end of julio. *[últimos de]*

8. Pero, ¿are you going to viajar solo o en grupo? *[¿va usted a]*

9. Estudiaré primero en algún lugar not far from Madrid y viajaré after terminar los estudios. *[no lejos de] [después de]*

10. You are right. En su lugar yo haría lo mismo. *[Tiene usted razón.]*

CHAPTER THREE

A. GRAMMAR AND IDIOM PRACTICE

Cuando salió Pedro el profesor se quedó pensando: "Este muchacho es serio y bueno, pero hasta ahora no ha estado nunca entre extraños, en una ciudad pequeña y desconocida. ¿Qué será de* él lejos de la influencia de su madre?" Don José trabajó un rato más; después volvió a su casa porque tenía hambre* y era hora de comer. Su esposa notó que estaba algo preocupado y le preguntó: 5

— ¿**Qué tienes,** hombre? ¿Qué te pasa?* Parece que has perdido a tu mejor amigo.

— Pasa que acabo de* convencer a Pedro Burk para que vaya¹ este verano a estudiar en España y no sé si he hecho bien.

— No hay motivo para estar preocupado. Ese muchacho no es un niño. 10 Tampoco es tonto. Estoy segura de que* no le pasará nada. Todo el mundo debe hacer algún viaje **de vez en cuando. Y a propósito,** ¿te gusta la sopa?

— Sí, está muy buena. Tú conoces a Pedro — dijo el marido volviendo a la misma conversación — y sabes que es un poco reservado y un poco raro en la selección de sus amigos. ¿Crees que le será posible hacer amistades en 15 España?

— ¡Qué tonto eres! En primer lugar habrá allí otros norteamericanos, quizá con menos conocimientos que él. En segundo lugar tú siempre has dicho que los españoles son la gente más amistosa del mundo. Por otra parte,* como tú vas a España también, puedes ir a Segovia a ver si **le hace falta** algo. Estoy 20 segura de que en dos semanas ya está acostumbrado a aquella vida. **Sigue** comiendo y olvida el asunto.

Al fin terminó el año escolar y Pedro fué a despedirse del* profesor.

— Adiós, don José. Hasta el lunes, catorce de junio, cuando espero verle de nuevo en Madrid. 25

Estrechó la mano que el profesor le extendió y añadió:

— En España le daré un abrazo a la española.

---

¹ **para que vaya** to go

— Sí, y hablaremos siempre en español. **Haga el favor** de avisarme el día de su llegada. Adiós y hasta la vista.*

El profesor salió en avión* el primero de junio y Pedro embarcó en Nueva York el siete del mismo mes en un barco italiano. Desembarcó en Barcelona y de allí fué a Madrid. Llamó por teléfono* a don José, pero como le dijeron que no estaba en casa continuó el viaje a Segovia con dos o tres compañeros de su grupo. Al regresar **a casa** y decirle la criada que un extranjero había telefoneado aquella noche, exclamó:

— Ya sé quién es. ¡Pobre muchacho! Le esperé todo el día* y creía que no llegaba hoy. Diga, María, ¿dónde está ese hombre ahora?

— No sé, señor. **No** entendí **más que** tres palabras: "¿Está don José?"

B. IDIOMS AND PHRASES

¿**qué será de** (él)?   *what will become of* (him)?

tenía hambre   *he was hungry*

¿**qué tienes**?   *what is the matter with you?   what's wrong?*

¿**qué te pasa**?   *what is the matter with you?*

acabo de (convencerle)   *I have just* (convinced him)

estoy segura de (que no le pasará nada)   *I am sure* (that nothing will happen to him)

de vez en cuando   *occasionally*

a propósito   *by the way*

por otra parte   *on the other hand*

le hace falta (algo)   *he needs* (something)

sigue (comiendo)   *keep on* (eating)

al fin   *finally*

despedirse de (1 profesor)   *to say good-by to* (the professor)

haga el favor de (avisarme)   *please* (let me know)

hasta la vista   *so long*

en avión   *by plane*

llamó por teléfono   *he phoned*

a casa   *home*

todo el (día)   *the whole* (day)

no (entendí) **más que** (tres)   (I understood) *only* (three)

36

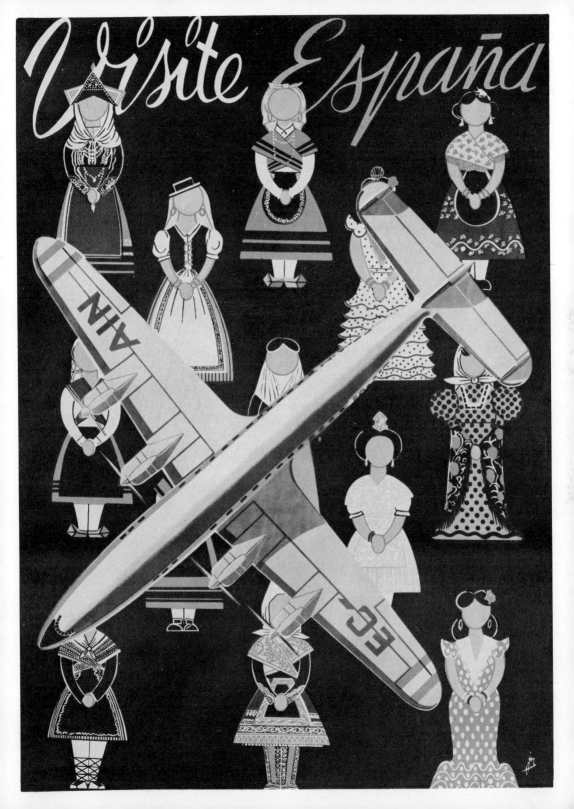

C. GRAMMAR REVIEW

12. Uses of Ser.

Ser is used:

(1) With predicate (*a*) nouns, (*b*) pronouns, and (*c*) adverbs or (*d*) infinitives used as predicate nouns.

(*a*) La vida **es** sueño.	Life *is* a dream.
(*b*) **Soy** yo;[1] **somos** nosotros;[1] **es** él.	*It is* I; *it is* we; *it is* he.
(*c*) Aquí **es** donde vivo.	Here *is* where I live.
(*d*) Ver **es** creer.	Seeing *is* believing.

(2) Before adjectives which denote a characteristic or a quality that is inborn or unlikely to change. Such adjectives are often those of class (such as nationality), shape, size, and color. Included here are **joven** *young;* **viejo** *old;* **pobre** *poor;* **rico** *rich;* and **feliz** *happy.*

Pepe **es** inteligente pero perezoso.	Joe *is* intelligent but lazy.
Vd. **es** muy amable.	You *are* very kind.
Son ciegos y mudos.	They *are* (born) blind and dumb.
¿Eran franceses?	*Were* they French?
La mesa **es** redonda.	The table *is* round.
El árbol **es** grande y viejo.	The tree *is* large and old.
Ellos **son** pobres, Vds. **son** ricos.	They *are* poor, you *are* rich.
Son muy jóvenes y felices.	They *are* very young and happy.

(3) With the preposition **de** to denote (*a*) origin, (*b*) ownership, or (*c*) material.

(*a*) **Somos de** Nueva York.	We *are from* New York.
(*b*) El sombrero **es de** mi hermano.	The hat *is* my brother's.
(*c*) La corbata **es de** seda.	The necktie *is* (made of) silk.

(4) In time expressions.

Es la una de la tarde.	*It is* one o'clock in the afternoon.
Son las ocho de la noche.	*It is* eight p.m.

---

[1] *It is* with a personal pronoun (*It is* I, *It is* we, etc.) is rendered by a form of the verb agreeing in *person* and *number* with the predicate pronoun.

se hace tarde - its getting late

(5) With past participles to form the passive voice.

Fué despertado por el despertador.   *He was* awakened by the alarm clock.

le   •   •   •

(6) In impersonal expressions.

Es tarde. *It is late.*   **Es** probable. *It is probable.*
Era posible ir. *It was possible to go.*   **Es** fácil ver. *It is easy to see.*

Es mentira - it's a lie.

13. Uses of Estar.

Estar is used:

(1) To express location or position, whether permanent or temporary.

Mi habitación **está** arriba.   My room *is* upstairs.
La iglesia **está** cerca de la estación.   The church *is* near the station. *estar + para = impending action*

(2) To denote a state or condition that is temporary or accidental. **Estar** implies that there has been a change or that there can be a change.

La taza **está** llena.   The cup *is* full.
El café **está** caliente.   The coffee *is* hot. ⟵ *always thought of as hot.*
Estoy bueno (bien) hoy.   *I am* well today.

The state or condition often results from an action.

Action (**ser**) *passive*	→	Resultant condition (**estar**)

Las cartas **fueron** escritas ayer.   →   Ya **están** escritas.
 The letters *were* written yesterday.   They *are* written now (already).
La puerta **fué** abierta ayer.   →   La puerta **está** abierta ahora.
 The door *was* opened yesterday.   The door *is* open now.

 Some conditions expressed by **estar** are permanent. ⟵

El perro **fué** matado.   →   El perro **está** muerto. *implies a change?*
 The dog *was* killed.   The dog *is* dead.

(3) To form the progressive tenses.[1]

Estamos buscando algo.   We *are* looking for something.
Estaban colocando flores en el vaso. They *were* placing flowers in the vase.

(over)

---

[1] Note that the present participles of **ser, estar, ir, venir, tener,** and **haber** *do not* appear as the second
member of the progressive forms. Avoid saying **Estoy viniendo,** etc.

Verbs of motion may replace **estar** as the auxiliary in the progressive tenses.

Va cantando.	He *is* (goes) singing.
Seguimos leyendo.	We *are* (continue) reading.

(4) With certain adjectives **estar** is used to denote *taste, appearance,* or *a personal reaction.*

¡Qué buena **está** la sopa hoy!	How good the soup *is* today!
¡**Estás** muy alto, muchacho!	You *are* very tall, boy!
El día **está** muy triste.	The day *is* very dismal.

(5) Often the meaning of an adjective varies according to the verb with which it is used.

	With **ser**	With **estar** <u>temporary</u>
alegre	*gay* (by nature)	*gay, merry*
bueno	*good, kind*	*well* (health); *good* (taste)
callado	*silent* (taciturn)	*silent* (not speaking)
cansado	*tiresome*	*tired*
cierto	*authentic, true*	*certain, sure*
divertido	*amusing*	*amused*
joven	*young* (actually)	*young* (in appearance)
rico	*rich* (person)	*wealthy; delicious* (foods)
viejo	*old* (actually)	*old* (in appearance)

14. The Personal *A.*

(1) The preposition **a** (which is not translated) is required in Spanish before a direct object designating a specific (definite) person (or, sometimes, an intelligent animal). It does not appear before unstressed pronouns (Chapter IV) or after **tener** *to have.*

Veo **a mi amigo** todos los días.	I see *my friend* every day.
Espantaron **al (el) perro.**	They frightened *the dog.*

But:

Veo mucha gente en la calle.	I see many people in the street.
Le veo. I see him.	Tengo dos hijos. I have two children.

40

querer a — love

(2) **A** is required also before the indefinite pronouns **alguien, nadie,** and before **alguno, ninguno, otro,** and **uno,** referring to persons, when they are used as direct objects.

¿Vió Vd. **a alguien** en el cuarto?	Did you see *someone* in the room?
No vi **a nadie** allí.	I saw *no one* there.

D. VERB REVIEW

Hacer *to do, make; have* (someone do something); **hacerse** *to become;* **querer** *to want, wish; care for* (someone); *be willing, will; try.*

Hace viento.[1] *It is* windy.	**Hace** mucho[2] sol. *It is* very sunny.
Hace calor. *It is* hot.	**Hace** mucho frío. *It is* very cold.
Hace buen (mal) tiempo.	*It is* fine (bad) weather.
Le vi **hace**[3] ocho días. ⎫	I saw him a week *ago.*
Hace ocho días **que** le vi. ⎭	
Hace[4] ocho días **que** está aquí.	He has been here for a week.
No **hacen caso de** la broma.	They *pay no attention to* the joke.
¿Le **hace falta** algo?	Do you *need* something?
Haga el favor de llenar el vaso.	*Please* fill the glass.
Le **hice** una pregunta.	I *asked* him a question.
Le **hice** borrar lo escrito.	I *had* him erase what was written.
Se hizo[5] rey.	He *became* king.
No **quería** hacerlo.	He *would not* (did not want to) do it.
No quiso hacerlo.	He *refused* to do it.
Quiere mucho **a** sus sobrinos.	He *loves* his nephews very much.
Quise abrir la ventana.	I *tried* to open the window.
¿Qué **quiere decir** eso?	What *does* that *mean?*

---

[1] **Hacer** is used with certain nouns to indicate states of the weather.

[2] Note that *very* in these idioms is translated by **mucho, -a.**

[3] **Hace** here means *ago;* if it precedes the main verb **que** is required.

[4] **Hacer** is used before an expression of time with the *present indicative* in Spanish to translate the *present perfect* of English whenever the action began in the past and is still continuing in the present.

[5] **Hacerse** means *to become* when the change involved is the result of one's own effort.

41

E. GRAMMAR EXERCISES

1. *Translate:*

1. I do. *yo hago*
2. They made it. *ellos lo hicieron*
3. Do it now! *hágalo ahora*
4. He has made. *Ella hecho*
5. She will do it. *ella lo ~~hará~~ hará (irregular)*
6. You wish. *Ud. quiere*
7. We wished (= tried). *nosotros ~~quisimos~~ quisimo*
8. I shall wish. *yo ~~querré~~ querré*
9. We should wish. *nosotros queríamos*
10. (That) God will it. *~~que~~ Dios ~~que~~ quiera.*

2. *Fill in the blanks with the proper form of* **ser** *or* **estar:**

place where
1. Allí *está* mi criado.
2. El señor Gómez *es* profesor.
origin, place where
3. Pablo *es* del Brasil pero ahora *está* en el Canadá.
condition
4. Mi abuelo *está* vivo (*alive*). *temporary*
5. Su hija menor *es* viva (*lively*).
6. El vestido *es* verde. *inherent quality*
7. Haga el favor de *ser* bueno. *to be good (character)*
8. El chocolate *está* frío. *temporary*
9. El papel *está* sucio. *temporary*
10. Nuestros amigos *son* ricos pero no *son* felices. *lasting condit.*
11. Su compañero *es* bajo. *short inherent quality*
12. El *wall* muro *está* hecho *made of* de ladrillos. *condition*
13. El ruso *es* difícil. *inherent quality*
14. La muchacha *es* joven. = ser
15. Él *está* tranquilo ahora. ~ quiet - vs. taciturn
16. El hielo *es* frío. *inherent quality*
17. Un alumno *es* francés. *nationality*
18. El libro *está* ~~todo es~~ escrito en inglés. ?
19. La obra *es* de mi hermano. *origin*
20. Las puertas *fueron* cerradas ayer por el profesor. *action progressive passive*
21. Las puertas *están* cerradas ahora.
22. Mi reloj *es* de plata. *material*
23. *Es* necesario pasar a la izquierda. *impers. Express.*
24. Él *es* ciego a causa de la explosión. *permanent*
25. Hoy *es* viernes.
26. *Son* las cuatro de la tarde.
27. *Es* más fácil reír *(laugh)* que llorar *(cry)*.
28. El edificio *fue* destruido ayer por el huracán.
29. Ellos *están* hablando ahora.
30. La nieve *es* fría.

The world was created in 7 days

ser.
agent

42

3. *Replace the dashes by* **a** *where necessary:*

1. Veo *a* Carlos.
2. No visité *a* nadie.
3. Tiene *ok* tres hijas.
4. Busco *a* mi criado. *own. personal*
5. Busco *ok* un criado. *anyon.*
6. ¿Vió Vd. *a* alguien en la calle?
7. Castigó *al* el perro.
8. El médico curó *al* el dueño de la tienda.
9. Juan come *ok* carne.
10. Quiero *ok* mi mamá.
11. Leo *a* la comedia.
12. ¿*a* quién pegó él?

4. *Translate:*

(a)

1. Do you know the teacher? He is young and (e) intelligent.
2. He is from Spain, but now he is in the United States.
3. In spite of his youth he is highly (**muy**) respected by (**de**) his colleagues.
4. He had met Don José in America some time before.
5. He was thinking that Pedro had never been outside of the country.
6. How is (tastes) the soup? It is cold but it has a very good taste. *¿Cómo está la sopa? fría un muy gusto*
7. And how is the weather? Is the sun shining?
8. Pedro's suitcase is [made] of black leather.
9. It was his father's.
10. It was full because it was not large.

(b)

1. Don José is still young (*in appearance*). *joven*
2. Pedro is serious but also a little queer. *serio*
3. I am sure (of) that he is not poor either.
4. The professor is worried although Pedro is not a child.
5. Spaniards are very friendly people.
6. How is (tastes) the dessert today?—It is very good.
7. When he knocked (called), a voice asked: Who is [that]? *(leave out!)*
8. It is I, Pedro Burk, he answered.—Is Don José [at home]?
9. No, he is not at home. He has not arrived yet.
10. Where is he? It is quite late already.

✓ F. EXERCISE ON IDIOMS AND PHRASES

1. *Translate the words underlined:*

1. Volvió home porque he was hungry. *a casa* *tenía hambre*
2. El profesor hizo el viaje by plane y Pedro by boat (**en barco**). *en avión* *en barco*
3. ¿What's the matter with you? Keep on comiendo. *¿Qué tienes?* *sigue*
4. ¿What will become of him si no entiende a la gente? *¿Qué será de él?*
5. I have just hablar con él y only entendió algunas palabras. *no más que*
6. On the other hand es bueno ver otros países occasionally. *Por otra parte* *de vez en cuando*
7. I am sure que él sabe pedir lo que he needs. *Estoy seguro* *le hace falta*
8. El último día fué a say good-by del profesor. *despedirse*
9. By the way, please avisarme el día de su llegada. *A propósito* *haga usted el favor de*
10. So long, D. José. I'll phone on llegar á Madrid. *Hasta la vista* *llamaré por teléfono*

2. *Translate:*

He spoke again of the matter. I am at your disposal. Otherwise we
Volvió a hablar del asunto. Estoy a su disposición. De lo contrario no
cast come.. That's why he is unable to do it. after a while he greeted
podremos venir. Por eso es incapaz de hacerlo. Después de un rato me
Next summer I will go abroad. Finally he finished the school year.
saludó. El verano próximo iré al extranjero. Al fin terminó el año escolar.
I waited for him all day. What is the matter with you dear? Do you like coffee?
Le esperé todo el día. ¿Qué tienes, muchacho? ¿Te gusta el café? Trabajó
He worked a while longer. Already it is time to eat. He will not spending I am sure.
un rato más. Ya es hora de comer. No le pasará nada, estoy segura.
He's not foolish. In the first place he invited him to eat dinner.
? Tampoco es tonto. En primer lugar le invitó a comer.

CHAPTER FOUR

Translate for Fri, Oct. 11

A. GRAMMAR AND IDIOM PRACTICE

Un día don José llegó a su casa muy cansado. Hacía calor* y se quitó la chaqueta y los zapatos. Después se sentó en el sitio más fresco de la casa y pensó en* Pedro.

— A mí me parece* que ese muchacho debe estar enfadado conmigo. No he oído de él desde que llegó a Segovia, **hace** ya dos semanas. Voy a escribirle 5 una carta ahora mismo* para saber qué es de su vida y para preguntarle si quiere venir a Madrid un fin de semana a visitarme. Al mismo tiempo le diré, para animarle, que en mi viaje al norte me detendré en Segovia para hacerle una visita.*

Estaba escribiendo cuando vino a su cuarto la criada con una carta en la 10 mano. La abrió, vió que era de Pedro y la leyó de prisa.*

— Querido maestro: — decía la carta. — A mí no me gusta escribir cartas, **es decir,** no me gusta escribir cartas en una lengua que no sé bien. Pero como le he prometido escribirle en español, intentaré darle algunas impresiones de este lugar. Voy a hablarle **con** franqueza. Me gusta la ciudad pero no me gusta 15 la vida en ella. Me gusta la abundancia de luz y color, me gusta el azul intenso del cielo, me gusta el clima, **por lo menos** hasta ahora. He dado muchos paseos* por las calles de la ciudad y por sus afueras, la mayoría de* las veces solo, y he podido admirar el imponente acueducto romano, el soberbio alcázar y las numerosas iglesias con arcadas románicas. 20

También hemos hecho una excursión a un pueblo llamado Turégano. Vd. me habló de él, ¿recuerda? Es un pueblo de viejas casas y de vieja historia, con un castillo medieval que, aunque casi en ruinas, todavía conserva fuerte y esbelta la silueta.

Vd. sabe que me encantan las cosas viejas y legendarias, pero después de 25 haberlas visto Segovia **ya no** tiene interés para mí. La vida es muy monótona y mis compañeros son gente poco interesante. Siento tener que decirle estas cosas. Apenas hablo con ellos porque no tenemos nada en común. Algún día **45** le contaré quiénes son y de dónde vienen. Por ahora* bástele saber que la mayor parte de* mis compañeros tienen más edad que yo.

Me acuerdo de* Vd. **muchas veces** y me gustaría verle para hacerle mil preguntas más.

Su amigo y discípulo, *pupil*

Pedro Burk

B. IDIOMS AND PHRASES

hacía calor *it was warm*
pensó en (Pedro) *he thought about* (Pedro)
me parece *I think*
hace (dos semanas) (two weeks) *ago*
ahora mismo *right now*
hacer una visita *to pay a visit*
de prisa *hurriedly, in a hurry*
es decir *that is to say*
con (franqueza) frank(*ly*)
por lo menos *at least*

he dado paseos *I've taken walks*
la mayoría de (las veces) *most of the* (times)
ya no *no longer*
por ahora *for the present*
la mayor parte de (mis compañeros) *most of* (my companions)
me acuerdo de (Vd.) *I remember* (you)
muchas veces *often*

C. GRAMMAR REVIEW

15. Uses of the Subject Pronouns. (See §75.)

Usted and **ustedes** (**Vd., Vds.; Ud., Uds.**) are the usual pronouns for *you* and are conjugated with the *third* person of the verb. They are expressed more frequently than the other subject forms, but usually not more than once in the same sentence. The other subject personal pronouns are normally expressed only for emphasis, contrast, or clarity.[1] **Tú** *thou, you* and **vosotros**[2] *you*, conjugated with the second person of the verb, are used among members

---

[1] *It is I* is translated **soy yo;** see §12 (1) note.

When *I* or *we* forms part of a compound subject, the verb is placed in the first person plural; when the subject is made up of the second and third persons, the verb is in the second person plural. To determine the person of the verb in these situations, insert a superfluous subject pronoun: *You and I (we) read.* **Vd. y yo (nosotros) leemos.** *You and they (you) are afraid.* **Vosotros y ellos (vosotros) tenéis miedo.**

[2] In Spanish America, **vosotros** has been replaced by **ustedes.**

SPAIN

A NEW
SHORTER
SPANISH
REVIEW
GRAMMAR

GRAMMAR
REVIEW

of the same family and in addressing intimate friends, children, servants, and animals. Subject pronouns often accompany infinitives and present participles.

Yo hago las preguntas, **Vd.** no.	*I* ask the questions, not *you.*
Él es alto, **ella** es baja.	*He* is tall, *she* is short.
¿Cómo está **ella?** Está bien.	How is *she?* She is well.
Pepe, ¿qué lees?	Joe, what are you reading?
¿Entienden **Vds.** las reglas?	Do *you* understand the rules?
por ser **ella** inglesa	because *she* is English
siendo **yo** inglés	*I* being English

16. Uses of the Object Pronouns. (See §75.)

Object pronouns may be the objects of verbs or prepositions. The unstressed forms (**me, le, nos,** etc.) are the direct or indirect objects of *verbs*, and the stressed forms (**mí, él, nosotros,** etc.) are objects of *prepositions*.

17. Position of the Unstressed Pronouns (Direct and Indirect Objects).

These pronouns (whether one or two) (*a*) normally precede the verb. They follow and are attached, however, (*b*) to infinitives, (*c*) to present participles, and (*d*) to those forms of the verb that express *affirmative* wishes or commands (imperative or subjunctive mood; see Chapter XII). In literary style the object pronouns are sometimes attached (*e*) to any form of the verb near the beginning of a clause.

(*a*) **Me** mira.	He looks at *me.*
(*b*) Puede mirar**me** *or* **Me** puede mirar.	He can look at *me.*
(*c*) Está mirándo**me** *or* **Me** está mirando.	He is looking at *me.*

Note that when an infinitive is preceded by a modal auxiliary (**querer, poder, deber, ir a**), the object pronoun may precede the auxiliary *or* be attached to the infinitive. Similarly, with the progressive forms, the object pronoun may precede both verbs *or* be attached to the present participle.

Note also that sometimes the graphic accent is necessary when a pronoun is attached in order to retain the original stress on the verb.

(*d*) Mírame (tú). (*imperative*)   Look at *me*.
Míreme Vd. (*subjunctive*)   Look at *me*.
(*e*) Al entrar, quitóse el sombrero.   On entering, he took off his hat.

When there are two object forms, both precede or both follow the verb in accordance with the rule above. (*a*) **Se** always precedes *all* other object forms; (*b*) in all other instances, the indirect form precedes the direct. When both forms are of the third person, the *indirect* (**le** or **les**) becomes **se.** A stressed form of the pronoun may be added for clearness or emphasis.

(*a*) **Se me** presentó.   He introduced *himself to me*.
(*b*) **Nos lo** contaban.   They were telling *it to us*.
Voy a comprár**selo** a él.   I am going to buy *it from him*.

I know – yo sé

18. Use of the Neuter Pronoun *Lo*.
(1) The neuter pronoun **lo** refers to a previously expressed idea.

Llegamos tarde y **lo** sentimos.   We arrived late and we regret it.

(2) **Lo** accompanies **decir, pedir, preguntar, saber,** etc., for the sake of completeness. *verbs of communication.*

Ya **lo** sé. I know (*it*).   Me **lo** dice. He tells me (*it*).
Se **lo** pedimos. We ask him (for *it*).   Pregúnte**selo**. Ask him (*it*).

(3) **Lo** is used as a complement after **estar, ser, parecer,** etc., to refer to both nouns and adjectives. English *it* and *so* often correspond to **lo.**

¿Es maestra?—**Lo** es.   Is she a teacher?—She is.
¿Son estudiantes?—Sí, **lo** son.   Are they students?—Yes, they are.
Están cansados pero no **lo** parecen.   They are tired but don't seem *so*.

19. Uses of the Indirect Object (Dative) Forms.
The indirect object forms of the pronoun are used to indicate (*a*) interest or concern, (*b*) separation, and (*c*) possession (when the definite article replaces the possessive adjective).

(*a*) **Me** cerraron la puerta.   They closed the door "*on me*."
(*b*) **Me** quitó el paraguas.   He took the umbrella away *from me*.
Nos compró un caballo.   He bought a horse *from us*.
(*c*) **Le** lavé las manos.   I washed *his* hands.

49

A NEW
SHORTER
SPANISH
REVIEW
GRAMMAR

GRAMMAR
REVIEW

20. Uses of the Stressed (Prepositional) Forms. (See §75.)

The stressed forms are used as objects of prepositions. **Ello** (like **lo**) refers to a previously expressed idea.

Iré con **él,** no con **Vd.**	I shall go with *him,* not with *you.*
Es para **mí** (para **ella,** para **ellos**).	It is for *me* (for *her,* for *them*).
No se presentó ayer; me acuerdo de **ello** ahora.	He did not appear yesterday; I remember *it* now.

The preposition **con** combines with **mí, ti,** and **sí** to form respectively **conmigo, contigo,** and **consigo.**

Venga **conmigo.** Come *with me.*	Lo lleva **consigo.** He takes it *with him.*

(1) The verb is sometimes understood:

¿A quién ve Vd.? ¿A **él?**—No, a **ella.**	Whom do you see? *Him?*—No, *her.*
Se lo diré a Vd., no a **él.**	I shall tell you, not *him.*

(2) The stressed forms are used redundantly in addition to the unstressed forms in order to clarify or emphasize:

Se lo da a Vd. (a **él,** a **ella,** a **ellos**).	He gives it to you (to *him, her, them*).
Se lo preguntamos a **él.**	We asked *him.*

21. Redundant Use of the Unstressed Forms.

(1) When an object precedes the verb, an unstressed object pronoun is inserted before the verb. This word order adds emphasis to the object.

Este chiste **lo** oí anoche.	This joke I heard last night.
A Jorge **le** di dos pesetas.	I gave two pesetas to George.
¿A mí **me** hablas así?	You speak that way to me?

(2) It is inserted especially when an indirect object referring to a person follows the verb.

Le dimos el papel a Jaime.	We gave the paper to James.

(3) When **todo** is used as an object, **lo** always accompanies the verb.

50 Cree que **lo** sabe todo.	He thinks he knows everything.

D. VERB REVIEW

Know for Monday

Decir *to say; tell;* **venir** *to come.*[1]

Digo **que sí (no).** I say *so (no).*	**Es** decir. *That is* to say.
Viene **a** molestarme.	He is coming *to* bother me.
Viene llorando.	*He is* (comes along) crying.
Se viene conmigo.	He is coming *along* with me.

E. GRAMMAR EXERCISES

1. *Translate:*

1. I tell. *digo*
2. He says. *dice*
3. They tell. *dicen*
4. She said. *dijo*
5. We shall tell. *diremos*

#6. Tell me. *dígame usted.*
*7. They have said. *han dicho*
8. I am coming. *vengo*
9. She comes. *ella viene*
10. Coming. *viniendo*

11. We came. *vinimos*
12. Come tomorrow. *Venga Vd. mañana*
13. They will come. *vendrán*

2. *Replace the nouns by pronouns and place them in the proper order:*

1. *le lo* Vi a Pepe cerrando la puerta.
2. *Las* Escribo cartas para enviar noticias a los interesados. *se las*
3. *se les* Entrego los libros a los amigos.
4. *Se lo* Toca el piano para complacer a la madre.
5. Tiraron piedras a los perros. *a ellos* (*refers to which is replaced by se*)
6. Es preciso poner *se lo* un telegrama a los padres. (*a ellas*)

3. *Replace the nouns by pronouns and add redundant forms:*

1. *se la a ella* Escribe una carta a la señorita.
2. *se lo a ella* Jorge mandó un regalo a su tía.
3. *se la a él* Lee la frase al señor.
4. *se los a él* Compré periódicos al vendedor.
5. *se la a él* Mostró la herida al médico.
6. Le gusta a Pedro regalar *se los* dulces a los niños. *a ellos* *a él*

4. *Translate the pronouns in parentheses and add the graphic accent where necessary:*

1. Van a vender (*it to me*). *me lo*
2. Vengo a dar (*them to them*). *se los*
3. Les gusta cantar (*it to you*). *se lo*
4. Están diciendo (*it to us*). *nos lo*
5. Se lo llevó con (*him*). *sigo*
6. ¿Quiere Vd. hablar con (*me*)? *migo*

---

[1] Conjugated like **venir: convenir** *to be proper, be well.*

A NEW
SHORTER
SPANISH
REVIEW
GRAMMAR

GRAMMAR
EXERCISES

7. Diga *(it to her)* (a ella)
8. Presente *(her to me)*.

9. Haga *(it for me)* en seguida.
10. Escriba *(it to him)*.

5. *Translate:* DO!

(a)

1. It seemed to Don José that he was angry with him.
2. He had not written to him since he arrived.
3. The city was small and there was little life in it.
4. After having *(inf.)* seen it, it no longer had any interest for him.
5. When he returned home he began to *(a)* think about him.
6. For this reason he invited him to *(a)* come to *(a)* visit him.
7. He doesn't know it yet but later his friends will tell him.
8. Have you learned everything already?
9. He regretted to have to tell Don José such things.
10. His sister had spoken of it to him.

(b)

1. When Don José arrived home, the servant *(f.)* took off his shoes.
2. I am going to write him a letter to *(para)* invite him to *(a)* come.
3. This boy, it seems to me, must be angry with me.
4. He was thinking about him when the servant entered with a letter in her hand.
5. It was a long letter from him.
6. In it he told *(contar)* many things about Segovia.
7. I seldom speak to them; they do not interest me.
8. I would like to see you in order to ask you several questions.
9. Is life here very different?—Yes, it is.
10. It will be necessary for me to learn more.

F. EXERCISES ON IDIOMS AND PHRASES

1. *Translate the words underlined:*
1. It was warm aquel día.
2. Llegó ago dos semanas.
3. I remember you often y me gustaría pay you a visit.
4. At least conozco a most of mis compañeros.
5. Voy a escribirle right now.
6. I think que salió de aquí in a hurry.
7. La ciudad no longer tiene interés para mí.

Es decir

8. That is to say, la vida en Segovia tiene pocos atractivos.

Por ahora

9. For the present mi única distracción es to take walks. *estar paseos*

La mayoría de

10. Most of los días Pedro thought about sus padres. *pensó en*

CHAPTER
FOUR

EXERCISES
ON
IDIOMS
AND
PHRASES

2. *Fill in the blanks with the proper form of* **deber, estar, haber, hacer, ser,** *or* **tener:**

1. Este café *está* caliente.
2. Ellos *tienen* mucha sed hoy.
3. Vd. no *debe* descansar tanto (*moral obligation*).
4. *Hace* seis años que le conocemos.
5. Él *tiene* que comer carne.
6. Hoy *hace* mal tiempo.
7. Ellas *deben* de presentarse esta noche (*futurity*).
8. ¡Cuánto tiempo *hace* que no le veo!
9. *Haya* que dormir la siesta de vez en cuando (*impersonal*).
10. Ella *es* muy contenta con el resultado de los exámenes.
11. El pobre *ha sido* ciego desde su nacimiento.
12. En el otoño no *hace* calor (*weather*).
13. Él *ha había* de llegar ayer.
14. La nieve *es* fría.
15. Vds. *deben* (*ought*) escribir a sus mamás.

The "Fiesta de toros"
IN
SPAIN

CHAPTER FIVE

A. GRAMMAR AND IDIOM PRACTICE

El profesor se puso* triste al leer la carta de Pedro. El muchacho no estaba contento y hasta cierto punto él era responsable. Trató de* olvidar el asunto pero no pudo. Una y otra vez* se preguntaba, mientras fumaba un cigarrillo:

— ¿Por qué no le gusta la vida en Segovia? ¿Quiénes eran aquellos compañeros sin ningún interés para él? ¿Por qué no decía nada de las clases que 5 tenía y de los profesores que le enseñaban?

Dejó pasar varios días y **por fin** escribió a Pedro. En la carta le decía que el 15 de julio pensaba pasar por Segovia. También le indicaba la hora de llegada del tren y le invitaba a venir a Madrid, si podía o quería hacer el viaje. Pedro no fué a Madrid, pero el día señalado estaba esperando al profesor en 10 la estación de Segovia. En el camino al hotel contó a don José que acababa de regresar de un viaje a Navarra. El profesor, sorprendido, le preguntó:

— ¿Por qué fué Vd. a Navarra? ¿No **tenía** nada **que** hacer aquí? ¿Cuánto tiempo* duró la excursión?

— Duró cosa de* una semana. Estaba tan aburrido aquí que decidí ir a ver 15 las fiestas de San Fermín, en Pamplona. Hace tiempo leí en una novela de Hemingway que durante la segunda semana de julio se celebra el encierro de reses bravas y se sueltan toros por las calles durante las primeras horas de la mañana. Como es natural sentía curiosidad por observar la habilidad de los jóvenes (toreros improvisados de un día) delante de* un toro y a la vista de 20 las muchachas que presencian el espectáculo desde los balcones de sus casas.

De repente Pedro soltó una carcajada* y dijo:

— Me río de* algo que me contaron. Parece que uno de los toros se separó de los demás y entró en un café donde sólo había dos personas: el dependiente y un parroquiano. El primero se escondió detrás del* mostrador al ver al 25 animal, pero el pobre hombre, que estaba sentado a una mesa, **empezó a** temblar y no sabía qué hacer. Se puso de pie* automáticamente y, muerto de **55**

to death

miedo, no se movió del lugar. El toro le miró un rato y después volvió a la
calle donde le esperaban los muchachos con sus capas. *waited for him* *capes.*

— Sí, un nuevo Don Tancredo — dijo el profesor sonriendo. — Si no fué *smiling*
✱ atacado por el toro se debe sin duda a que la bestia creyó que era una estatua. *attacked* *beast* *statue.*

5 Ahora ya lo sabe Vd. Si **de pronto, algún día, se encuentra con** un toro *all of a sudden* *you come upon*
en los caminos de España y quiere salvar la vida, no se mueva. *streets* *to save* *do not move.*

✱ En el hotel el profesor se lavó la cara, cambió de* camisa y de corbata y *changed his* *shirt* *necktie*
dijo: *I am inviting him to eat*

— Le invito a cenar conmigo. Son las nueve y media de la noche y no he
10 comido nada desde la una.

— Yo ya comí, pero como en este país siempre tengo hambre acepto su *always*
invitación. Además, me quedan* muchas cosas que preguntarle. *Besides, I have many things to ask you.*

B. IDIOMS AND PHRASES

se puso (triste) *he became* (sad)
trató de (olvidar) *he tried to* (forget)
una y otra vez *again and again*
por fin *finally*
¿(no) **tenía** (nada) **que** (hacer)? *did
    you* (not) *have* (anything) *to* (do)?
¿cuánto tiempo? *how long?*
cosa de (una semana) *about* (a week)
delante de *in front of*
de repente *suddenly*
soltó una carcajada *he burst out
    laughing*
me río de (algo) *I am laughing at*
    (something)

detrás de *behind*
empezó a (temblar) *he began to*
    (tremble)
se puso de pie *he stood up*
de pronto *all of a sudden*
se encuentra con (un toro) *you
    come upon* (a bull)
cambió de (camisa) *he changed*
    (his shirt)
me quedan (muchas cosas) **que**
    (preguntarle) *I have* (many
    things) *left to* (ask you)

C. GRAMMAR REVIEW

22. Uses of the Imperfect (Past Descriptive) Tense.

The activity or state observed by this tense is actually "imperfect," that is,
unfinished or of *indefinite* duration. The imperfect tense gives no indication as
to when the action or state *began* or *ended*.[1] Its principal uses therefore are:

---

[1] Only three verbs are irregular in the imperfect indicative: **ser: era, eras, era, éramos, erais, eran;
ir: iba, ibas, iba, íbamos, ibais, iban; ver: veía, veías, veía, veíamos, veíais, veían**

(1) To denote what was *customary, habitual,* or *repeated* in the past, usually translating the English *used to, was accustomed to,* and on occasions *would,* followed by an infinitive.

Vivía en la Calle Quince.   He *used to live* on 15th Street.
Siempre me **saludaba** cuando me **veía**.   He always *greeted (was accustomed to, would, greet)* me when he *saw* me.

(2) To describe actions and states *in progress* when something else *was happening*. (Both verbs are in the imperfect tense; the translation here is *was* + *-ing* or *were* + *-ing*.)

Él fumaba mientras yo **hablaba**.   He *was smoking* while *I was talking*.
Yo **leía** mientras **llovía**.   I *was reading* while *it was raining*.

(3) To describe an action which was *in progress* when another action *took place* (preterit). (Again the English translation is usually *was* + *-ing* or *were* + *-ing*.)

Nevaba cuando entré.   *It was snowing* when I came in.
Escribía cuando se abrió la puerta.   *He was writing* when the door opened.

(4) To give the time of day in the past.
Eran las seis cuando llegaron.   It *was* six when they arrived.

(5) To express mental action or state of indefinite duration in the past with verbs as **creer, desear, esperar, querer,** and **saber.**

No **quería** venir conmigo.   He *did* not *want* to come with me.
Ella no lo **sabía**.   She *did* not *know* (it).

(6) To describe the background of an action.
Era una hermosa mañana de primavera.   It *was* a beautiful spring morning.

23. Uses of the Preterit (Narrative Past) Tense.

Many actions (and states) in the past are single, instantaneous, fully completed, or definitely ended, regardless of duration. These are expressed by the preterit tense. No emphasis is placed on their continuance but simply on the fact that they took place or existed. Repeated actions, when considered as an undivided unit, are represented by the preterit. Similarly, the preterit tense

A NEW
SHORTER
SPANISH
REVIEW
GRAMMAR

GRAMMAR
REVIEW

regularly appears with **nunca.**[1] It corresponds usually to the English simple past, *I spoke,* and to the emphatic past tense, *I did speak.*[2]

El tren **llegó** a las siete.	The train *arrived* at seven o'clock.
Vino[3] a mi casa todos los días.	He *came* to my house every day.
Las vacaciones **duraron** tres meses.	The vacation *lasted* three months.
¿**Escribió** Vd. la lección de ayer?	*Did* you *write* yesterday's lesson?
Nunca **estuve** enfermo en la Habana.	I *was* never ill in Havana.

24. Differences in the Values of the Imperfect and Preterit Tenses.

Care must be taken to differentiate between the uses of these two tenses. Every action or state has a beginning, a middle, and an end. The imperfect portrays only the middle phase, describing what was going on or existing in the past, and gives no indication that the action or state ever began or ended. The preterit, on the other hand, reports that the action or state, regardless of its duration, definitely began or definitely ended. Not only does the preterit record a single act or state in the past (regardless of its duration) but it may portray a series of acts or a prolonged state, so long as these are considered to be one single act and to have definitely ended.

IMPERFECT	PRETERIT
Leía la Biblia todas las noches.	**Leyó** la Biblia varias veces.
He *read* the Bible every night.	He *read* the Bible several times.
Me **visitaba** con frecuencia.	Me **visitó** varias veces.
He *visited* me frequently.	He *visited* me several times.
Vivía allí cuando le conocí.	**Vivió** allí toda su vida.
He *lived* there when I met him.	He *lived* there all his life.
Estaba en España el año pasado.	**Estuve** en España el año pasado.
I *was* in Spain last year.	I *was* in Spain last year.

---

[1] The preterit of **deber, poder, querer, ser,** and **haber** (impersonal) is regularly used when the accompanying verb is in the preterit.

[2] A few verbs may have a different meaning in the preterit: **supe** I *learned, found out;* **conocí** I *met;* **tuve** I *received;* **fuí** I *became, had been:* Lo **supe** anoche. I *found* it *out* last night. La **conocí** en Madrid. I *met* her in Madrid. **Tuvo** un cero. He *received* a zero. La señorita **fué** su maestra. The young lady *became* (or *had been*) his teacher.

[3] **Venía,** also correct, would stress the fact that the action was repeated or customary.

Carlos III **era** rey de España.
  Charles III *was* king of Spain.
Era un buen rey.
  He *was* a good king.

↑

Note that the action or state continued over an indefinite period of time with no indication that it ever ended.

Carlos III **fué** rey de España.
  Charles III *was* king of Spain.
Fué rey por 25 años.
  He *was* king for 25 years.

↑

Note the assumption that the action or state has definitely ended.

25. Negation.

(1) A verb is made negative by placing **no** before it. Only an object personal pronoun may stand between **no** and the verb.

No escribe cartas.
No se lo pregunté.

He does *not* write letters.
I did *not* ask him.

(2) In addition to **no,** there are other negative expressions.

nada *nothing, not . . . anything*
nadie *nobody, no one, not . . . anyone*
ninguno *no one, none*
ni *not, not . . . or*

ni . . . ni . . . *neither . . . nor*
nunca, jamás *never, not . . . ever*
tampoco *not . . . either*

When any of these terms follows the verb, **no** is required before it.

No llega **nunca** a tiempo.
Ella **no** canta **tampoco.**

He *never* arrives on time.
She does *not* sing *either.*

When they precede the verb, **no** is not required.

Ninguno habla. *No one* is speaking.
Nadie canta. *Nobody* is singing.

Tampoco lee. He does *not* read *either.*
Nunca corre. He *never* runs.

(3) When the verb is not expressed, **no** generally follows the word it accompanies.

¿Lo ha leído Vd.?—Todavía **no.**

Have you read it?—*Not* yet.

(4) *Anyone, ever, someone, something* are translated by their corresponding negatives after (*a*) comparatives and (*b*) **sin** *without.*

(a) mejor que **nunca**
   más alto que **nadie**
(b) sin decir **nada** a **nadie**

better than *ever*
taller than *anyone*
without saying *anything* to *anyone*

59

A NEW
SHORTER
SPANISH
REVIEW
GRAMMAR

GRAMMAR
REVIEW

26. The Passive Voice.

When the subject receives the action of the verb, the action or voice is said to be passive. The passive voice is formed in Spanish with **ser** and the past participle of the principal verb, which agrees in gender and number with the subject. It is used mainly when the subject is a person and when the agent is expressed or clearly implied; *it always denotes action.* When the subject is a thing and when no agent is expressed, the reflexive is more usual as a substitute for the passive. (See §29.7a.) The agent is regularly expressed by **por**; with mental actions and states, and with **acompañar** *to accompany*, **rodear** *to surround*, and **seguir** *to follow*, **de** is usual.

La frase **fué escrita** por el alumno. (*action*)	The sentence *was written* by the student.
Cf. La frase ya **está escrita.** (*state*)	The sentence *is written* now. no agent
Ella **es amada de** todos.	She *is loved by* all.

D. VERB REVIEW

Poder *to be able, can, could; be possible, may, might;* **poner**[1] *to put, place, set;* **ponerse** *to become;*[2] *to put on; set.*

No **podía** hacerlo.	He *couldn't* (wasn't able to) do it.
No **pudo** hacerlo.	He *couldn't* (tried but failed to) do it.
No **puedo menos de** mirarla.	I *can't help* looking at her.
Se pone triste.	She *becomes* sad.
Se pone los guantes.	He *puts on* his gloves.
Se pone el sol.	The sun *sets.*
Se pone a saltar.	He *begins to* jump.

E. GRAMMAR EXERCISES

1. *Translate:*

   1. He can. *Puede*
   2. You will be able. *usted podrá*
   3. They used to be able. *Ellos podían*
   4. We could. *podríamos*
   5. Being able. *podiendo*
   6. Put it there! *¡póngalo usted allí!*
   7. I place. *yo pongo*
   8. He should put. *el podría*
   9. (That) I might place. *que yo pusiera*
   10. You have put. *usted ha puesto*

[1] Conjugated like **poner: componer** *to compose,* **disponer** *to arrange,* **exponer** *to express,* **imponer** *to impose,* **oponer** *to oppose,* **proponer** *to propose,* **suponer** *to suppose.*

[2] **Ponerse** with an adjective usually means *to become* when there is an (involuntary) change in physical, mental, or emotional states.

2. *Identify and translate:*

1. vayan *ir*
2. uniéramos *unir*
3. señalaron *señar*
4. significará *significar*
5. satisfaré *satisfacer*
6. puesto *poner*
7. tuvieran *tener*
8. íbamos *ir*
9. quiso *querer*
10. hayamos *haber*
11. haría *hacer*
12. dijésemos *decir*
13. él vino ~~vino~~ *venir*
14. pondrá *poner*
15. puedo *poder*
16. venga *venir*
17. dije *decir*
18. tuvo *tener*
19. hay *haber*
20. estuvo *estar*
21. supieron *saber*
22. puse *poner*
23. habrá luna *haber*
24. fuesen *ir or ser*
25. sea la luz *ser*
26. pusimos *poner*
27. vendrán *venir*
28. pude *poder*
29. fué *ir or ser*
30. supe *saber*

CHAPTER
FIVE

GRAMMAR
EXERCISES

3. *Give the imperfect or preterit of the verbs in italics as required by usage:*

1. Él (*fumar*) cuando yo (*entrar*).
2. (*Ser*) las ocho en punto cuando ellos (*llegar*).
3. Ella (*venir*) a mi casa todos los días.
4. Yo (*comprar*) una corbata que no me (*gustar*).
5. Los (*conocer*) en Segovia hace tiempo.
6. ¿Qué (*hacer*) Vd. mientras yo (*estudiar*)?
7. El vapor (*llegar*) a Nueva York en diciembre.
8. Ayer (*llover*).
9. La lucha (*durar*) sólo diez minutos.
10. Yo no lo (*saber*).
11. Pedro (*estudiar*) alemán cinco años.
12. Ellos no (*saber*) quiénes (*ser*) nosotros.
13. Lo (*saber*) ayer tarde.
14. Me (*ver*) cuando (*visitar*) a los vecinos.
15. Ella (*declarar*) que yo la (*engañar*).
16. ¿Dónde (*nacer*) Vd.?
17. (*Haber*) mucha gente en el autobús.

la is only a direct obj. not a direct obj.

4. *Translate:*

(*a*)

1. He used to write home often.
2. One day he was reading a letter when someone entered.
3. Pedro told her that he was surprised by (**de**) her visit.
4. He tried to (**de**) forget her but he could not.
5. It was five o'clock and the sun was setting already.

61

A NEW
SHORTER
SPANISH
REVIEW
GRAMMAR

GRAMMAR
EXERCISES

6. Without saying (*inf.*) anything to her he went out. *salió.*
7. No one wanted to accompany her without being (*inf.*) invited. *Nadie*
8. But in Pamplona he was invited by many people to a dance. *a un baile.*
✱ 9. He wasn't left alone a single instant. *no le dejaban solo ni siquiera un instante.*
10. The trip lasted about eight days. *duró cosa de ocho días.*

(*b*) *Mientras* *cigarillo* *en él.*
1. While he was smoking a cigarette, he thought about him.
2. Evidently Pedro was not happy in that place. *Por lo visto* *contento*
3. Why didn't he like the city? *gustaba*
4. Why didn't he mention the subjects that he was studying? *mencionó*
✱ 5. He informed him in a letter that he expected to see him very soon. *informó* *pensaba* *pronto.*
6. His trip to Pamplona lasted a week.
7. He went there because he was bored in Segovia. *aburrido*
8. They told him that a bull entered a café. *dijeron* *en un café.*
9. One of the men disappeared, the other didn't know what (**qué**) to do. *no sabía*
10. If he was not attacked, it was because the bull was afraid of him. *Si no fue atacado* *miedo*

F. EXERCISE ON IDIOMS AND PHRASES

Translate the words underlined:

1. He came upon un amigo en la calle y became muy contento. *se puso*
2. Suddenly él began to reír. *De repente* *empezó*
3. El amigo también burst out laughing. *soltó una carcajada.*
4. How long duró su viaje? *¿Cuánto tiempo*
5. About tres horas. I had nada to do allí y di la vuelta. *cosa de* *Tenía* *hacer*
6. En el hotel Pedro changed ropa. *cambió de*
7. Después he stood up in front of un espejo y tried to afeitarse. *Se puso de pie delante de* *y trató de*
8. Finally se sentó y began to escribir. *Por fin* *empezó a* *hacerle.*
9. I have todavía muchas cosas left to do. *me quedan* *que hacerle.*
10. All of a sudden oyó un ruido behind él. *De pronto* *detrás de*

CHAPTER SIX

A. GRAMMAR AND IDIOM PRACTICE

Bajaron al comedor del hotel y se sentaron a una mesa. Al poco rato* se acercó el camarero y el profesor preguntó a Pedro si le gustaba el gazpacho y si se atrevía a beber vino con la comida.

— **A veces** las comidas españolas no me sientan bien* — contestó — pero estoy dispuesto a probarlas todas. En cuanto a* vinos me gusta el Valdepeñas 5 que, según dicen, "es bueno de entrar y malo de salir."

Don José se sonrió al oír tales palabras en boca de un muchacho que en los Estados Unidos no estaba acostumbrado a beber vino. Después le explicó que gazpacho era una especie de sopa de verduras, muy refrescante y muy sana. Para estar bien hecho debe contener migas de pan, aceite, tomate, un 10 poco de ajo y agua. Luego añadió:

— No sé si le gustará. Pero si no le gusta no importa,* me lo tomaré yo. Y ahora, como tardarán bastante en* servirnos — continuó don José — puede empezar a contarme sus impresiones de esta ciudad. Me marcho mañana y no nos queda mucho tiempo para hablar. 15

— Segovia es una ciudad muy antigua, y Vd. ya sabe que todo lo viejo y legendario me interesa mucho. Ahí tiene Vd., **por ejemplo,** ese magnífico acueducto romano, de más de un kilómetro de largo.* Pues bien,* ¿sabe Vd. por qué le llama la gente "Puente del Diablo"? (*El profesor no contestó y Pedro continuó.*) Le llaman así porque se cree que sólo el Diablo pudo construirlo. 20 Se cuenta que una joven segoviana muy bella bajaba **todos los días** al río a buscar agua y estaba muy cansada. Hasta que un día se le apareció el Diablo y le dijo que si se casaba con* él sería capaz de hacer un milagro. Ella, en broma* y para librarse de él, le prometió su mano si lograba traer agua a su casa. Se separaron, y aquella noche el Diablo reunió a una multitud de diablillos 25 que trabajaron sin parar un momento. **Al día siguiente** ya estaba terminado el acueducto y el Diablo se presentó a la joven para exigirle el cumplimiento de su promesa. Cuando la muchacha vió de nuevo al "Enemigo" se desmayó. **63**

Pero al volver en sí* se le ocurrió hacer la señal de la cruz y el "Espíritu del Mal" huyó **para siempre** de esta tierra.

Iba a decir algo el profesor, pero se calló al ver llegar al mozo con la comida. Pedro se comió el gazpacho y los demás platos. También se bebió dos
5 vasos de vino y se sentía bastante contento.

— **¿A ver** qué hora tiene Vd.? — preguntó don José. — Se me olvidó el reloj arriba, en el cuarto.

— Son casi las once — dijo Pedro. — Hora de acostarse, pues estará Vd. muy cansado del viaje.

10 — ¡No, hombre! En España no se acuesta uno tan temprano. Vamos a **dar una vuelta** por la ciudad.

— Acuérdese de que esto no es Madrid — explicó Pedro. — A estas horas* ya no hay gente por las calles. **De noche** ésta es una ciudad casi muerta. Yo debiera acostarme, pero si Vd. quiere dar un paseo, **vamos.**

B. IDIOMS AND PHRASES

al poco rato *shortly afterwards*
a veces *at times*
(las comidas no) **me sientan bien** (the meals don't) *agree with me*
en cuanto a (vinos) *as for* (wines)
no importa *it doesn't matter*
tardarán en (servirnos) *they will be long in* (serving us)
por ejemplo *for example*
(un kilómetro) **de largo** (a kilometer) *long*
pues bien *well then, well*

todos los (días) *every* (day)
se casaba con (él) *she would marry* (him)
en broma *as a joke, jokingly*
al día siguiente *on the following day*
volver en sí *to come to*
para siempre *forever*
a ver *let's see*
dar una vuelta *to take a stroll*
a estas horas *at this* (late) *hour*
de noche *at night*
vamos *let's go, come on*

C. GRAMMAR REVIEW

27. Reflexive Verbs.

A verb is called reflexive when the action is directed back, reflected, upon the subject. The subject and the object are the same person or thing, thus, **me**
64 **levanto** *I rise, I get up,* literally means *I raise myself.* Since almost any verb

SPAIN

get married ~~with~~ someone
con

in Spanish can be made reflexive, the reflexive construction is much commoner in Spanish than in English.

TRANSITIVE	REFLEXIVE
Miro **al niño.** I look at *the child.*	**Me** miro en el espejo. I look at *myself* in the mirror.
Invitó **a María.** He invited *Mary.*	**Se** invitó. He invited *himself.*

28. Reflexive Pronouns.

	SINGULAR			PLURAL	
Unstressed		*Stressed*	*Unstressed*		*Stressed*
me	*myself*	**mí**	**nos**	*ourselves*	**nosotros, -as**
te	*yourself*	**ti**	**os**	*yourselves*	**vosotros, -as**
se	*yourself, himself* *herself, itself*	**sí**	**se**	*yourselves* *themselves*	**sí**

Like other object pronouns, the unstressed forms are used as objects of verbs, and the stressed forms as objects of prepositions.

Me lavo. I wash (myself).   **Se** baña. He bathes (himself).

The plural forms, **nos, os,** and **se,** may have reciprocal force.

Nos entendemos bien (uno a otro). We understand *each other* well.

29. Types and Uses of Reflexive Verbs.

(1) Many verbs are reflexive in Spanish and not in English. Common verbs of this type are **apresurarse** *to hurry,* **atreverse** *to dare,* and **quejarse** *to complain.*

No **me atrevo** a decir nada.   I don't *dare* say anything.
Nunca **se queja** de sus notas.   He never *complains* of his grades.

(2) Some verbs in Spanish when used reflexively assume a different meaning. Frequent verbs of this type are **acostar** *to put to bed,* **acostarse** *to go to bed, lie down;* **casar** *to marry* (off), **casarse** *to get married, marry;* **encontrar** *to find,* **encontrarse** *to be* (by effort); **hacer** *to do, make,* **hacerse** *to become;* **poner** *to put, place,* **ponerse** *to become* (involuntary); **sentar** *to seat,* **sentarse** *to sit down.*

66

reír – to laugh

TRANSITIVE	REFLEXIVE
Acostó al niño. *He put the child to bed.*	**Se acostó** con el niño. *He went to bed with the child.*
Casó a la criada con el chófer. *He married the servant to the chauffeur.*	**Se casó con** la criada. *He married the servant.*
Le **sentó** en la silla. *He seated him in the chair.*	**Se sentó** en la silla. *He sat down in the chair.*

(3) The reflexive pronoun is used with many intransitive verbs to indicate interest or concern, on the part of the subject, in the action or state. Common verbs of this type are **irse, marcharse** *to go away,* **quedarse** *to stay,* **reírse** *to laugh.*

Se va en seguida.	He is going away immediately.
Me marcho mañana.	I am leaving tomorrow.
Nos reímos de él.	We laughed at him.

(4) Similarly, with verbs that are originally transitive, the various states of (*a*) interest, concern, (*b*) separation, and (*c*) possession (Cf. §19) are naturally expressed by the reflexive pronoun when the subject of the verb is involved in the action or state. Often this construction contains in English the adverbs *up, off, on,* etc., and in other cases it may convey subtle shades of meaning impossible of direct translation.

(*a*) **Se** bebió todo el chocolate.	He drank (*up*) all the chocolate.
(*b*) (*c*) **Me** quito la chaqueta.	{ I take *off my* coat. { (I take the coat *off* me.)
(*c*) **Me** pongo el sombrero.	I put *on my* hat.

(5) Some reflexive verbs are used idiomatically or impersonally, that is, the English subject becomes the Spanish indirect object, and the English object becomes the Spanish subject.

Se me olvida el libro.	{ *I forget* the book. { (The book forgets itself to me.)
No **se le ocurre** nada.	{ *He thinks of* nothing. { (Nothing occurs itself to him.)
Cf. **Me** gusta el libro.	*I like* the book.

(6) The reflexive **se** with the third person singular of the verb regularly expresses an indefinite subject, equivalent to English *one, we, they, people, somebody, you* (indefinite), etc. **Uno** is also used as an indefinite subject; see §30.

Se trabaja mucho aquí.	*We work* very much here.
No se duerme bien de día.	*You don't sleep* well in the daytime.
Se come bien allí.	*People eat* well there. (Good meals are served there.)

(7) (*a*) The reflexive construction serves very frequently as a substitute for the passive voice, especially when the subject is a *thing* and no agent is expressed. The verb is in the singular or plural according to the number of the subject, which often follows the verb.

Aquí **se vende** "La Gaceta."	"The Gazette" *is sold* here.
Aquí **se venden** periódicos.	Newspapers *are sold* here.

(*b*) The reflexive construction in the third person singular may also serve as an equivalent of the passive voice when the subject in English is a *person*. The English *subject* becomes the *direct object* in Spanish and is usually preceded by the preposition **a** (§14). **Le** and **les** are the pronouns regularly used in the third person.

Se invitó a Tomás.	Thomas *was invited.*
Se le invitó (a él).	He *was invited.*
Se nos estima.	We *are esteemed.*

30. Other Methods of Expressing an Indefinite Subject.

As in English, an indefinite subject may be expressed in Spanish (*a*) by **uno** *one* and (*b*) by the third person plural. The latter construction is used very frequently as a substitute for the passive voice when the passive subject is a living being.

(*a*) ¿Qué puede hacer **uno?** (¿Qué **se** puede hacer?)	What can *one* do?
Uno no debe asustarse tanto.	*One* should not get so scared.
(*b*) **Mataron** al ladrón.	The robber *was killed.* They *killed* the robber.
Eso es lo que me **dicen.**	That is what *they* tell me.
(Eso es lo que **se me dice.**)	(That is what *I am told.*)

Since in many cases the passive voice construction involves an indefinite, unnamed agent, it can be seen in review that the following constructions are more or less equivalent to each other.

El profesor **fué invitado** a un baile. ⎤
Se invitó al profesor a un baile. ⎟
Se le invitó (al profesor) a un baile. ⎬ The professor *was invited* to a dance.
Invitaron al profesor a un baile. ⎦

D. VERB REVIEW

Spelling-Changing Verbs. Class I. buscar *to look for, hunt for; get;* **pagar** *to pay, pay for;* **alcanzar** *to reach, attain.*

Busqué a mi hermano.	*I looked for* my brother.
Pague Vd. la comida, por favor.	*Pay for* the dinner, please.
Pagué cinco pesetas **por**[1] el regalo.	*I paid* five pesetas *for* the present.
Alcancé mi deseo.	*I attained* my desire.

Other common verbs of **Class I** are: *ar – 1st sing. pret. changes* / *er + ir – 1st sing. indicative changes*

acercarse (a) *to approach*	**llegar (a)** *to arrive, get to*
colocar *to put, place*	**negar (ie)** *to deny*
explicar *to explain*	**obligar (a)** *to oblige, force*
indicar *to indicate, show*	**pegar** *to stick; fasten; beat*
sacar *to take out; get*	**rogar (ue)** *to ask, request*
tocar *to touch, play* (an instrument)	**comenzar (ie) (a)** *to commence*
entregar *to deliver, hand over*	**cruzar** *to cross*
jugar (ue) *to play* (a game)	**empezar (ie) (a)** *to begin*
juzgar *to judge*	**gozar (de)** *to enjoy*

E. GRAMMAR REVIEW

1. *Insert the proper letters to form the preterit or present subjunctive and translate:*

   1. (acercar) Me acer__é al teatro.
   2. (buscar) Busquémoslo.
   3. (explicar) Explícamelo.
   4. (sacar) Saqué el pañuelo del bolsillo.
   5. (tocar) Toque el violín, por favor.

---

[1] **Por** translates *for* with **pagar** when the amount (or **¿cuánto?**) is indicated.

A NEW
SHORTER
SPANISH
REVIEW
GRAMMAR

GRAMMAR
REVIEW

6. (entregar) Entré*ga*me el billete.
7. (jugar) Ju*gu*é tres partidas.
8. (juzgar) No me juz*gu*e mal.
9. (llegar) Lle*gu*emos a tiempo.
10. (pegar) No pe*gu*e al animal.
11. (obligar) Le obli*gu*é a asistir.
12. (comenzar) Comen__é a reñir.
13. (empezar) Empié*c*elo ahora mismo.
14. (gozar) Go*c*é de la vida.

Él se iba lejos (imp.)
" se fué " (pret.)
se irá " (fut.)
se iría " (cond.)
se ha ido " (pres. perf.)
se había ido " (pluperfect)

2. *Give a synopsis of* **Él se va lejos** *in the other tenses of the indicative.*

se habrá ido " (fut. perf.)
se habría ido " (cond. perf.)

3. *Give the proper form of the verb in parentheses:*
1. Ellos siempre (*apresurarse*) a contestar a las preguntas. *apresura*
2. Ellas nunca (*atreverse*) a pasear de noche. *atreve*
3. Nuestros amigos (*casarse*) el próximo mes. *se casarán*
4. Ella (*hacerse*) un vestido de lana. *se hace*
5. Ellas (*llamarse*) María y Luisa. *se llaman*
6. Ellos (*ponerse*) a cantar anoche a las diez. *se pusieron*
7. Él (*ponerse*) los zapatos y (*irse*). *puso* *se fué*
8. Él (*quedarse*) dormido en el cine. *se quedó*
9. Ella siempre (*quejarse*) de su mala suerte. *se queja*

4. *Write the following sentences in three ways, as in the model:*

He was killed: **fué matado, le mataron, se le mató:**
1. They were invited. *fueron invitados, los invitaron, se les invitó.*
2. She was called. *fué llamada, le llamaron, se le llamó.*
3. He was respected. *fué respetado, le respetaron, se le respetó.*
4. We are hated. *fueron odiados nos odiamos, se los odió*
5. You are admired. *usted fué admirado, le admiran, se le admiró.*
6. I was received. *Era recibido, me recibieron, se recibió.*
7. He was nominated. *Era nombrado, le nombraron, se le nombró.*

5. *Translate:*

(a)
1. The bed in the hotel was hard but he didn't complain. *dura* *no se quejó.*
2. They say that in Spain wine is drunk with (the) meals. *Se bebe vino*
3. It appears that young people seldom go to bed early.
4. One sleeps better at night if one works in the daytime. *Se duerme* *de noche* *de día.*
5. They sat close to the window. *ventana.*
6. It occurred to her to shut the door. *cerrar la puerta*
7. The young lady and the gentleman looked at each other for a long time. *se miraron uno a otra mucho tiempo.*

8. According to him, she was greatly (**muy**) admired.
9. She was told that they would miss her.
10. We forgot to say that they married the following year.

(b)

con él

1. Don José sat down with him at a small table.
2. Don't you like the gazpacho? They serve good meals (one eats well) here.
3. Do you dare to drink a bottle of wine with me?
4. Pedro did not eat (up) all the gazpacho, but drank (up) almost all the wine. *se bebió*
5. What time is it? I forgot to bring my watch. *traer*
6. When one is tired, he should go to bed.
7. People believe that the aqueduct was built by the devil.
8. It is said that it was built in one night.
9. Did you know that we are not allowed to smoke in the Residencia?
10. I was invited yesterday but I could not go. *ayer*

F. EXERCISE ON IDIOMS AND PHRASES

1. *Translate the words underlined:*

A veces *no me sientan bien.*
1. At times las comidas don't agree with me.
a ver *a estas horas.*
2. Let's see si es posible comer at this late hour.
no importa *en broma.*
3. Si no le gusta it doesn't matter; me la comeré yo—dijo jokingly.
Todas las noches
4. Every night doy un paseo antes de cenar.
de *largo.*
5. El acueducto tiene about un kilómetro long.
Tardarán en *de noche*
6. They will be long in servirnos; at night hay mucha gente aquí.
Pues, al poco rato
7. Well, shortly afterwards apareció el camarero.
volvió en sí *no se casar*
8. Ella came to y decidió not to marry él.
Al día siguiente
9. On the following day desapareció.
dar un paseo, vamos.
10. Si Vd. quiere take a stroll, let's go.

2. *Translate:*

Most of the time I go for a walk alone. *He is older than we.* *I also*
La mayoría de las veces pasea solo. Tiene más edad que nosotros. Todavía
love to ask him many questions. *As for myself, I don't like to write letters.*
tengo que hacerle muchas preguntas. A mí no me gusta escribir cartas. El
The waiter approached the table. *I forgot my watch.* *I left it with the*
camarero se acercó a la mesa. Se me olvidó el reloj. Se separó de los
rest. *He did not dare drink wine.* *Yes, I*
demás. No se atrevió a beber vino. No nos queda mucho tiempo. Sí, me
am waiting for a friend. *I have just finished returning from a trip.* *He looked at me for a*
espera un amigo. Acababa de regresar de un viaje. Me miró durante un
short time. *It is 9.00 at night.* *I arrived at my house, very tired.* *He went to*
rato. Son las nueve de la noche. Llegó a mi casa muy cansado. Iba a decir
Say something but he kept still.
algo pero se calló.

71

SPAIN

Guy Georget

CHAPTER SEVEN

A. GRAMMAR AND IDIOM PRACTICE

Era una noche muy clara. Desde un lugar alto se podía distinguir **a lo lejos** la extensa llanura castellana bañada por la luz de la luna. Después de tomar un refresco en un café céntrico volvieron a casa y **por último** se despidieron en frente del hotel. Antes de* dirigirse al* antiguo palacio donde vivían los estudiantes extranjeros, Pedro dijo: 5

— Como Vd. no se marcha hasta por la tarde,* le invito a comer conmigo en el comedor de la Residencia. Así conocerá a algunos de mis compañeros.

— Acepto con mucho gusto* — exclamó don José. — Por la mañana, mientras Vd. está en sus clases, puedo pasear y **a la vez** sacar algunas fotografías* del incomparable alcázar, del acueducto romano y de las magníficas 10 iglesias que hay aquí. No se preocupe por mí.* Conozco la ciudad y no me perderé. **A las** doce y media en punto* estaré en su "palacio."

Don José llegó a* la Residencia un poco después de las doce y Pedro, que le esperaba, le llevó a su cuarto. Era un cuarto **más bien** pequeño, pero con mucha luz y bien ventilado. Desde el balcón se veía la plaza del mercado y la 15 alta torre de una de las iglesias.

— Querían poner a otro estudiante en esta habitación conmigo, pero se convencieron de que no era posible. No hay más que un armario y ya ve Vd. que está lleno con la poca ropa que he traído.

— ¡Es lástima! — dijo el profesor. — Con un compañero de cuarto tendría 20 más oportunidad de hablar español. ¿No se siente muy solo aquí?

— **Al contrario,** estoy más contento **de** esta **manera.** El estudiante que querían poner aquí es un francés que pronuncia el español peor que yo. Además voy a confesarle toda la verdad, señor profesor, y **es que** nunca podré decir como Carlos V que el español "es la lengua para hablar con Dios." No 25 lo podré decir porque nunca aprenderé esta lengua. Ahora vamos a comer; ya ha sonado la campanilla.

73

Las declaraciones de Pedro causaron gran sorpresa a don José. En el comedor se sentaron solos a una mesa y hablaron inglés mientras comían. En otras mesas habría unos veinticinco o treinta estudiantes, cada cual hablando la lengua de su preferencia. La comida no era mala, aunque tampoco era muy
5 abundante. Primero sirvieron un pedazo de tortilla española, hecha a base de patatas y huevos, y después un filete un poco duro. De postre* había melocotones y queso de cabra muy sabroso.

— Dígame Vd., Pedro — preguntó don José — ¿no les obligan a hablar español mientras están en la casa? ¿Qué clase de Escuela es ésta?
10 — No le falta a Vd. razón. Como nadie nos obliga, algunos de nosotros no hacemos ningún esfuerzo. Hablamos un poco en la clase de conversación, pero en las otras clases el profesor **ni siquiera** nos hace preguntas. Da su conferencia y al final de* la hora se marcha. Como tampoco entiendo todo lo que dice, a veces dedico el tiempo a escribir extensas cartas a la familia y a los amigos
15 íntimos. ¿Está Vd. desilusionado conmigo?

— Sí, mucho — contestó don José. — Yo creía que tenía Vd. más fuerza de voluntad. ¡No necesitaba venir a España para hablar inglés! ¿Quién es la persona encargada del* grupo de estudiantes norteamericanos? Me gustaría hablar con ella.

B. IDIOMS AND PHRASES

a lo lejos *in the distance*
por último *finally*
antes de (dirigirse) *before* (going)
dirigirse a(l palacio) *to go to* (the palace)
hasta por la tarde *until (this) afternoon*
con mucho gusto *very gladly*
a la vez *at the same time*
sacar fotografías *to take pictures*
no se preocupe por (mí) *don't worry about* (me)
a las (doce y media) **en punto** *at* (half-past twelve) *sharp*

llegó a (la Residencia) *he reached* (the residence hall)
más bien *rather*
al contrario *on the contrary*
de (esta) **manera** *in* (this) *way*
es que *the fact is, that is*
de postre *for (as) dessert*
ni siquiera *not even*
al final de (la hora) *at the end of* (the hour)
encargada de *in charge of*

C. GRAMMAR REVIEW

31. The Adjective.

Adjectives are used to qualify nouns. In English, adjectives have the same form whether they modify a masculine, feminine, singular, or plural noun. In Spanish, adjectives vary in form to agree in gender and number with the noun they modify. If one noun is feminine and the other masculine, the adjective is put in the masculine plural form.

una taza y un vaso **llenos**	a *full* cup and glass
Tiene la boca y los ojos **pintados.**	Her lips and eyes are *painted.*

32. Feminine of Adjectives.

The feminine of most adjectives is formed by changing **-o** to **-a.** If the masculine form ends in a consonant or **-e,** the masculine and feminine forms are identical.

un hombre **viejo** an *old* man	una mujer **vieja** an *old* woman
un paso **fácil** an *easy* step	una lección **fácil** an *easy* lesson
un dicho **común** a *common* saying	una falta **común** a *common* error
un viejo **fuerte** a *strong* old man	una voz **fuerte** a *loud* voice

Adjectives of nationality, however, that end in a consonant, and those that end in **-or** (except comparatives) add **-a** to the masculine to form the feminine.

el pueblo **español** *Spanish* people	la tierra **española** *Spanish* land
un pobre **inglés** a *poor* Englishman	una palabra **inglesa** an *English* word
un nombre **alemán** a *German* name	una esposa **alemana** a *German* wife
una francesa **encantadora**	a *charming* French girl

But:

mi **mejor** amiga my *best* friend	mi hermana **mayor** my *oldest* sister

33. Plural of Adjectives.

The plural of adjectives is formed the same as of nouns, with the same peculiarities of spelling-change and the addition or loss of the graphic accent. (Review §10.)

negro, -os, -a, -as *black*	**feliz, felices** *m.* and *f.* *happy*
andaluz, andaluces ⎫ *Andalusian*	**joven, jóvenes** *m.* and *f.* *young*
andaluza, andaluzas ⎭	**cortés, corteses** *m.* and *f.* *courteous*

75

A NEW
SHORTER
SPANISH
REVIEW
GRAMMAR

GRAMMAR
REVIEW

34. Position of Adjectives.

(1) Numerical, demonstrative, possessive, and indefinite (*another, some, many, all*, etc.) adjectives precede the noun.

tres árboles *three* trees	**otra** vez *again*
esta vez *this* time	**algún** día *some* day
su abuelo *her* grandfather	**muchos** viajes *many* trips

(2) Adjectives which distinguish a noun from other nouns of the same class regularly *follow* the noun. Among these are adjectives of size, color, shape, nationality, long adjectives, those modified by adverbs, and past participles used as adjectives.

un sitio **pequeño** a *small* place	un espejo **redondo** a *round* mirror
una hoja **verde** a *green* leaf	vinos **franceses** *French* wines
una historia **interesante**	an *interesting* story
un punto muy **delicado**	a very *delicate* matter
un alumno **aplicado**	a *diligent* student

(3) Certain common adjectives, although they may differentiate, usually precede the noun.

bello *beautiful*	**gran(de)** *great*	**mayor** *greater, greatest*
buen(o) *good*	**mal(o)** *bad, wicked; wrong*	**mejor** *better, best*

peor

(4) Distinguishing adjectives *precede* the noun when they denote an inherent or logical characteristic, a trait that is usual, well-known, already established, or expected. Adjectives used as rhetorical ornaments or that refer to the poetic or figurative sense of the noun likewise precede.

santa fe *holy* faith	la **blanca** nieve the *white* snow
mudas estatuas *silent* statues	el **fiero** león the *savage* lion
el **famoso** autor de *Don Quijote*	the *famous* author of *Don Quijote*

(5) A few adjectives change their meaning according as they precede or follow:

AFTER NOUN (literal meaning)	BEFORE NOUN (figurative meaning)
un marido **pobre** a *poor* (not rich) husband	un **pobre** marido a *poor* (unfortunate) husband
un hombre **grande** a *big* (tall) man	un **gran** hombre a *great* man
la viuda **misma** the widow *herself*	la **misma** viuda the *same* widow
un traje **nuevo** a (brand-)*new* suit	un **nuevo** traje a *new* (different) suit

It is to be noted that when the adjective follows the noun, the adjective is emphatic; when the noun follows the adjective, the stress is on the noun.

(6) When two or more adjectives modify the same noun, each is placed before or after the noun in accordance with the rule that governs each.

otro ejemplo **difícil**	*another difficult* example
muchos generales **españoles**	*many Spanish* generals

(7) In English one noun is often used as an adjective to qualify another noun. In Spanish **de** must precede the second noun.

un reloj **de oro** a *gold* watch	una taza **de plata** a *silver* cup
un pañuelo **de seda**	a *silk* handkerchief

35. Apocopation (Shortening) of Adjectives.

(1) The following adjectives drop their final **-o** before a masculine singular noun: **bueno, malo, alguno, uno, ninguno, primero,** and **tercero. Algún** and **ningún** acquire the graphic accent when **-o** is dropped. An adjective may intervene between **algún, ningún, primer, tercer,** or **un** and the noun.

un **buen** amo a *good* master	¡de **ningún** modo! by *no* means!
un **mal** carácter a *bad* character	el **primer** golpe the *first* blow
algún otro cargo *some* other office	el **tercer** juego the *third* game

(2) **Grande** becomes **gran** before a masculine or feminine singular noun, and usually means *great:*

un **gran** servicio a *great* service	una **gran** mujer a *great* woman

Santo becomes **San** before names of saints, except those beginning with **To-** or **Do-** (**Santo Tomás, Santo Domingo**):

San Francisco *St.* Francis	**San** José *St.* Joseph

Ciento becomes **cien** before a noun of either gender, and before a number larger than itself: *101 = ciento y uno*

cien oficiales *100* officers	**cien** batallas *100* battles
cien mil *100,000*	**cien** millones *100,000,000*

But:

ciento cincuenta oraciones	*one hundred* and fifty prayers

Cualquiera may become **cualquier** before a noun of either gender.

cualquier medio   *any* means   **cualquier** duda   *any* doubt

36. Uses of Adjectives.

Adjectives are used:

(1) As nouns.

Un **ciego** nos pidió pan.   A *blind man* asked us for bread.

(2) As adverbs.

Se acercaron **rápidos.**   They approached *rapidly*.

37. Indefinite Pronouns, Adjectives, and Adverbs.

(1) Pronouns.

algo   *something, anything*   **nada**   *nothing*
alguien   *someone, somebody*   **nadie**   *nobody, no one*
alguno   *someone, anyone, some, any*   **ninguno**   *no one, none*

Alguien and **nadie** refer to persons not previously mentioned; **alguno** and **ninguno** refer to a person or thing already mentioned or understood.

Toma **algo.**   He drinks *something*.   No dice **nada.**   He says *nothing*.
Alguien llegó.   *Someone* arrived.   **Nadie** habla.   *No one* speaks.
Algunos lo creen.   *Some* believe it.   **Ninguno** fuma.   *No one* smokes.

already mentioned or thought of

(2) Adjectives.

alguno   *some, any*; pl. *a few*   **ninguno**   *no*
Me prestó **algún** dinero.   He lent me *some* money.
No tiene **ningún** interés.   He has *no* interest.

(3) Adverbs.

algo   *somewhat*   **nada**   *(not) at all, (not) a bit*
Está **algo** cansado.   He is *somewhat* tired.
Ella no es **nada** bonita.   She is not *at all* pretty.

D. VERB REVIEW

Spelling-Changing Verbs. Class II. conocer *to be acquainted with, know; recognize; meet;* **conducir**[1] *to conduct, lead; drive;* **vencer** *to conquer, overcome, defeat.*

Other common verbs of **Class II** are:

agradecer *to thank for, be grateful for*	**nacer** *to be born*
aparecer *to appear*	**ofrecer** *to offer*
carecer (de) *to be lacking, lack*	**parecer** *to seem, appear; look like*
convencer *to convince*	**placer** *to please*
crecer *to grow, increase*	**reconocer** *to recognize*
merecer *to deserve, be worthy of*	**traducir**[1] *to translate*

Le **agradezco** su invitación.　　　　*I thank you for your invitation.*

La **conocí** anoche.　　　　*I met her last night.*

Me **parece** que se han marchado.　　　　*I think that they have left.*

E. GRAMMAR REVIEW

1. *Supply the missing letters and translate:*

with cer & cir if have a vowel before the ending, then changes to zc.

1. (*agradecer*) Le agrade__zc__o su atención.
2. (*aparecer*) Deseo que Vd. apare__zc__a mañana. *look*
3. (*carecer*) Yo care__zc__o de varias cosas.
4. (*conducir*) Desean que yo condu__zc__a su coche. *drive*
5. (*conocer*) Deseo que Vds. cono__zc__an a mi hermano.
6. (*convencer*) Yo siempre le conven__zc__o.
7. (*merecer*) Yo no lo mere__zc__o.
8. (*obedecer*) Es preciso *necessary* que Vd. me obede__zc__a. *beg*
9. (*ofrecer*) Yo se lo ofre__zc__o. *offer*
10. (*parecer*) Dicen que me pare__zc__o *I look like* a mi abuelo. *grandfather*
11. (*reconocer*) Es posible que yo le recono__zc__a. *recognize*
12. (*traducir*) Tradúz__c__ame esta frase *sentence*, por favor. *translate*
13. (*vencer*) Yo nunca le ven__z__o.

2. *Place the adjective before or after the noun, according to usage:*

1. (*mexicano*) Visitamos a una señora. *mejicana*
2. (*pobre* penniless) La señorita se encuentra enferma. *pobre*

---

[1] Has an irregular preterit and imperfect subjunctive.

A NEW
SHORTER
SPANISH
REVIEW
GRAMMAR

GRAMMAR
REVIEW

3. (*mudo*) Se arrodillaron *mudos* ante las imágenes.

4. (*negro*) Ella tiene los ojos. *negros*

5. (*alto*) Se encontraron en *alta* mar (*fem.*).

6. (*mucho, bueno, magnífico*) Hay *muchos* cuadros *buenos* en el museo. *magnífico*

7. (*fácil*) Nos gustan las lecciones. *fáciles*

8. (*hermoso, árabe*) Compraron un *hermoso* caballo. *árabe*

9. (*mismo*) El profesor *mismo* me lo dijo.

10. (*mejor*) Espera *mejor* suerte en vano. *better*

11. (*cinco*) Estudiamos la lección *cinco*

12. (*blanco, hermoso*) Vimos la nieve *blanca* y las flores. *hermosas*

13. (*inmóvil*) Se detuvieron delante de la estatua. *inmóvil*

14. (*célebre, español*) Velázquez era un pintor. *célebre* *español*

15. (*santo*) Lee la *santa* Biblia a menudo.

16. (*redondo*) Compraron una mesa. *redonda*

17. (*pobre* unfortunate) El *pobre* chico tenía hambre.

18. (*santo*) Su hermano es un hombre. *santo*

19. (*francés*) Conduce un auto. *francés*

20. (*brillante*) Pronunció un discurso. *brillante*

3. *Fill in the blank with the adjective, shortening it where necessary:*

1. (*grande*) Washington fué un hombre *grande* y también un *gran* hombre.

2. (*alguno*) Seremos más felices *algún* día.

3. (*tercero*) Al *tercer* día de haber salido, volvieron.

4. (*ciento*) Llegaron *cien* hombres y *cien* mujeres.

5. (*ninguno*) No lo haríamos de *ningún* modo.

6. (*malo*) Es un hombre de *mal* genio.

7. (*bueno*) Estaban de *buen* humor.

8. (*santo*) ¿Dónde está *San* Francisco?

9. (*primero*) Faltó a la clase el *primer* día.

4. *Translate:*

(*a*)

1. He bought no book until the third day.

2. Nobody had told him that long lessons are sometimes easy.

3. He was somewhat preoccupied and not at all sure of himself.

4. One day someone introduced him to two French girls.

5. They could not find some words in the small Spanish dictionary.

6. If you (*pl.*) have any doubt I'll help you.

7. Then he took them to a very expensive restaurant.

8. He was talking seriously but they wouldn't believe him.
9. After dinner they disappeared rapidly.
10. The silver watch that he had received from his mother also disappeared.

(b)

1. It was a very pleasant summer evening.
2. From (**desde**) the tall tower of the cathedral one [can] see the whole city.
3. Most of the foreign students lived in an old palace.
4. Some of my companions are young Americans.
5. Don José went to see the beautiful Romanesque churches.
6. Afterwards Pedro took him to a small room on the second floor.
7. In the dining room some students were talking in their own languages (*sing.*).
8. Some of us do not make any serious effort.
9. In the afternoon someone telephoned to Pedro.
10. Who is it? I don't know anyone in (the) town.

F. EXERCISE ON IDIOMS AND PHRASES

Translate the words underlined:

1. Finally acabó de comer y went to su cuarto.
2. Pero before entrar he took a picture.
3. He reached su casa at doce y media.
4. Don't worry about her; conoce bien la ciudad.
5. ¿Está ella in charge of todos los estudiantes?
6. No, ella doesn't even forma parte del grupo.
7. The fact is es una mujer rather callada.
8. On the contrary, me gustaría conocerla y at the same time hablar con ella.
9. En las comidas tenemos siempre queso for dessert.
10. Acepto very gladly su invitación.

SPAIN

CHAPTER EIGHT

A. GRAMMAR AND IDIOM PRACTICE

— La directora de nuestro grupo — contestó Pedro — es una señora española muy simpática y amable. Vive en un hotel de la ciudad, no muy lejos del suyo, y la vemos muy pocas veces.* Un amigo mío dice que se pasa el tiempo escribiendo cartas a su esposo y a sus hijos. **Al principio** asistía a* nuestra clase de conversación y nos animaba diciendo que estábamos adelantando mucho.

— Dígame, amigo mío — continuó preguntando el profesor — ¿quiénes son los otros norteamericanos que forman parte de su grupo? ¿Cuántos son Vds.? ¿Dónde se reúnen las clases?

— Somos diez u once en nuestro grupo, pero de distinta edad todos. Nuestra preparación y nuestro interés también son distintos. En su hotel vive una familia de California que ha venido sólo a divertirse; el padre ha estado en Sudamérica y habla español bastante bien, la madre no habla nada y los dos hijos — una muchacha de diez y seis años y un muchacho de quince — saben sólo unas palabras que aprendieron en la escuela superior. Mis otros compañeros son cuatro maestras solteronas y dos viejecitos que se han retirado de sus negocios y quieren gozar de* su descanso en Europa. En la Residencia hay dos jóvenes de mi edad, que han venido por cuenta propia y son mis mejores amigos. Todas las clases tienen lugar* en la Biblioteca Provincial.

— ¡**Dios mío**! — exclamó don José. — ¡Qué desilusión! Si me lo hubieran dicho en América, no lo habría creído. Yo me imaginaba un grupo bien organizado de jóvenes universitarios, como Vd., deseosos de aprender y divertirse. Claro que* la culpa no es toda suya, pero creo que si demostrara más interés aprendería más.

De vuelta en el hotel, el profesor recogió algunas cosas con mucha prisa, las metió en la maleta, se puso* el sombrero y se disponía a* salir de* la habitación cuando Pedro preguntó:

— Allí veo algo. ¿Es de Vd. aquel paquete?

83

—Sí, es mío. ¡He perdido la cabeza **por completo!** Si llego a casa de mi amigo sin este paquete, estoy seguro de que sus niñitas no querrán recibirme.

Mientras el profesor pagaba la cuenta, Pedro llamó un taxi. Entraron los dos en* él y se dirigieron a la estación. En el camino Pedro dió las gracias a* 5 don José por su visita y por sus buenos consejos.

— Siento no haber conocido a sus profesores, a sus compañeros y a la directora del grupo. **De todos modos** me alegro de* ver que Vd. disfruta de* buena salud y que la vida aquí no le es **del todo** insoportable. Dígame, ¿han hecho más excursiones?

10 — Sí, señor — contestó Pedro. — Fuimos un día a Ávila, ciudad notable por las murallas medievales que la rodean; a la Granja, cerca de* aquí, donde tenían los reyes un palacio de verano; y al Escorial, famoso por su imponente monasterio. Pero de este último lugar puedo contarle muy poco porque me puse enfermo. Me dolía todo el cuerpo y di la vuelta* en el primer tren. Pero 15 le prometo volver por allí antes de abandonar España.

B. IDIOMS AND PHRASES

pocas veces seldom

al principio at first

asistía a (la clase) she used to attend (the class)

gozar de (su descanso) to enjoy (their rest)

(las clases) **tienen lugar** (the classes) are held, take place

¡Dios mío! Dear me! Good Heavens!

claro que of course

de vuelta back

se puso (el sombrero) he put on (his hat)

se disponía a (salir) he was getting ready to (leave)

salir de (la habitación) to leave (the room)

por completo completely

entraron en (el taxi) they got into (the taxi)

dió las gracias a (don José) he thanked (Don José)

de todos modos at any rate

me alegro de (ver) I'm glad to (see)

disfruta de (buena salud) you enjoy (good health)

del todo completely

cerca de (aquí) near (here)

di la vuelta I turned back

84

38. Possessive Adjectives.

agrees with the thing possessed, not the person doing it.

(1) UNSTRESSED FORMS		STRESSED FORMS *These come after noun possessed.*	
mi, mis	*my*	**mío,-a,-os,-as**	*my, of mine*
tu, tus	*your*	**tuyo,-a,-os,-as**	*your, of yours*
su, sus	{ *your, his* { *her, its*	**suyo,-a,-os,-as**	{ *your, of yours, (of) his* { *her, (of) hers, etc.*
nuestro,-a,-os,-as	*our*	**nuestro,-a,-os,-as**	*our, of ours*
vuestro,-a,-os,-as	*your*	**vuestro,-a,-os,-as**	*your, of yours*
su, sus	{ *your* { *their*	**suyo,-a,-os,-as**	{ *your, of yours* { *their, of theirs*

(2) Possessive adjectives in Spanish agree in gender and number with the noun they modify, the thing possessed, and *not with the possessor* as in English. The unstressed forms precede the noun and are generally repeated before each noun they modify.

mi boca *my* mouth	**su** cara *his* face
su madre y **su** padre *his* mother and father	**nuestras** clases *our* classes
	sus cuentas *your* bills

(3) The stressed forms, which always follow the noun, are used (*a*) in direct address, (*b*) to translate *of mine, of yours*, etc., and (*c*) in exclamations and oaths.

(*a*) Querido amigo **mío:**   *My* dear friend: (in a letter)
¿Qué tienes, hijo **mío?**   What is the matter, *my* son?

(*b*) una carta **mía** a letter *of mine*   un sobrino **suyo** a nephew *of his*
Son cosas **suyas.**   They are things of *his* (*hers*, etc.)

(*c*) ¡Dios **mío!**   Dear me! *My* goodness!

(4) The meaning of **su** and **suyo** (*your, his, her, its, their*) can be made clear by the use of **de Vd., de él,** etc., after the noun. **Su** is often, but not always, replaced by the definite article.

su caballo *or*	*your* (*his, her, their*) horse
su caballo (**el** caballo) **de Vd.** (**de él, de ella,** etc.)	
Son amigos **suyos.** *or*	} They are *your* (*his, her,* etc.) friends.
Son amigos **de Vd.** (**de él, de ella,** etc.).	

85

A NEW
SHORTER
SPANISH
REVIEW
GRAMMAR

GRAMMAR
REVIEW

It is important to note that these prepositional forms replace mainly **suyo** and not the other possessive adjectives.

39. The Use of the Definite Article for the Possessive Adjective.

The definite article regularly replaces the possessive adjective with parts of the body, articles of personal wear or something habitually associated with the subject.

Levantaron **la** mano.[1]	They raised *their* hand*s*.
Se quita **el** sombrero.	He takes off *his* (own) hat.
Le duele **la** cabeza.	*His* head aches.
Le corté **el** dedo.	I cut *his* finger.

40. Possession.

Ownership is expressed in Spanish by **de** plus a noun or pronoun.

la letra **de María**	*Mary's* handwriting
La carta es **de él.**	The letter is *his.*

41. Possessive Pronouns.

The possessive pronouns are formed in Spanish by prefixing the definite article to the stressed forms of the possessive adjectives. **El suyo** is clarified by replacing it with **el de Vd., el de él, el de ella,** etc.

(Dos coches:) **El mío** es negro, **el suyo (el de ella)** es rojo.	(Two cars:) *Mine* is black, *hers* is red.
(Padres:) **Los nuestros** son españoles, **los suyos (los de ellos)** son alemanes.	(Parents:) *Ours* are Spanish, *theirs* are German.
(Plumas:) **La mía** es una estilográfica, **la suya (la de él)** no lo es.	(Pens:) *Mine* is a fountain pen, *his* is not.

Note that at times *his* is **la suya (la de él),** *hers* may be **el suyo (el de ella);** *ours* may be singular: **el nuestro,** etc., since in Spanish the pronoun agrees with the object possessed and not with the possessor as in English.

After **ser,** the definite article is not used with the possessive pronoun when mere ownership (identification) is involved.

¿De quién es este libro? — Es **mío.**	Whose book is this? — It is *mine.*

---

[1] Note the use of the singular in Spanish when one single object is possessed by each member of a group.

But to differentiate ownership, after **ser,** the definite article is used with the possessive pronoun.

¿Cuál es su libro? — Éste es **el mío.** Which is your book? — This is *mine, i.e.,*
                                This is the one that belongs to me.

42. Uses of the Future and Conditional Tenses.[1]

These two tenses are generally used as in English. Neither, however, follows **si** meaning *if.*

Estudiaré si Vd. me ayuda. *I shall study* if you (will) help me.
Estudiaría si Vd. me ayudara *I would study* if you would help me.
    (*imperfect subjunctive*).

(1) Meanings of *will, would,* and *should.* In English these auxiliaries do not always refer to the future or conditional ideas. *only use "ra" form on deber, querer, + poder.*

¿**Quiere Vd.** cerrar la puerta? *Will you close* the door? (*a wish, not futurity*)

No quisieron venir. They *would not come.* (*a refusal, not conditional*)

Siempre me **hablaba** cuando me veía. He *would* always *speak* when he saw me. (*customary action, not conditional*)

Si Vd. **escuchara,** aprendería. If you *would listen* (*contrary to fact, not conditional*), you would learn.

Debo (debiera) estudiar. I *should* study. (*moral obligation*)

"If" clause uses past subjunctive.

[1] The endings of the future tense and those of the conditional tense are the same for all verbs, regular or irregular. When the future tense is irregular, the conditional tense always has the same irregularity. This irregularity always consists in a modification of the infinitive element:

Five verbs drop the **e** of the infinitive element:

INFINITIVE:	**haber**	**poder**	**querer**	**saber**	**caber**
FUTURE:	*habré,* etc.	*podré,* etc.	*querré,* etc.	*sabré,* etc.	*cabré,* etc.
CONDITIONAL:	*habría,* etc.	*podría,* etc.	*querría,* etc.	*sabría,* etc.	*cabría,* etc.

Five verbs replace the **e** or **i** of the infinitive ending by **d:**

INFINITIVE:	**poner**	**salir**	**tener**	**valer**	**venir**
FUTURE:	*pondré,* etc.	*saldré,* etc.	*tendré,* etc.	*valdré,* etc.	*vendré,* etc.
CONDITIONAL:	*pondría,* etc.	*saldría,* etc.	*tendría,* etc.	*valdría,* etc.	*vendría,* etc.

learn

Two verbs contract the infinitive element:

INFINITIVE:	**decir**	**hacer**
FUTURE:	*diré,* etc.	*haré,* etc.
CONDITIONAL:	*diría,* etc.	*haría,* etc.

A NEW
SHORTER
SPANISH
REVIEW
GRAMMAR

GRAMMAR
REVIEW

(ser—to be)
(estar—to be)

(2) The future tense is used to express probability, supposition, or conjecture concerning an action or state in the present time. These ideas are expressed in English by *must, can, probably, I wonder,* etc. The conditional expresses the same notions concerning past action or state.

¿Qué hora **será**?	{ *I wonder* what time *it is?* / What time *can it be?*
Será la una.	*It is probably* one o'clock.
Será él.	It *must be* he.
¿Dónde **estarán** mis llaves?	*I wonder* where my keys *are.*
¿Qué hora **sería?**	*I wonder* what time *it was?*
Serían las dos.	*It was probably* two o'clock.

(3) After **si** meaning *whether,* both future and conditional are used.

No sé si **vendrá.**	I don't know whether he *will come.*
No sabía si **vendría.**	I didn't know whether he *would come.*

D. VERB REVIEW

Spelling-Changing Verbs. Class III. coger *to catch, gather;* **fingir** *to pretend;* **distinguir** *to distinguish.* *change g to j when followed by the letter o or a.*

Other verbs of **Class III** are:

escoger *to choose*
recoger *to pick (up); gather*
dirigir *to direct*
   dirigirse *to make one's way*
   dirigirse (a) *to address; apply*

elegir (i) *to choose, elect*
exigir *to demand, require*
conseguir (i) *to obtain, get*
seguir (i) *to follow; go on, keep on*

Me dirijo a la tienda. *I go to the store.*
Diríjase al dueño. *Apply to the owner.*
Consigo hacerlo. *I succeed in doing it.*
Siga trabajando. *Keep on working.*

drop the "u" after a "g" when followed by o or a.

E. GRAMMAR EXERCISES

1. *Give the first person singular present indicative and the* ~~third~~ 1st *person singular present subjunctive of:*

1. escoger *escojo escoja*
2. distinguir *distingo, distinga*
3. fingir *finjo finja*
4. recoger *recojo, recoja*
5. dirigir *dirijo dirija*
6. exigir *exijo exija*
7. conseguir *consigo consiga*
8. coger *cojo coja*
9. seguir *sigo, siga*

será — it is 30 o'clock
sería — it was

2. (a) *Translate the possessives and place them in the proper position:*

1. (*My*) vestido es más bonito que (*hers*). *[suyo] (el de ella)*
2. (*Your*) piso tiene más habitaciones que (*theirs*). *el de ellos* *[su]*
3. (*My*) querido amigo: (*My*) querida madre: *mía*
4. Un pariente (*of his*) compró aceite para (*his*) coche no para (*mine*). *[de suyo] [su] mío.*
5. ¿Qué haces, (*my*) amiga? *mía*
6. Son amigos (*of yours*)? *[suyo]*
ok 7. Es una casa (*of ours*). *nuestra.*
8. ¡(*My*) Dios, qué de prisa habla Vd.! *[mío]*
9. (*Our*) alumnos estudian más que (*his*). *nuestros [los suyos]*
10. La pluma es (*yours*), Carlos. *[suya]*
11. Un traje (*of mine*) está roto. *[mío]*
12. Un primo (*of hers*) me saludó. *[de ella]*

el de plus 3rd sing or 3rd plural only

(b) *Replace the words in parentheses by possessive pronouns:*

1. Él dice que (*su casa*) es más grande que (*mi casa*). *[la suya] [la mía]*
2. Ella ofrece (*su coche*) pero Vd. prefiere (*su coche*). *ok [el suyo] [el de usted]*
3. (*Nuestro perro*) y (*el perro de ellos*) están en la calle. *ok [el nuestro] [el de ellos]*
4. (*Su amigo de él*) trabajó con (*su padre de ella*). *ok [el de él] [el de ella]*
5. (*Nuestro jardín*) está al lado de (*su jardín de ellas*). *ok [el nuestro] [el de ellas]*
6. (*La madre de él*) se casó con (*el padre de ella*). *[la de él] [el de ella]*
7. (*El reloj de Vd.*) vale más que (*mi reloj*). *[el de usted] [el mío]*

3. *Translate:*

(a)

1. (I wonder) where the Spanish lady is?
2. She probably lives in the hotel behind yours. (*use future tense*)
3. If our hotel is near hers, where is yours?
4. A friend of mine says that she writes letters to her children every day.
5. She attends their class, not ours. *no la nuestra*
6. My son, are you telling me the truth? *¿está usted? familiar*
7. A companion of yours wants to use my camera. Where can his be? (*future tense*)
8. Theirs is probably too old to (**para**) take good pictures.
9. I bought mine before the war. When did you buy yours?
10. My parents write to her once every week; do yours write often?

(b)

1. She spends her (the) time writing to her husband and her children.
2. Some of my classmates don't even attend their classes.
3. My friend, (I wonder) who your companions are? (*future tense*)
4. Two boys from California are my best friends.

5. In our group all are Americans, but our preparation is very different.
6. That package must be yours. — No, mine is in my suitcase.
7. I can't go to my friend's house without taking (*inf.*) a present for his daughters.
8. As a rule my health has been good, only one day I cut my finger.
9. Oh! Another day, when we went to El Escorial, my whole body ached.
10. Don José, I wish to thank you for your advice (*plur.*) and for your visit.

F. EXERCISE ON IDIOMS AND PHRASES

Translate the words underlined:

1. At first yo didn't enjoy nada y me era imposible enjoy la vida.
2. I used to attend a las clases pero seldom entendía al profesor.
3. Of course la culpa es mía completely.
4. Las clases are held (take place) en un viejo edificio near aquí.
5. He thanked him for su visita antes de leaving el hotel.
6. I'm glad verle tan alegre.
7. He was getting ready to acostarse cuando alguien entered la habitación.
8. ¡Good Heavens! ¿Qué hace Vd. aquí, D. José?
9. He tenido que turn back porque olvidé el paquete.
10. Pedro put on los zapatos y le acompañó al hotel.

CHAPTER NINE

A. GRAMMAR AND IDIOM PRACTICE

El tren venía retrasado y pudieron hablar un rato más.

— Tengo todavía que hacerle una pregunta, Pedro. ¿Qué impresiones ha recibido Vd. de España hasta ahora?

— Realmente no puedo decir mucho, **ni** bueno **ni** malo, de este país. ¡He visto tan poco y he hablado con <u>tan</u> pocos españoles! Pero, **en general** me 5 parece que es un país interesantísimo que ofrece los mayores contrastes. Esta meseta castellana, seca y sin árboles, me ha impresionado más que <u>nada</u>.* Viéndola comprendo mejor la novela de Cervantes, *Don Quijote*. También me <u>he dado cuenta de</u>* que España es un país agrícola más que industrial. Con <u>frecuencia camina</u> uno por horas sin ver una sola casa en el campo. Porque 10 aquí los <u>campesinos</u> no viven en el campo como en nuestro país, sino en pueblos a donde regresan después del trabajo. Estos campesinos que trabajan la tierra desde la salida del sol hasta que anochece y que <u>utilizan</u> instrumentos tan primitivos me han impresionado quizá más que otra cosa.* Cuando los he visto pasar montados en sus burros o mulas, graves y serenos, siempre saludan al 15 extraño con la <u>mayor</u> cortesía.

— Es Vd. **sin duda** muy buen observador — dijo don José. — Siga hablando; me interesa lo que dice.

— Lo que más me gusta de esta región — continuó Pedro — es la abundancia de <u>luz</u> y la <u>intensidad azul</u> de su <u>cielo</u>, apenas sin nubes. El clima es 20 verdaderamente delicioso en esta época del año. Creo que es el clima más seco del mundo, un clima que me recuerda el de Arizona y Nuevo México. Le digo con toda sinceridad que si no hubiera sido por el clima, ya me habría marchado de* aquí.

— Afortunadamente — dijo el profesor — en menos de dos semanas 25 terminan las clases y **quedará** Vd. libre. No olvide que otras regiones de España son <u>tan interesantes como</u> ésta.

91

—Sí, ya lo sé. Por eso, la semana que viene pienso hacer otra escapada para ver Burgos, la tierra del Cid Campeador. Más tarde voy a separarme del grupo por unos diez o doce días a fin de* ver, en compañía de los dos amigos de California, otros lugares que me interesan. La mayor parte de mis compañeros desean salir cuanto antes* para Italia, en avión. Me reuniré con* ellos de nuevo en Bruselas o en Londres. ¿Tiene más preguntas que hacerme?

— Sí, muchas más, pero ya no hay tiempo. ¡Qué tristes son las despedidas! ¿verdad?* Pero lo más triste aún es que no volveremos a vernos en España. Me quedaré en el norte **unos cuantos** días y a mi regreso* ya no estará Vd. **por aquí.**

— Bueno, así es la vida.* En menos de dos meses nos veremos en la universidad. Entonces le contaré las aventuras más extraordinarias que Vd. ha oído en su vida — añadió Pedro sonriendo.

El profesor se sonrió también y se dispuso a subir al* tren.

— Mi último consejo — dijo don José — es que tome Vd. las cosas con más calma, que coma y beba con moderación y que huya de las malas compañías. Adiós y mucha suerte en sus viajes.

El tren partió a los pocos minutos.* Por la ventanilla el profesor pudo ver a Pedro que desde el andén le decía adiós con un pañuelo blanco que tenía en la mano.

B. IDIOMS AND PHRASES

ni (bueno) **ni** (malo)   *neither* (good) *nor* (bad)

en general   *as a rule*

más que nada   *more than anything*

me he dado cuenta de (que es)   *I've realized* (that it is)

otra cosa   *anything else*

sin duda   *doubtless*

me habría marchado de (aquí)   *I would have left* (here)

quedará Vd. (libre)   *you will be* (free)

a fin de (ver)   *in order to* (see)

cuanto antes   *as soon as possible*

me reuniré con (ellos)   *I'll join* (them)

¿verdad?   *aren't they?*

unos cuantos   *a few*

a mi regreso   *on my return*

por aquí   *around here*

así es la vida   *such is life*

subir a(l tren)   *to get on* (the train)

a los pocos (minutos)   *in a few* (minutes)

92

C. GRAMMAR REVIEW

43. Adverbs.

Adverbs of manner are formed by adding **-mente** to the feminine singular of the adjective. If the adjective has a graphic accent, the accent is retained. Adverbs are also commonly formed by **con** and a noun.

claro: **claramente** clear, *clearly*   fácil: **fácilmente** easy, *easily*
feliz: **felizmente** happy, *happily*   frío: **fríamente** cold, *coldly*
con cariño affectionate*ly*   **con** ruido noisi*ly*

44. Comparison.

(1) The comparative of equality is expressed by **tan** (+ an adjective or adverb +) **como** as . . . as, so . . . as or by **tanto, -a, -os, -as** (+ a noun +) **como** as (so) much . . . as, as (so) many . . . as. (Never say **tan mucho**.)

Ella es **tan** joven **como** él.   She is *as* young *as* he.
Él habla **tan** despacio **como** yo.   He speaks *as* slowly *as* I.
Tengo **tanto** dinero **como** Vd.   I have *as much* money *as* you.
Él lee **tantos** libros **como** ella.   He reads *as many* books *as* she.

(2) Comparison of Inequality. The comparative and superlative degrees are expressed by placing **más** or **menos** before the adjective or adverb. English usage determines whether the degree is comparative or superlative.

más corto shor*ter* (short*est*)   **menos** ancho *less (least)* wide
más despacio *more (most)* slowly   **menos** rápido *less (least)* swiftly

Than is usually expressed by **que.**[1]

Este lápiz es más corto **que** aquél.   This pencil is shorter *than* that one.
Él se marchó más tarde **que** yo.   He left later *than* I.

---

[1] When *than* is followed by a clause and the point of comparison is an adjective or adverb, it is translated by **de** followed by **lo que:**
Ella es más rica **de lo que** Vd. cree.   She is richer *than* you think.

It will be noticed that the second verb is usually one of thinking or believing.

When the comparison involves a noun in the main clause, *than* may be expressed by **de** followed by **el que, la que, los que,** or **las que,** according to the gender and number of the noun.

94 Gana más dinero **del que** gasta.   He earns more money *than* he spends.

De translates *than* before numerals in affirmative sentences.

Ganó más **de** cuarenta dólares. He earned more *than* forty dollars.

But:

No gastó **más** que veinte. He did not spend more *than* twenty.

In after a superlative is usually rendered by **de.**

el cuento más largo **del** libro the longest story *in* the book

45. Irregular Comparison.

There are five irregular comparative (or superlative) forms of adjectives and four of adverbs.

ADJECTIVES

Positive		*Comparative-Superlative*
bueno	*good*	**mejor** *better, best*
malo	*bad*	**peor** *worse, worst*
poco	*little*	**menos** *less, fewer, least*
grande	{ *large*	**más grande** (in size) *larger, largest*
	{ *great*	**mayor** (in importance, age) *greater, greatest; older, oldest*
pequeño	*small*	{ **más pequeño** (in size) *smaller, smallest*
		{ **menor** (in importance, age) *younger, youngest; less, least*

ADVERBS

mucho	much	**más**	more, most	**bien**	well	**mejor**	better, best
poco	little	**menos**	less, least	**mal**	bad	**peor**	worse, worst

el **mejor** uso   the *better* use

más o **menos**   more or less

Cortó el árbol **más grande.**

Su hija **mayor** ha llegado.

No es de la **menor** importancia.

Recibió **más** de la mitad.

Él pronuncia **mejor** que nosotros.

la **peor** suerte   the *worst* luck

lo **menos** posible   the *least* possible

He cut down the *largest* tree.

His *older* daughter has arrived.

It's not of the *slightest* importance.

He received *more* than half.

He pronounces *better* than we.

Note. **Más bien** translates *rather.*

A NEW
SHORTER
SPANISH
REVIEW
GRAMMAR

GRAMMAR
REVIEW

After a comparative, affirmative terms such as **alguien, alguno, algo,** etc., are replaced by their corresponding negative forms: **nadie, ninguno, nada,** etc. (Cf. §25.4.)

Canta mejor que **nunca.**	He sings better than *ever.*
Es más alto que **nadie.**	He is taller than *anyone.*

46. The Absolute Superlative.

A high degree of quality, without implying comparison, is expressed by placing **muy** before the adjective or adverb or by adding **-ísimo, -a, -os, -as** to the adjective. When **-ísimo** is added the final vowel is dropped.[1] **Muchísimo** is the regular form for *very much.* (Avoid **muy mucho.**)

muy útil *very* useful	**muy** seguro *very* safe, certain
dulce sweet; **dulcísimo** *very sweet*	puro pure; **purísimo** *very pure*

47. Uses of the Present Participle.

The present participle *never occurs after prepositions* and is never inflected. It is used:

(1) To form the progressive tenses with **estar** or its many substitutes—verbs of motion as **ir, andar, venir,** which retain something of their original meaning, and **seguir, continuar,** etc. (Cf. §13.3.)

Grito, **estoy** gritando. I *am* shouting.	**Viene** fumando. He *is* smoking.
Va pensando. He *is* thinking.	**Anda** espiando. He *is* spying.

The present participles of **ir** and **venir** seldom appear in the progressive tenses.

(2) After verbs of perception, in vivid descriptions.

Le vi **llorando.** I saw him *crying.*	La oí **leyendo.** I heard her *reading.*

(3) To express the idea of *time, manner, condition,* and the like with the subject expressed or understood.

---

[1] To retain the sound of the final consonant, it is sometimes necessary to make spelling-changes when **-ísimo** is added: final **c** becomes **qu: fresco: fresquísimo** *very cool;* final **g** becomes **gu: largo: larguísimo** *very long;* final **z** becomes **c: feliz: felicísimo** *very happy;* others retain their Latin forms: **bueno: bonísimo** *very good;* **notable: notabilísimo** *very remarkable;* **antiguo: antiquísimo** *very ancient,* etc.

Él pasa el tiempo **pintando**.	He spends his time *painting*.	CHAPTER NINE
Preguntando se llega a Roma.	*By asking* one reaches his goal.	
Hablando se aprende a hablar.	*By talking* one learns to talk.	GRAMMAR REVIEW

48. Conditional Sentences.

In conditional sentences, the tense and mood of Spanish and English coincide except in one important particular. Whenever *would* appears in the *main* clause, the verb in the if-clause in Spanish must be put in the imperfect subjunctive (either the **-ra** or the **-se** form). If the tenses are compound, the pluperfect subjunctive is used in the **si**-clause. *for imp. subjunctive drop the "ron" of 3rd person plural of preterit tenses + add endings.*

	PRESENT INDICATIVE	PRESENT INDICATIVE
He *learns* if he *studies*.	**Aprende**	si **estudia**.

	FUTURE INDICATIVE	PRESENT INDICATIVE
He *will learn* if he *studies*.	**Aprenderá**	si **estudia**.

	CONDITIONAL INDIC.	IMPERFECT SUB.
He _would_ learn { if he *studied*. / if he *would study*. / if he *were to study*. }	**Aprendería**	si { **estudiara**. / **estudiese**. }

contrary to fact

I *would* not *do* it if I *were* you.	No lo **haría**	si **fuese** Vd.

	CONDITIONAL PERF. IND.	PLUPERFECT SUB.
He *would have learned* if he *had studied*.	**Habría aprendido**	si **hubiera estudiado**.

The future and conditional tenses seldom appear after **si** meaning *if*. *If he will study tomorrow* becomes *If he studies tomorrow:* **Si estudia mañana.** As explained above, *If he would study* is rendered by the imperfect subjunctive.

49. Word Order in Questions.

In general, Spanish word order is very flexible; no word, however, (*a*) may intervene between the two elements of a compound tense. In questions (*b*) the usual word order is: verb + noun object (predicate adjective, or adverb) + subject. Normally (*c*) when the subject is shorter than the noun object with its qualifying terms, the subject follows the verb immediately.

(*a*) No **ha leído** todavía el periódico.	He *has* not yet *read* the paper.	
(*b*) ¿**Come pan** Alberto?	Does Albert *eat bread?*	
¿**Es verde** el lápiz?	*Is* the pencil *green?*	**97**

But:

(c) ¿**Comió Vd.** la manzana roja?   *Did you eat* the red apple?

D. VERB REVIEW

Spelling-Changing Verbs. Class IV. enviar *to send;* **continuar** *to continue.* **Class V. huir** *to flee.*

Like **enviar:**

confiar *to confide, entrust; trust*	**fiar** *to trust;* **fiarse (de)** *to trust*
criar *to bring up, raise*	**guiar** *to guide; drive* (a vehicle)
criarse *to grow up*	

Like **huir:**

concluir *to conclude, finish*	**construir** *to build, construct*
constituir *to constitute*	**destruir** *to destroy*

Le **confío** este asunto a Vd.	*I entrust* this matter to you.
El chico **se cría** sano.	The child *is growing up* healthy.
Nunca **se fía** de sus amigos.	He never *trusts* his friends.
El guía después de consultar la guía **guía** con cuidado.	The guide after consulting the guidebook *drives* carefully.

Continúa correspondiendo con ella.	He *continues* to correspond with her.
Destruyeron todos mis planes.	They *destroyed* all my plans.
Huye siempre del mal, hijo mío.	Always *flee* evil, my son.

E. GRAMMAR EXERCISES

1. (a) *Give the third person singular present indicative and present subjunctive of:*

1. confiar   3. fiar   5. continuar   7. destruir   9. construir
2. criar   4. guiar   6. constituir   8. concluir

(b) *Translate:*

1. I build.
2. He destroys.
3. They trust.
4. You continue.
5. She sends.
6. You grow up.
7. (That) they may send.
8. (That) she may destroy.

2. (a) *Form adverbs with the following words, using* **-mente** *with the*
   adjectives and **con** *with the nouns:*

1. inútil *inútilmente*   4. noble *noblemente* 7. cuidado *con cuidado*   10. confianza *con confianza*
2. absoluto *absolutamente* 5. débil *débilmente*   8. dolor *con dolor*   11. paciencia *con paciencia*
3. afortunado *afortunadamente*   6. infeliz *infelizmente*   9. cariño *con cariño* 12. ruido *con ruido*

(b) *Form the absolute superlative by adding* **-ísimo** *to:*

1. loco *loquísimo*   3. suave *suavísimo*   5. alto *altísimo*
2. feo *feísimo*   4. largo *larguísimo*   6. rico *riquísimo*

3. *Translate the words in parentheses:*

1. Este vino es (*as* **tan**) dulce (*as* **como**) aquél.
2. Esta calle es (*less* **menos**) ancha que la otra.
3. Aquel cortaplumas corta (*better than* **mejor que**) el mío.
4. Ganaron (*more than* **más que**) diez pesetas por día.
5. Mi mujer es (*older than* **mayor que**) yo.
6. Ésta es la (*best* **mejor**) universidad (*in* **en**) el país.
7. Alfonso XII reinó (*fewer* **menos**) años (*than* **que**) su hijo.
8. Su hijo (*younger* **menor**) es el novio de la hija (*youngest* **menor**) del señor Torres.
9. Lo pronunció con la (*greatest* **mayor**) dificultad.
10. Nunca aprendió (*so much* **tanto**).
11. Gastó (*as much* **tanto**) dinero (*as* **como**) yo.
12. No leyeron (*more than* **más que**) veinte páginas.
13. Comieron (*more than* **más que**) cuatro (*two ways*).
14. Es el (*oldest* **mayor de**) estudiante (*in*) la clase.
15. Nuestra ciudad es (*smaller than* **más pequeño que**) Bogotá.
16. No hablamos (*so* **tan**) lentamente (*as* **como**) ellos.

(4) *mejor*

4. *Give the proper form of the infinitive in parentheses:*

1. Si Vd. lee despacio, nosotros (*entender* **entenderemos**).
2. Si yo (*tener* **tuviera**) bastante dinero, iría al cine.
3. Si (*llover* **llueve**) no saldremos de casa.
4. Si (*llover* **lloviera**) no saldríamos de casa.
5. Si él hubiera estudiado anoche, lo (*haber* **habría**) aprendido.
6. Si lo (*tener* **tuviera**) ahora, nos lo daría.
7. Si él (*venir* **veniera**) mañana, me lo traería.

subj. — cond.

A NEW
SHORTER
SPANISH
REVIEW
GRAMMAR

GRAMMAR
EXERCISES

? 8. Si yo (*ser*) *era* Vd., no lo (*hacer*) *haría*.

OK 9. Dígamelo si Vd. lo (*saber*) *sabe*.

OK 10. Ella no (*estar*) *estaría* tan gorda si (*comer*) *comiera* menos.

5. *Translate:*

(*a*)

1. More than fifteen of your classmates are Americans, aren't they?
2. Your roommate was not the worst student in the world.
3. He studied as many subjects as any other student.
4. No one reads Spanish more easily than he.
5. Nothing is of greater importance than [to] read without translating (*inf.*).
6. In fact, his grades are better than yours.
7. Up to now he has earned the best grades.
8. By asking many questions he has learned more than we about Spanish life and customs.
9. If I paid more attention, I would be able to answer the questions better.
10. I have less to (**que**) fear than before.

(*b*)

1. I think that Spain is a most interesting country and that it offers the greatest contrasts.
2. And Spaniards show the greatest courtesy to foreigners.
3. It seems to me that Castile has the driest climate in Europe. It is as dry as our southwest.
4. Seeing it (*fem.*), I recall (remember) the landscape of New Mexico.
5. Now I can understand better Cervantes' great novel.
6. Some of my classmates are older and speak more clearly than I.
7. You must always remember that by talking one learns to (**a**) talk.
8. Well, in less than three weeks you will finish and will be happier than ever.
9. The worst thing is that I will not see you again.
10. From (**desde**) the train Don José saw Pedro waving his white handkerchief.

F. EXERCISE ON IDIOMS AND PHRASES

1. *Translate the words underlined:*
1. *En general*
   As a rule no le interesan *ni* neither las iglesias *ni* nor las catedrales.
2. Ahora *me doy cuenta de* realize que España es un país agrícola.

CHAPTER
NINE

EXERCISE
ON
IDIOMS
AND
PHRASES

Saliré *cuanto antes.*
3. I'll leave Segovia as soon as possible.

unos cuantos *estaré*
4. En a few días I shall be libre.

a mi regreso *sin duda* *por aquí.*
5. On my return Vd. doubtless no estará around here.

a los pocos minutos.
6. El tren partió in a few minutes.

a fin de ver
7. Fué a Madrid in order to see el Museo del Prado.

¿no es verdad?
8. Las despedidas siempre son tristes, aren't they?

subía al
9. He got on el tren porque ya era tarde.

me reuniré
10. Me separo de mis amigos pero I'll join ellos la semana que viene.

2. *Translate:*

This way you will learn more. *He arrived a little after 12:00.*
De esta manera Vd. aprenderá más. Llegó poco después de las doce. Le
I will talk to him frankly & tell him the whole truth. *He goes to his classes in*
hablaré con franqueza y le diré toda la verdad. Va a sus clases por la
the morning. They never force us to speak Spanish. At any rate, you
mañana. No nos obligan nunca a hablar español. De todos modos, Vd.
show little interest. At times life here is unbearable.
demuestra poco interés. A veces la vida aquí es del todo insoportable.
Now you pronounce & speak rather well. You always do things hurriedly.
Ahora pronuncia y habla bastante bien. Siempre hace las cosas con mucha
Today my whole body aches. The landscape impressed me more than
prisa. Hoy me duele todo el cuerpo. El paisaje me impresionó más que
anything. My roommate is French. She says that I am progressing much.
nada. Mi compañero de cuarto es francés. Ella dice que adelanto mucho.
They still converse a while more. We get up at 7:00 sharp.
Todavía conversaron un rato más. Nos levantamos a las siete en punto.

PUBLISHED BY THE SPANISH STATE TOURIST DEPARTMENT · MADRID

SPAIN

CHAPTER TEN

A. GRAMMAR AND IDIOM PRACTICE

El tren expreso venía lleno de gente que iba a las playas del norte a veranear.
El mozo que había subido la maleta del profesor le condujo a su asiento. En el
otro asiento, junto a* la ventanilla, viajaba un señor que **por lo visto** leía algo
muy interesante. Levantó los ojos del libro para dar las "Buenas tardes"* al
recién llegado y continuó leyendo. Don José se sienta, cierra los ojos y piensa 5
en las horas pasadas con Pedro.

— Ese muchacho — se dijo — está perdiendo el tiempo.* Me arrepiento de
haberle recomendado Segovia, porque allí ni aprende ni se divierte gran cosa.*
Por eso cuando se encuentra demasiado aburrido hace escapadas a otras partes
de vez en cuando. 10

Don José siente el calor de la tarde, se quita* la chaqueta y duerme durante
unos minutos. Pero al poco rato le despiertan los chillidos de los niños y los
gritos de hombres y mujeres. Unos quieren tener las ventanas cerradas a causa
del* polvo que entraba, otros prefieren abrirlas para no morirse de calor. El
señor que estaba leyendo se levantó y dijo **en voz alta**: "Esto parece un 15
gallinero." Luego dirigiéndose a* don José le preguntó:

— ¿Quiere Vd. acompañarme al bar?

— Ah, ¿pero tienen bar aquí? — no lo sabía. Bueno, vamos. Le sigo.
El bar estaba en medio del* vagón. Consistía en una estrecha mesa colocada
a lo largo de* una ventana de cristales, con banquillos a un lado. Todos los 20
vagones tenían el mismo arreglo, de modo que* era fácil salir a tomar un
refresco.

— He advertido que Vd. está leyendo un libro en inglés. ¿Conoce Vd. esa
lengua?

— No es inglés lo que leo — contestó sonriendo — sino "americano," que 25
es una lengua muy diferente. El inglés de Inglaterra lo entiendo bastante bien,
pero esta novela del hampa americana contiene muchas palabras que no encuentro
en mi diccionario.

103

Entonces mostró a don José un pequeño diccionario de *pocket* bolsillo, y el profesor le dijo:

— Esa clase de novelas suele emplear una *jargon* jerga especial, es decir, palabras que no se encuentran aun en diccionarios de mayor *size* tamaño que el suyo. Si Vd.
5 quiere yo puedo *help* ayudarle a* *settle* resolver algunas *doubts* dudas.

— Es Vd. muy amable. ¿Fuma Vd.? — preguntó *offering* ofreciéndole un cigarrillo.

— Sí fumo, pero prefiero mis propios cigarrillos. ¿Los conoce?

— *I think so* Creo que sí. Son americanos, ¿no? Aquí también se venden, pero cuestan *they are* un ojo de la cara.* *terribly expensive* Pruebe Vd. uno de los míos — insistió.

10 ➤ Encendieron ambos el cigarrillo y siguieron charlando. El desconocido, que se llamaba* Carlos Noriega, era un hombre de negocios que vestía con elegancia, hablaba con perfección el castellano y había viajado mucho por *almost* casi toda Europa.

— Ahora *I dream* sueño con* hacer un viaje algún día a los Estados Unidos. Todos
15 los españoles sentimos gran curiosidad por conocer *that* ese gran país de donde Vd. viene. *Unfortunately* Por desgracia,* a la *majority* mayoría nos impide realizar este *dream* sueño la falta de dólares. Las *foreign exchanges* divisas están *controlled* controladas por el gobierno y es muy difícil *to attain* conseguir esa moneda.

as there were Como había varias personas esperando a la puerta del bar, los nuevos amigos
20 se levantaron y volvieron a sus respectivos asientos.

B. IDIOMS AND PHRASES

junto a   next to
por lo visto   apparently
dar (las "Buenas tardes")   to wish
  ("Good afternoon")
está perdiendo el tiempo   he is
  wasting his time
no . . . gran cosa   not . . . very much
se quita (la chaqueta)   he takes off
  (his coat)
a causa de   because of, on account of
en voz alta   out loud, in a loud voice
dirigiéndose a (don José)   turning to
  (Don José)
en medio de   in the middle (midst) of

a lo largo de   along
de modo que   so that
ayudarle a (resolver)   to help him to
  (solve)
creo que sí   I think so
cuestan un ojo de la cara   they are
  terribly expensive
que se llamaba (Carlos)   whose name
  was (Charles)
sueño con (hacer)   I dream of
  (making)
por desgracia   unfortunately

C. VERB REVIEW

50. Radical-Changing Verbs.

In certain verbs and under certain conditions the last vowel of the stem (**e** or **o**) changes. The endings of such verbs are always regular. These verbs fall into three classes.

Class I. The verbs of this class belong to the first (**-ar**) and the second (**-er**) conjugations. The stem vowel **e,** *when stressed,* becomes **ie,** and **o,** *when stressed,* becomes **ue.** Note that these changes occur only in four forms of the present indicative and of the present subjunctive (throughout the singular and in the third plural of each tense) and in the singular imperative.

pensar *to think*[1]   **contar** *to count*   **entender** *to understand*   **mover** *to move*

PRESENT INDICATIVE

pienso	cuento	entiendo	muevo
piensas	cuentas	entiendes	mueves
piensa	cuenta	entiende	mueve
pensamos	contamos	entendemos	movemos
pensáis	contáis	entendéis	movéis
piensan	cuentan	entienden	mueven

PRESENT SUBJUNCTIVE

piense	cuente	entienda	mueva
pienses	cuentes	entiendas	muevas
piense	cuente	entienda	mueva
pensemos	contemos	entendamos	movamos
penséis	contéis	entendáis	mováis
piensen	cuenten	entiendan	muevan

IMPERATIVE SINGULAR

piensa (tú)	cuenta (tú)	entiende (tú)	mueve (tú)

Other common verbs of **Class I** are:[2]

acordarse (de) *to remember*
acostar *to lay down, put to bed;*
  acostarse *to lie down; go to bed*

almorzar[3] *to eat lunch, have lunch*
cerrar *to close; lock, fasten*
comenzar[3] *to commence*

---

[1] *To think (= to believe)* = **creer:** Creo que va a llover; *to think of (= to have an opinion of)* = **pensar de:** ¿Qué **piensa Vd. de** él?; *to think of (= to have in one's mind)* = **pensar en;** Pienso en ella; *I think (= it seems to me)* = **me parece:** Me parece que va a llover.

[2] For less frequent verbs of **Class I,** see §76.   [3] Has a spelling-change also; see Chapter VI.

A NEW
SHORTER
SPANISH
REVIEW
GRAMMAR

VERB
REVIEW

contar *to count; tell* (a story)
  contar con *to count on*
costar *to cost*
despertar *to awaken, wake up*
  despertarse *to wake up*
doler *to ache*
empezar[1] **(a)** *to begin*
encender *to light, kindle*
encontrar *to find; come upon*
  encontrarse *to be*
  encontrarse con *to meet*
jugar[2] *to play; gamble*
  jugar a *to play* (cards)
llover *to rain*
mostrar *to show, display*

negar[1] *to deny*
  negarse (a) *to refuse*
nevar *to snow*
perder *to lose; ruin; waste*
  perderse *to get lost*
probar *to prove; test; try out*
recordar *to recall; remember; remind*
rogar[1] *to ask, request*
sentar *to seat*
  sentarse *to sit down*
soler *to be accustomed*
sonar *to sound, ring*
soñar (con) *to dream (of)*
volver *to turn; return; bring back*
  volver a + inf. *again to . . .*
  volverse *to turn around; become*

Cuenta con Vd. *He counts on* you.
Se encuentra solo.
Vuelve a leer la página.

Me **duelen** los oídos. My ears *ache*.
He is (happens to be) alone.
He reads the page *again*.

Class II. The verbs of **Class II** are *all* of the third conjugation and their endings are regular.

(*a*) *When stressed,* the stem vowel **e** becomes **ie** and **o** becomes **ue,** exactly as in Class I.

(*b*) When the stem is *unstressed,* **e** becomes **i** and **o** becomes **u** if the next syllable contains a stressed **a, ie,** or **-ió.**

	sentir *to feel; regret*		**dormir** *to sleep*	
(*a*) PRESENT INDICATIVE	siento	sentimos	duermo	dormimos
	sientes	sentís	duermes	dormís
	siente	sienten	duerme	duermen
IMPERATIVE SINGULAR	siente (tú)		duerme (tú)	
PRESENT SUBJUNCTIVE	sienta		duerma	
	sientas		duermas	
	sienta		duerma	

[1] Has a spelling-change also; see Chapter VI.

[2] Conjugated as though the stem vowel, when stressed, were still **o** rather than **u;** it has a spelling-change also; see Chapter VI: Pres. ind. **juego,** etc.; Pres. subj. **juegue,** etc.; Imperative sing. **juega.**

(b)		sintamos		durmamos
		sintáis		durmáis
(a)		sientan		duerman
(b)	PRESENT PARTICIPLE	sintiendo		durmiendo

PRETERIT	sentí	sentimos	dormí	dormimos
	sentiste	sentisteis	dormiste	dormisteis
	sintió	sintieron	durmió	durmieron
IMPERFECT SUBJUNCTIVE	sintiera, etc.		durmiera, etc.	
	sintiese, etc.		durmiese, etc.	

The following common verbs belong to **Class II:**

adquirir[1] *to acquire, gain*
advertir *to warn, tell; notice*
consentir (en) *to consent (to); permit*
convertir *to convert; change*
  convertirse en *to change into*
divertir *to amuse*
  divertirse *to have a good time*
dormir *to sleep*
  dormirse *to fall asleep*

herir *to wound, strike*
mentir *to lie, tell a falsehood*
morir(se) *to die*
preferir *to prefer*
referir *to refer; relate, tell*
sentir(se) *to feel*

Me divierto mucho. *I am having a very good time.*
Se durmió en el auto. *He fell asleep in the car.*
Ella no **se siente** bien. *She doesn't feel well.*
Prefirieron quedarse en casa. *They preferred to stay home.*

Class III. All verbs of **Class III** are of the *third* conjugation and all have the stem vowel **e.** There are no **o**-stem verbs in this group. All endings are regular.

  (a) When *stressed,* the stem vowel **e** becomes **i.**
  (b) When the stem is *unstressed,* **e** again becomes **i** if the next syllable contains a stressed **a, ie,** or **-ió.**

servir *to serve*

(a) PRESENT INDICATIVE		IMPERATIVE SINGULAR	PRESENT SUBJUNCTIVE	
sirvo	servimos	sirve (tú)	sirva	(b) sirvamos
sirves	servís		sirvas	(b) sirváis
sirve	sirven		sirva	(a) sirvan

---

[1] Conjugated as though the **i** of the stem, when stressed, were still **e.**

(*b*) PRESENT PARTICIPLE PRETERIT IMPERFECT SUBJUNCTIVE

sirviendo	serví	servimos	sirviera, etc.
	serviste	servisteis	sirviese, etc.
	sirvió	sirvieron	

Other common verbs of **Class III** are:

conseguir[1] *to obtain; succeed in*

despedir *to dismiss, discharge*

　despedirse (de) *to say good-by (to)*

elegir[1] *to elect, choose*

impedir *to prevent, hinder, keep from*

pedir[2] *to ask, ask for*

reír[3] *to laugh*

　reírse (de) *to laugh (at)*

Sigue riendo. *He keeps on laughing.*

Ella **se viste** de blanco.

Se despidieron de ella.

rendir *to subdue; yield*

　rendirse *to surrender; get tired*

reñir[4] *to scold; quarrel*

repetir *to repeat; recur*

seguir[1] *to follow; keep on*

servir de *to serve as*

sonreír[3] *to smile*

vestir(se) *to dress*

Sirvió de guía. *He served* as a guide.

She *dresses* in white.

They said good-by to her.

D. EXERCISES ON VERBS

1. *Fill in the blanks with the proper vowel(s)* (**ie, i, ue, u, e, o**), *with accents, when necessary, and translate:*

(*a*)

1. (*cerrar*) Yo c<u>ie</u>rro.
2. (*comenzar*) ¡Com<u>ie</u>ncelo!
3. (*despertar*) Nos desp<u>e</u>rtamos.
4. (*empezar*) Él emp<u>ie</u>za.
5. (*encender*) ¡Enc<u>ie</u>ndalo!
6. (*negar*) Nosotros n<u>e</u>gamos.
7. ¡No lo n<u>ie</u>gue!
8. (*nevar*) N<u>ie</u>va.
9. (*perder*) ¡No lo p<u>ie</u>rda!
10. (*sentar*) S<u>e</u>ntémonos.
11. ¡S<u>ie</u>ntese!
12. (*acordar*) No me ac<u>ue</u>rdo.
13. (*almorzar*) Alm<u>o</u>rcemos.
14. (*encontrar*) Me enc<u>ue</u>ntro con él.

---

[1] Has a spelling-change also; see Chapter VIII.

[2] **Pedir** means *to ask, request, ask for* (something); *to order* (a meal); **preguntar** means *to ask* (a question); **preguntar por** *to ask for, inquire* (concerning someone).

[3] In verbs ending in **-eír** of **Class III**, the **i** of the stem merges with the **i** of the endings **-ie-** and **-ió** so that there are never two **i**'s in succession. Stressed **i** bears the graphic accent: **reír**: Pres. ind. **río**, etc.; Pres. part. **riendo**; Pres. subj. **ría**, etc.; Preterit **rió, rieron**, etc.

[4] The **ñ** of this type of verb absorbs an unstressed **i**: **reñí** but **riñó, riñeron**, etc.

15. (*jugar*) Juega al golf.
16. (*llover*) Llueve.
17. (*mostrar*) ¡Muéstremelo!
18. (*recordar*) ¿Recuerda Vd.?
19. (*rogar*) Se lo ruego.
20. (*soñar*) ¡Sueñe conmigo!

(*b*)

1. (*consentir*) Consienten en venir.
2. (*dormir*) ¡No se duerma Vd.!
3. Se durmió.
4. Están durmiendo.
5. Durmámonos.
6. Duermo.
7. (*divertirse*) Vds. se divirtieron.
8. ¡Diviértanse Vds.!
9. Se está divirtiendo.
10. (*mentir*) Mintió.
(*to lie*) e

11. ¡No mienta!
12. Mentí.
13. (*morir*) Se está muriendo.
14. Me muero de sed.
15. (*preferir*) Prefiramos.
16. Prefirió.
17. (*sentir*) Lo siento.
18. Se sintió enfermo.
19. Sintiéramos.
20. Sentimos.

(*c*)

1. (*conseguir*) Lo consigo.
2. (*despedirse*) Se despide.
3. Despidámonos.
4. Se despidieron.
5. (*elegir*) ¡Elija uno!
6. (*impedir*) ¡No me lo impida!
7. (*reírse*) Me río.
8. ¡No se ría de mí!
9. Se rió.
10. ¡No nos riamos!
11. (*repetir*) ¡Repítalo!
12. Repito.
13. Vd. lo repitió.

14. Estoy repitiendo.
15. (*seguir*) (Que) no sigamos.
16. ¡Siga Vd.!
17. Está siguiendo.
18. Sigue.
19. (*servir*) Sirvo.
20. ¡Sírvase!
21. Sirvieron.
22. (*vestir*) Me visto.
23. ¡Vístase Vd.!
24. Me estoy vistiendo.
25. (*pedir*) ¡No me lo pida!

2. *Replace the dash by the proper form of the verb in parentheses:*

1. (*negarse*) Ahora él se *negó* a devolvérmelo.
2. (*sentir*) Ellos lo *sintieron* mucho (*preterit*).
3. (*dormirse*) Ella estaba cansada y se *durmió*.
4. (*sentir*) Ahora me *siento* enfermo.
5. (*elegir*) El año pasado ellos le *eligieron* presidente.
6. (*costar*) Me *cuesta* trabajo montar a caballo.
7. (*impedir*) Anoche su padre les *impidió* salir.

8. (*despertarse*) Cada mañana ellas se *despiertan* a las cinco.
9. (*pedir*) Anoche él me *pidió* un cigarrillo.
10. (*seguir*) Vds. *siguen* hablando del viaje.
11. (*divertirse*) Es mejor que Vds. *diviertan* (*pres. subj.*) mientras son jóvenes.
12. (*morir*) Estoy *muriendo* de hambre.

3. *Translate:*

(*a*)

1. I don't understand why you always have lunch in the same place.
2. Because they serve good meals there.
3. They don't cost very much and they taste good.
4. I remember when you laughed and scolded the waiter because he kept on repeating that the food was *era* excellent.
5. I don't deny that you always have a good time.
6. Yes. I play golf even when it rains.
7. Does your arm ache today?
8. No, I don't feel any pain.
9. When I go to bed I close my eyes and soon fall asleep.
10. He dressed in a hurry and said good-by to Pedro.

(*b*)

1. Pedro went to bed and slept for two hours.
2. For his part, Don José sits down in the chair, closes his eyes and thinks about him.
3. Then he sleeps for a while, that is, until the children wake him.
4. Some say that they prefer to travel with the windows closed. *cerradas*
5. His traveling companion lights a cigarette and offers him one.
6. Why don't you try one of mine? *uno de míos. le ofrece uno*
7. Thank you. I don't feel well today.
8. By the way, do you understand English?
9. I can read it and I can understand a little, but I don't speak it very well.
10. Sometimes I get lost because some words I can't find (them) in this dictionary.

E. EXERCISE ON IDIOMS AND PHRASES

Translate the words underlined:
1. *A causa de* On account of el calor los hombres *se quitaron* took off la chaqueta.
2. *Por lo visto* Apparently mi compañero de viaje, sentado *junto a* next to la ventana, no entendía inglés.

ayudarle (a usted) ?

? 3. Si Vd. me lo permite yo puedo help you to traducir algunas palabras.

? 4. Con mucho gusto, pues I'm wasting my time sin diccionario. _estoy perdiendo el tiempo_ _distinguiéndola_

5. Después, turning to D. José, le ofreció un cigarrillo. _Por desgracia_

6. Unfortunately estos cigarrillos deben be terribly expensive en España. _estar un ojo de la cara_

? 7. His name was Carlos y hablaba in a loud voice. _Se llamaba_ _voz alta_ _Creo que sí_

8. ¿Desea Vd. acompañarme a tomar un refresco? — I think so; tengo sed.

9. In the middle of el vagón había varios asientos, so that era casi imposible _En medio de_ _de modo que_ salir.

10. I'm dreaming of visitar su país en el otoño. _Sueño con_

SPAIN

Villemot

CHAPTER ELEVEN

A. GRAMMAR AND IDIOM PRACTICE

El profesor explicó a su nuevo amigo el significado de algunas palabras como "bum," "bluff," "thug," y otras por el estilo.* Después el Sr. Noriega cerró el libro y dijo:

— Dejemos esto y cuénteme muchas cosas de su país. ¡Cuánto me alegro de tenerle de compañero de viaje! ¿Es Nueva York verdaderamente tan interesante 5 como dicen?

— Bueno, — contestó don José con una sonrisa — Nueva York es **en efecto** muy interesante para los que tienen dinero y muy triste, también, para los que no lo tienen. Pasa como en todas las grandes ciudades del mundo. Con dinero allí se come bien y se pueden hacer muchas cosas. Lo que me extraña es por 10 qué todos los extranjeros desean visitar Nueva York. Para mí hay ciudades más interesantes en los Estados Unidos, San Francisco, por ejemplo.

— Ya sé que hay otras ciudades importantes en su país, pero para nosotros Nueva York es símbolo de la grandeza y poder de Norteamérica: sus rascacielos, sus puentes gigantescos, sus grandes almacenes, su vida agitada y su animación. 15 ¡Qué diferente de estas ciudades españolas tan históricas y con frecuencia tan sin vida!

— **No obstante** también tienen su encanto — dijo el profesor.

El tren **se iba acercando a** una estación y había disminuido la marcha. Desde la ventanilla del tren, a muy poca distancia,* se veía un castillo 20 imponente. Don José, al verlo, no pudo contener una exclamación . . . "¡Qué maravilla! ¿Qué castillo es ése?" — preguntó.

— Es el castillo de la Mota, en Medina del Campo, donde se dice que murió la gran reina Isabel la Católica. (*El tren llega a la estación.*) Bajemos a estirar las piernas — propuso el Sr. Noriega. — En España no tenemos nunca prisa* 25 y el tren para aquí quince minutos **a lo menos.**

Dieron un paseo* por la estación y Noriega continuó haciendo preguntas sobre la vida en Norteamérica. Quería saber si **era verdad** que la Prensa **113**

was free or was under the control of the large trusts, if it was true
americana era libre o estaba sometida a los grandes "trusts," si era verdad
that the colored race would build a 2nd citizenship
que la raza de color constituía una segunda ciudadanía, si los Estados Unidos
wanted war. In short, he wanted to know what the thought
deseaban la guerra. **En fin,** quería saber lo que los norteamericanos pensaban
of Spain today.
de* España hoy.

Heavens! *many questions. I figure that will spend the night talking*
5 —¡Dios mío! ¡Cuántas preguntas! Me figuro que pasaremos la noche hablan-
since after answering your questions you will have to answer
do, pues después de contestar a sus preguntas Vd. tendrá que contestar a otras
many of mine about present conditions
tantas mías sobre España: sobre su gobierno actual y sobre las condiciones de

vida de los españoles.
That cannot be *smiling* *I am very sorry*
—Eso no podrá ser —dijo Noriega sonriendo. —Lo siento mucho* pero
there will not be time *I am going to the next station* *do*
10 no habrá tiempo porque me bajo en la próxima estación. Venga Vd. conmigo
there we will talk of everything.
a mi casa y allí hablaremos de todo.
What a pity! *they were not meeting me*
—¡Qué lástima! —exclamó don José. —Si no me estuvieran esperando
I would accept *Let them wait for you*
aceptaría su invitación.
Send *right away* *telegram tomorrow*
—Póngale un telegrama* **en seguida** a su amigo ¡Que le esperen mañana!
at *at midnight*
15 El tren llegó a Oviedo a las doce de la noche.* En la estación esperaban a
Rijos *waited*
don José su amigo Lorenzo, su esposa Adela, y sus dos niñas.
more strange thought *to see 2 little so small*
—¡Qué cosa más* rara! —pensó don José al ver a dos niñas tan pequeñas
in *At what hour do children go to bed in Spain?*
en la estación. —¿A qué hora se acuestan los chiquillos en España?
To the notice *the smallest child did not approach to greet him, he*
Al notar el profesor que la niña más pequeña no se acercaba a saludarle, le
said to her:
20 dijo:
Come, *approach* *Bring something for you but I won't give it to you if*
—Ven, Matilde, acércate. Traigo algo para ti pero no te lo daré si no me das
you don't give me a kiss before. Come don't be shy. *she refused*
un besito antes. Ven, no seas tímida.
her father. *go to bed*
—**No le hagas caso,** Pepe —dijo su padre. —No quiso acostarse porque
she said that she wanted to see her uncle for now she doesn't dare speak to you
decía que quería ver a "su tío," y ahora no se atreve a* hablarte. Ya verás
will see how tomorrow she will lose her fear little by little we will become good friends
25 cómo mañana pierde el miedo y **poco a poco** os hacéis* buenos amigos.

B. IDIOMS AND PHRASES

por el estilo *of that sort*

en efecto *as a matter of fact, in fact*

no obstante *however*

se iba acercando a (una estación)
  it was approaching (a station)

a muy poca distancia *at a very
  short distance*

tenemos prisa *we are in a hurry*

a lo menos *at least*

dieron un paseo *they took a stroll*

era verdad *it was true*

en fin *in short*

pensaban de (España) *they were
  thinking about* (Spain)

lo siento mucho *I'm very sorry*

ponga un telegrama *send a telegram*

en seguida *right away*
a las doce de la noche *at midnight*
¡qué (cosa) más (rara)! *what a (queer thing)!*
no le hagas caso *don't pay any attention to her*

se atreve a (hablarte) *she dares to (speak to you)*
poco a poco *little by little*
hacerse (amigos) *to become (friends)*

C. GRAMMAR REVIEW

51. Commands.

(1) Formal commands, affirmative and negative, are regularly expressed in Spanish by the present subjunctive. Contrary to English usage, the subject pronoun **usted (ustedes)** is usually expressed and is placed after the verb.

Cante Vd.[1] *Sing.*	**Canten** Vds. *Sing.*
No **cante** Vd. Don't *sing.*	No **canten** Vds. Don't *sing.*
Cántemela. *Sing* it to me.	No me **canten** Vds. Don't *sing* to me.

When object pronouns are attached to verbs, the graphic accent is sometimes required on the verb to retain the stress in its original position. In negative commands, the pronoun object always precedes the verb.

(2) The English indirect command, *let's,* is expressed by the first person plural of the present subjunctive.

Cantemos. *Let's sing.*	**Cantémos**la. *Let's sing* it.
No la **cantemos.** *Let's* not *sing* it.	No **nos levantemos.** *Let's* not *get up.*
Levantémonos. *Let's get up.*	**Sentémonos.** *Let's sit down.*

Note that when the reflexive **-nos** is attached to a reflexive verb, the final **-s** of the verb is dropped.

The present subjunctive of **ir: vayamos** *let's go,* may be reduced to **vamos.**

Vamos a casa. *Let's go* home.	**Vámonos.** *Let's be going.*

Vamos a + infinitive, *let's,* may substitute for the subjunctive in a command, especially when the act is about to be performed.

Vamos a cantar. *Let's sing.*	**Vamos** a bailar. *Let's dance.*

Vamos a ver may be reduced to **a ver** *let's see.*

---

[1] A command in Spanish is not so blunt as one in English, since **Cante Vd.** originally meant *May your Grace sing.* It is therefore not absolutely necessary to say *please* in Spanish for the sake of politeness.

A NEW
SHORTER
SPANISH
REVIEW
GRAMMAR

GRAMMAR
REVIEW

(3) Indirect commands in the third person, singular or plural, introduced in English by *let, have, may,* are introduced in Spanish by **que** followed by the subjunctive. In this construction the object pronouns precede the verb.

Que lo **cante** él. *Let* him *sing* it.	**Que** lo **haga** Jorge. *Let* George *do* it.
Que suba el baúl.	*Have him bring up* the trunk.

In some expressions **que** may be omitted.

¡Dios le **bendiga!**	(*May*) God *bless* you!
Dios se lo **pague.**	(*May*) God *reward* you.
¡**Viva** España!	*Long live* Spain!

(4) *Let* has still another value (*let me, let us,* etc.) which must be carefully distinguished from the foregoing ones. When *let* means *to allow, permit,* and does not introduce an indirect command, it must be translated by **dejar** or **permitir.**

Déjeme cantar. *Let me* sing.	**Permítame** cantar. *Let me* sing.
Déjele cantar. *Let him* sing.	**Permítales** cantar. *Let them* sing.
Déjenos cantar. *Let us* sing.	**Permítanos** cantar. *Let us* sing.

(5) A command in the *affirmative familiar* form is expressed by the imperative mood. Except for a few verbs given below,[1] the singular (**tú**) form of the imperative and the third person singular present indicative are identical: **Canta.** *He sings* or *Sing.* All negative commands are expressed by the second person present *subjunctive.*[2]

Canta (tú). *Sing.*	No **cantes.** Don't *sing.*
Cántala (tú). *Sing it.*	No la **cantes.** Don't *sing* it.

---

[1] The following verbs are irregular in the imperative singular:

decir: **di**	ir: **vé**	salir: **sal**	tener: **ten**	venir: **ven**
hacer: **haz**	poner: **pon**	ser: **sé**	valer: **val(te)** or **vále(te)**	

[2] The plural imperative of all verbs is formed by replacing the **-r** of the infinitive by **d.**

cantar: **cantad** *sing*	beber: **bebed** *drink*	vivir: **vivid** *live*
Cantadla (vosotros). *Sing it.*	No la **cantéis.** Don't *sing* it.	

The imperative plural of reflexive verbs drops its final **-d.**

Lavados becomes **Lavaos,** niños.	*Wash yourselves,* children.

Exception: **Idos.** *Go away.*

affirmative commands

−ar	−er	−ir
a	e	e
ad	ed	id

The following scheme illustrates the selection of the imperative or subjunctive mood:

AFFIRMATIVE		NEGATIVE
If *familiar*, the imperative mood, otherwise, the subjunctive.		Subjunctive only

SINGULAR

1. **Déjame** (tú) subir.	*(imperative)*	*Let me go up.*	No me **dejes** subir.
Déjeme Vd. subir.	*(subjunctive)*	*Let me go up.*	No me **deje** Vd. subir.
2. **Sube** (tú)	*(imperative)*	*Go up.*	No **subas.**
3. **Suba** Vd.	*(subjunctive)*	*Go up.*	No **suba** Vd.
Que suba él.	*(subjunctive)*	*Let him go up.*	Que no **suba** él.

PLURAL

1. **Subamos.**	*(subjunctive)*	*Let's go up.*	No **subamos.**
2. **Subid** (vosotros).	*(imperative)*	*Go up.*	No **subáis.**
3. **Suban** Vds.	*(subjunctive)*	*Go up.*	No **suban** Vds.
Que suban ellos.	*(subjunctive)*	*Let them go up.*	**Que** no **suban** ellos.

52. Interrogative and Exclamatory Terms.

¿qué? *what? which? what a . . . !*	**¿quién? ¿quiénes?** *who?*
¿cuál? ¿cuáles? *which (one)? what?*	**¿de quién?** *whose? of whom?*
¿cuánto, -a? *how much?*	**¿cuántos, -as?** *how many?*

cuyo is never used in a question.

To differentiate these forms from other parts of speech of identical spelling, the graphic accent is required. The accent remains in indirect questions.

Nos preguntaron **quién** era.	They asked us *who* he was.

53. Uses of Interrogative and Exclamatory Terms.

(1) **¿Qué?** *what? which? what a . . . !* is invariable. It is used as a pronoun or adjective. As a pronoun it is used as subject or object of a verb but *does not refer to persons.*

¿Qué pasó ayer?	*What* happened yesterday?
¿Qué desea Vd. ahora?	*What* do you want now?
¿Qué es poesía? (*definition*)	*What* is poetry?
¿Qué fecha tenemos hoy?	*What* date is it today?
¿Qué ciudad visitó Vd.?	*Which* city did you visit?
¡Qué hermoso castillo!	*What a* beautiful castle!

When the noun is modified by an adjective which follows in Spanish, **más** or **tan** is placed before the adjective for added emphasis.

¡**Qué** libro **más (tan)** interesante!   *What an* interesting book!

¡**Qué . . . !** before an adjective or adverb means *how . . . !*

¡**Qué** raro es su amigo!   *How* strange your friend is!
¡**Qué** despacio lee!   *How* slowly he reads!

What kind of . . . ? is usually ¿**qué clase de . . . ?**

¿**Qué clase de** madera es?   *What kind of* wood is it?

(2) ¿**Cuál?** ¿**cuáles?** *which (one)? what?* is usually a pronoun followed by **ser,** and refers to persons or things.

¿**Cuál** de ellas es su hermana?   *Which one* of them is your sister?
¿**Cuál** es la fecha?   *What* is the date?
¿**Cuál** es su número de teléfono?   *What* is your telephone number?
¿**Cuál** es la capital del Perú?   *What* (city) is the capital of Peru?

Note that ¿**cuál?** stresses choice and ¿**qué?** asks for a definition.

¿**Cuál** es su dirección?   *What* is your address?

But:

¿**Qué** es el átomo?   *What* is the atom?

(3) ¿**Quién?** ¿**quiénes?** *who?* is an interrogative pronoun and is used only of persons. After a preposition it means *whom?* ¿**De quién?** (*not* **cuyo**) means *whose?*

¿**Quién** llegó anoche?   *Who* arrived last night?
¿**A quién** vió Vd. esta mañana?   *Whom* did you see this morning?
Dime con **quién** andas.   Tell me with *whom* you associate.
¿**De quién** es ese jardín?   *Whose* garden is that?

(4) ¿**Cuánto, -a, -os, -as?** *how much? how many?* is used as a pronoun or adjective and is inflected. With a verb ¡**cuánto!** means *how!*

¿**Cuánto** tiene Vd.?   *How much* do you have?
¿**Cuántas** asignaturas estudia Vd.?   *How many* courses are you studying?
¡**Cuánto** me alegro de verle!   *How* glad I am to see you!

¿**A cuánto?** and ¿**a cómo?** are used in inquiring amounts.

¿**A cuántos** estamos? — Estamos a dos.   *What* is the date? — It's the second.

¿**A cómo** se vende este paño?   *What* is the price of this cloth?

(5) ¿**Cómo?** *how? (in what way?)* refers to manner.

¿**Cómo** se cortó Vd. el dedo?   *How* did you cut your finger?

¿**Cómo** le gustan los huevos?   *How* do you like your eggs (cooked)?

When *how do you like . . . ?* means *what is your opinion of . . . ?* it is translated by ¿**qué le parece . . . ?** or ¿**qué tal le gusta . . . ?**

¿**Qué le parece** mi coche? }
¿**Qué tal le gusta** mi coche? }   *How do you like* my car?

D. VERB REVIEW

Dar *to give; hit, strike; take; wish;* **ver** *to see.*

La puerta **da al** jardín.   The door *faces* the garden.
Dió con él en la calle.   He *found* him on the street.
Da cuenta de su viaje.   He *reports on* his trip.
Da un paso.   He *takes* a step.
Se da cuenta del error.   He *realizes* the mistake.
Le **di las gracias.**   I *thanked* him.
Di un paseo ayer.   I *took* a stroll yesterday.

A ver si puede Vd. hacerlo.   *Let's see* if you can do it.
Se ve engañado.   He *is* deceived.
Se ve que Vd. se engaña.   *It is clear* that you are mistaken.

E. GRAMMAR EXERCISES

1. *Translate:*

1. I give. *Yo doy*
2. I gave. *yo dí*
3. She gave. *ella dió*
4. They gave. *ellos dieron*
5. (That) he may give. *que dé él*
6. (That) we might give. *que diesemos nosotros*

7. I see. *Yo veo*
8. See me tomorrow. *Véame ud mañana*
9. They used to see. *ellos veían*
10. You were seeing. *ud. veya*
11. He has seen. *él ha visto*
12. (That) they may see. *que vean ellos* **119**

A NEW
SHORTER
SPANISH
REVIEW
GRAMMAR

GRAMMAR
EXERCISES

2. (a) *Give the polite (**usted**) forms for the following intimate forms:*

1. Dímelo. *dígamelo Vd.* ?
2. Acostaos. *acuéstense Vds.*
3. Sé bueno. *sea Vd. bueno*
4. Sígueme. *sígame Vd.* ?
5. No me los des. *no le los de* ?

6. Asomaos a la ventana. *Asómense a la vent*
7. No les escribas. *no les escriba Vd.*
8. No os lo pongáis. *no se lo pongan V*
9. Idos de aquí. *váyanse de aquí*
10. Dánoslo. *dénoslo Vd.*

(b) *Give the intimate (**tú**) forms for the following polite forms:*

1. Sea bueno. *Sé bueno.* ?
2. No me los dé. *no me los des*
6K 3. Muéstreme la falta. ?
4. No se duerma. *no te duerma*
5. Vístase ahora. *ite*

6. Pierda cuidado.
7. Venga mañana.
8. Póngaselo. *póntelo*
9. No se moleste por mí. *te se*
10. Salga ahora.

(c) *Give the affirmative form of the same person (in the subjunctive or imperative mood, as required) of:*

1. No te vayas. *vete* ?
2. No se quejen Vds. *quejen se Vds.*
3. No se lo prestes. *préstaselo*
4. No nos sentemos. *sentemonos*
5. No se la dé Vd. *désela Vd.*

6. No nos lo envíen Vds. *envíen los Vd.*
7. No te escapes. *escápete*
8. No nos lo pida Vd. *pídanoslo Vd.*
9. No nos levantemos. *levantemonos*
10. No se despierte Vd. *despiértese Vd.*

*1. no te rías
no os riáis
no se ría Vd.
no serían Vds.* ?

*2. diviértete
divertíos
diviértase Vd.
diviértanse Vds.*

*3. Díselo
Decídselo
Dígaselo Vd.
Díganselo Vds*

*4. Sal
Salid
Salga Vd.
Salgan Vds.*

*5. hazlo al instante
hacedlo " "
hágalo Vd. "
háganlo Vds. "*

*6. Ten
Tened
Tenga Vd.
Tengan Vds.*

*7. vete Váyase
Idos Váyanse*

3. *Translate the English words, using the familiar (**tú**) and the formal (**usted**) command forms in both the singular and plural:*

1. (*Do not laugh*) de nuestra situación.
2. (*Have a good time*) esta noche.
3. (*Tell*)selo.
4. (*Go out*) cuanto antes.
5. (*Do*)lo al instante.

6. (*Have*) paciencia.
7. (*Go away*) en seguida.
8. (*Put*)lo en el pupitre.
9. (*Come*) ahora mismo.
10. (*Be*) bueno.

4. *Translate the English words:*

1. ¿(*What*) anunció él? *Qué*
2. ¿(*Who*) arregló el asunto? *Quién*
3. ¿(*How much*) cuesta un par de zapatos? *Cuánto*
4. ¿(*What*) es el número de su calle? *Cuál*
5. ¿(*Who*) le asustaron? *Quién*
6. ¿(*Which*) es su primo de Vd.? *Cuál*
7. ¿(*What*) es justicia? *Qué*
8. ¿(*Whose*) es este traje? *De quién*

120

*8. Ponlo
Ponedlo Vd
Póngalo Vd
Pónganlo Vds.*

*9. Ven
Venid Vd.
Venga Vd.
Vengan Vds*

*10. se
Sed Vd
Sea
Sean Vds.*

9. ¡(*How*) feliz es Vd.! Qué
10. ¡(*What*) fortuna! Qué
11. ¿(*Whom*) llevó Vd. al baile? a quién
12. No sé (*who*) era. quién
13. ¡(*What a*) desgracia! Qué
14. ¿(*How*) podemos cruzar el río? Como
15. ¿De (*what*) color es su corbata? qué/
16. ¿(*How many*) meses piensa Vd. quedarse allí? Cuanto
17. ¿(*What*) es la capital de su estado? Cual,
18. ¿De (*whom*) recibieron tales noticias? quién
19. ¿(*What*) es su nombre? cual
20. ¡(*What*) mentiras dice él! que/

5. *Translate:*

(*a*)

1. Give me your address, please.
2. What's your telephone number at home?
3. Let's write to each other next year.
4. Let's go once more to the old café.
5. Let's see if you know how to order a meal in Spanish.
6. If you can't, let me do it for (**por**) you.
7. What a fine dinner you have chosen!
8. How much did you pay for it?
9. Which dessert did you like best (most)?
10. What a sweet voice the waitress had!

(*b*)

1. Tell me something about your country.
2. What a difference between your cities and ours!
3. What a beautiful castle! — exclaimed Don José.
4. Let's see if you know where we are!
5. Let's get off the train. I would like to see the station.
6. Let me invite you to (**a**) [have] a cup of coffee.
7. How strange to find a Spaniard who doesn't drink coffee!
8. Come to my house and let's continue our conversation there.
9. Let them meet you tomorrow. Send them a telegram.
10. Don José said to the child: — Come here, don't be shy.

(over)

F. EXERCISE ON IDIOMS AND PHRASES

Translate the words underlined:

1. El profesor y Noriega *hacerse* became buenos amigos right away. *en seguida*
2. *no obstante* However Carlos *se atrevió a* did not dare to hablar en público de cosas of that sort. *por el estilo.*
3. *a lo menos* At least Vd. podrá decirme lo que los españoles think of nosotros. *piensan de*
4. *Era verdad.* It was true. Se podía ver el castillo at a very short distance. *a muy poca distancia .*
5. *Poco a poco* Little by little el tren was approaching Medina del Campo. *se iba acercando a*
6. *dar un paseo* Vamos a take a stroll por la estación.
7. *En fin* In short, ¿viene Vd. conmigo a mi casa o are you in a hurry? *tiene usted prisa?*
8. ¿Por qué don't you send un telegrama a su amigo? *ponga un telegrama*
9. At midnight? I don't dare. *¿A las doce de la noche? yo no se atrevo.(?)*
10. *no hagas caso* Don't pay any attention de la hora. En España nadie se acuesta temprano.

CHAPTER TWELVE

A. GRAMMAR AND IDIOM PRACTICE

— ¡Es lástima que no te decidas a quedarte más días con nosotros! — le dijo
su amigo a don José. — La semana que viene tengo que ir a uno de los pueblos
más bonitos de la provincia y **de veras** me gustaría que me acompañaras.

— Entonces no hablemos más. Te acompaño. Deseo que me expliques muchas
cosas de esta hermosa tierra, pues es probable que no vuelva nunca a verla. 5

Por la tarde llegó una carta de Pedro que decía:

— Estimado maestro y amigo:

Espero que ésta le encuentre contento y feliz, **Tal vez** le sorprenda saber
que a los pocos días de* salir Vd. de Segovia determiné viajar también hacia
el norte, a Santiago de Compostela, en vez de* ir a Burgos como tenía planeado. 10
Permítame que le explique por qué he cambiado de planes. En primer lugar*
porque aquí, en Santiago, no hace tanto calor como en Burgos, y en segundo
lugar porque desde que leímos en su clase aquella novela *La casa de la Troya*
he sentido deseos de* ver esta ciudad. Además, mi profesor de Historia de
España en Segovia contó las glorias de Santiago, diciendo que durante la Edad 15
Media había sido una de las ciudades más importantes, un lugar de peregrinación a donde acudían peregrinos de todo el mundo.* Según una leyenda se
descubrió aquí, a principios del* siglo IX, el sepulcro del apóstol Santiago y
en el mismo lugar se edificó una ermita que más tarde se convirtió en
magnífica catedral. 20

Temo que se esté riendo de mí al leer estas cosas. Pero no me importa que
se ría. Me alegro de haber venido. El Pórtico de la Gloria de la catedral,
ejemplo magnífico del arte románico, es lo que más me ha impresionado hasta
ahora. Ayer, imitando a millares de peregrinos que han pasado por aquí, puse
los cinco dedos de la mano derecha en la columna central de este pórtico. 25
También fuí a ver la imagen del Apóstol detrás del altar mayor, pero no la
abracé ni besé como hacían otros.

123

Le ruego que siga leyendo porque aún debo contarle algo que me llamó
mucho la atención.* Dentro de la catedral vi que siete acólitos vestidos de*
rojos sayales sacaban un enorme incensario, lo colgaban de una cuerda y luego
lo elevaban hasta la bóveda. Después, tirando de* la cuerda lo sacudían a
5 manera de* péndulo y densas nubes de incienso se extendían por todo el
interior. Como es posible que Vd. no sepa el origen de este incensario, llamado
botafumeiro, voy a explicárselo. Se dice que en tiempos antiguos era necesario
derramar mucho incienso para combatir el mal olor producido por la aglomeración de tantos cuerpos sudorosos. **Hay que tener en cuenta** que estos

10 peregrinos venían a pie* de muy lejos y llegaban muy sucios.

En fin, Santiago es una ciudad muy interesante que le recomiendo visite, si
es que no la conoce. Si Vd. viene le aconsejo se fije en* una estatua arrodillada
que hay a la entrada. Cuentan que es la estatua del gran escultor que hizo todas
las figuras del Pórtico. Cuentan también que está tan gastada porque durante
15 siglos muchas madres han traído a sus niños para acercar sus cabezas a la del
artista y ver si **de** ese **modo** se les transmite parte del genio del creador.
Siguiendo la costumbre, acerqué también mi cabeza en la esperanza de que
aumentasen mis conocimientos de español, pero siento decirle que no he notado
mejora ninguna.
20 Acaso le escriba **otra vez** antes de salir de España, aunque no estoy seguro
de que le interesen las cosas que le cuento. Mientras tanto* cuídese y
diviértase.

Su buen amigo y mal alumno,

Pedro Burk

B. IDIOMS AND PHRASES

de veras *really, truly*
tal vez *perhaps*
a los pocos días de (salir Vd.) *a few days after* (you left)
en vez de *instead of*
en (primer) **lugar** *in the* (first) *place*
he sentido deseos de (ver) *I've had the desire to* (see)
de todo el mundo *from everywhere*

a principios de(l siglo) *at the beginning of* (the century)
(me) **llamó la atención** *attracted* (my) *attention*
vestido de (sayales) *wearing, dressed in* (sackcloth robes)
tirando de (la cuerda) *pulling* (the rope)

a manera de (péndulo) *like a*
  (pendulum)
hay que tener en cuenta *one must*
  (should) bear in mind
a pie *on foot*

fijarse en (una estatua) *to notice*
  (a statue)
de (ese) **modo** *in* (that) *manner*
otra vez *again*
mientras tanto *in the meantime*

C. GRAMMAR REVIEW

54. The Theory of the Subjunctive Mood.

(*a*) The indicative mood in a dependent clause expresses a *fact*. (*b*) To the subjunctive mood then falls the role of expressing in a dependent clause an action or state that is *uncertain* or that *has not been accomplished* at the time the speaker has in mind. (*c*) In those instances where a subjunctive expresses a fact, the emphasis is not on the fact but on the speaker's attitude or feeling toward it.

(*a*) Es cierto que él **está** aquí.	It is certain that he *is* here.
(*b*) No es cierto que él **esté** aquí.	It is not certain that he *is* here.
Deseo que él **esté** aquí.	I desire that he *be* here.
(*c*) Siento que él **esté** aquí.	I am sorry that he *is* here.

Note that the subjunctive is not used unless the subjects of the two clauses are *different*.

(Yo) deseo estar aquí.	I desire to be here.
(Yo) deseo que **él esté** aquí.	*I* desire that *he be* here.

55. The Subjunctive in Main Clauses.

While the principal use of the subjunctive is in dependent clauses, under certain conditions it may appear in a main clause:

(1) In commands; these are sometimes introduced by **que.** (See §51.)

Présteme su pluma. *Lend* me your pen. **Sentémonos** allí. *Let's sit* there.
¡Que lo **pase** bien! *Good luck!* **Perdone.** *Pardon* me.

(2) After **acaso, quizá(s), tal vez** *perhaps,* when doubt is implied.

Tal vez **salga** yo mañana. Perhaps I'll *leave* tomorrow.

(3) The imperfect subjunctive forms, **quisiera, debiera,** and **pudiera** are sometimes used in main clauses instead of the conditional or present indicative for politeness or to soften a statement.

Quisiera verle a Vd.	*I want (should like)* to see you.	**CHAPTER TWELVE**
Vd. **debiera** estudiar más.	You *ought to (should)* study more.	
Pudiera ser verdad.	It *could* be true.	

56. The Subjunctive in Noun (Dependent) Clauses.

The subjunctive mood is required after verbs expressing:

(1) Emotion (**alegrarse** *to be glad,* **esperar** *to hope,* **sentir** *to be sorry, regret,* **sorprender** *to surprise,* **temer, tener miedo** *to be afraid, fear,* **es lástima** *it is a pity,* etc.).

Espero que[1] Vd. **venga.**	I hope you *will come.*
Él teme que ellos no **escuchen.**	He is afraid they *aren't listening.*

(2) Desire (**desear** *to wish,* **gustar** *to please,* **preferir** *to prefer,* **querer** *to wish,* etc.).

Preferimos que Vd. lo **lea.**	We prefer that you *read* it.
Quieren que **escribamos.**	They want *us to write.*
Querían que **escribiéramos.**	They wanted *us to write.*

Note that the English infinitive must often be rendered by the present or imperfect subjunctive, the choice of tense depending upon the tense of the main verb. (See §57.)

(3) Necessity (**es necesario, es preciso** *it is necessary,* etc.).

Es necesario que **trabajemos.**	It is necessary that *we work.*
Es preciso que **salgamos.**	It is necessary *for us to leave.*

(4) Commands (**mandar** *to order,* **decir** *to tell,* **escribir** *to write*); requests (**pedir** *to ask,* **rogar** *to beg*); permission (**permitir, dejar** *to allow*); causation (**hacer** *to have, cause*); etc.

Le[2] mando que **se quede** en casa.	I order you *to stay* home.
Les rogamos que nos **visiten.**	We beg them *to visit* us.

---

[1] **Que** after an expression that governs a subjunctive is rarely omitted.

[2] In most cases, to be learned from observation, the pronoun object of a verb governing the subjunctive mood should be retained as the *indirect* object of this verb:

I tell *him* to come. **Le** digo que venga *rather than* Digo que **él** venga.

He asks *me* to come. **Me** ruega que venga *rather than* Ruega que **yo** venga.

Exceptions:

I want *him* to come. Quiero que **él** venga. (Don't say **Le** quiero que venga.)

He desires *me* to come. Desea que **yo** venga. (Don't say **Me** desea que venga.)

When say I don't doubt, you use regular tense.
When say I doubt, you use subjunctive tense.

(5) Possibility (**es posible** *it is possible*), etc.; probability (**es probable** *it is probable*); etc.

Es posible que **respondan.**	It is possible that they *will reply*.
Es probable que **entiendan.**	It is probable that they *understand*.

(6) Doubt (**dudar** *to doubt,* and frequently **no creer** *not to believe,* etc.).

Dudo que **estudien** mucho.	I doubt that they *study* very much.
No creo que **viva** (vive) allí.	I don't think he *lives* there.

(7) Approval, opinion, advisability, importance (**vale más** *it is better,* **importa** *it matters, it is important;* **basta** *it is enough*); etc.

Más vale que nos **marchemos.**	It is better that we *leave*.
	We had better *leave*.
Basta que Vd. lo **prometa.**	It is enough that you *promise* it.

57. Sequence of Tenses.

The Spanish future subjunctive is no longer in general use and has been replaced by the present subjunctive. There is no conditional subjunctive: the English auxiliaries *would* and *should* in dependent clauses usually indicate that the accompanying verb is in the imperfect subjunctive in Spanish. Except for these instances, the tense of the subjunctive in Spanish is usually that of English.[1]

I am afraid he is not *studying.*	
I am afraid he does not *study.*	**Temo** que no **estudie.**
I am afraid he will not *study.*	

I am afraid he did not *study.*	**Temo** que no **estudiara.**
I am afraid he has not *studied.*	**Temo** que no **haya estudiado.**

I was afraid he did not *study.*	
I was afraid he would not *study.*	**Temía** que no **estudiara.**
I was afraid he had not *studied.*	**Temía** que no **hubiera estudiado.**

---

[1] *I want you to study.* becomes
I want that you study. } **Deseo** que Vd. **estudie.**

He wanted you to study. becomes
He wanted that you should study. } **Deseaba** que Vd. **estudiara.**

58. Use of the Infinitive for the Subjunctive.

We have seen that the subjunctive is used when the subject of the dependent verb is different from that of the main verb.

(Yo) quiero bailar.	I want to dance.

But:

(Yo) quiero que **él** baile.	*I* want *him* to dance.

However, after a few verbs and expressions (to be learned from observation), the infinitive may be used instead of the subjunctive, provided the infinitive has a pronoun as its subject.

(1) This use of the infinitive for the subjunctive is particularly common with **ser** in the impersonal construction.

Me es imposible **quedar.** *rather than*
Es imposible que **yo quede.** } It is impossible *for me to stay.*

(2) If the subject of the infinitive is indefinite (not expressed), the infinitive, not the subjunctive, is the usual construction.

Es fácil **criticar.**	It is easy (*for one*) *to criticize.*

(3) After **dejar** *to allow,* **hacer** *to have, cause,* and **mandar** *to order,* the infinitive construction is more frequent than the subjunctive.

Déjele salir. *Let him come out.*		**Mándele** volver. *Order him to return.*

(4) After **permitir** *to permit* and **impedir** *to prevent,* the infinitive and subjunctive are used with equal frequency.

Nos permiten **ir.** *or*
Nos permiten que **vayamos.** } They permit *us to go.*

Le impido **saltar.** *or*
Le impido que **salte.** } I prevent *him from jumping.*

D. VERB REVIEW

Andar *to go, walk;* **oír** *to hear.*

Andamos buscando la llave.	*We are (go)* looking for the key.
Su reloj **anda** bien.	His watch *runs* well.
¡Oiga!	Listen!
Han **oído de** su belleza.	They have *heard of* her beauty.

129

E. GRAMMAR EXERCISES

1. *Translate:*

1. He went. *él fué*
2. We walked. *anduvimos* (b)
3. (That) she might go. *que fuera ella*
4. I hear. *yo oigo*
5. He hears. *oye*
6. We heard. *oímos*

7. I heard. *yo oí*
8. We have heard. *hemos oído*
9. Listen! *escuche usted*
10. Let us hear. *oigamos nosotros*
11. (That) we might hear. *que oyéramos nosotros*

2. *Change the infinitive in parentheses to the subjunctive or indicative when necessary.*

1. Tal vez yo (*volver*) mañana. *vuelva*
2. Por favor, (*preparar*) Vds. dos lecciones para el lunes. *preparen*
3. Me alegro de que ellas (*encontrarse*) mejores. *se encuentran mejores*
4. Es verdad que ellos (*estar*) en el centro. *están*
5. Él temía que ella no le (*ver*) anoche. *viera*
6. Sentimos que ellos lo (*perder*). *perdieran*
7. Desean que Vds. (*oír*) lo que están diciendo. *oigan*
8. Es lástima que ella no (*poder*) hallarlo. *pueda*
9. Querían que nosotros le (*escribir*) todos los días. *escribiéramos*
10. Era preciso que él nos (*visitar*). *visitara*
11. Es imposible que Jorge lo (*hacer*). *haga*
12. Dudamos que ellos (*ser*) sinceros. *sean*
13. Basta que Vd. me lo (*decir*). *diga*
14. Más vale que ella no (*hablar*) tanto. *hable*
15. Es imposible que yo (*quedar*) (*two ways*). *quede* *quedara?*
16. Nos permitieron que (*fumar*) (*two ways*). *fuma* *fumáramos ?*
17. Me dice que (*subir*) al coche. *suba*
18. Le pidió que (*callarse*). *se callara*
19. ¡Que Vd. (*gozar*) de mejor salud! *goce*
20. Es probable que él no (*tener*) dinero. *tenga*
21. Me sorprendió que él (*decir*) eso. *dijera*
22. Siento no (*poder*) ir. *poder* (b)
23. Escríbale que nos (*enviar*) dinero. *envíe*
24. ¡Que él (*descansar*) en paz! *descanse*
25. Que ella la (*cantar*) ahora. *cante*
26. Le rogué que me (*permitir*) fumar. *permitir*

3. *Translate:*

(*a*)

1. I am glad that you have lost your (the) fear.
2. He doubted that many were wholly satisfied.
3. It does not matter to me whether (that) you tell the truth or not.
4. Pardon me, sir, lend me your pen, please.
5. It was necessary for him to tear the paper.
6. Their mother asked them to pick up their clothes from the floor.
7. It was not enough that they promised to do it.
8. It was a pity that he decided not to stay longer.
9. It was probable that the professor would not return there.
10. He was afraid that his feet would attract attention.

(*b*)

1. I am sorry you are not staying longer with us.
2. It is impossible for me to stay more than a week.
3. I would like you to accompany me on a trip that I intend to take.
4. Then let's go. Perhaps I shall never return to Asturias.
5. Pedro's letter began: I was glad to see you last week.
6. Allow me to tell you what (**lo que**) I have done since you left Segovia.
7. It is possible that you have not seen Santiago.
8. I hope you can come here some day.
9. Do you wish me to explain to you the origin of the *botafumeiro?*
10. I don't believe that you will be back in Madrid until August 15th.

F. EXERCISE ON IDIOMS AND PHRASES

1. *Translate the words underlined:*

1. One must pensarlo in the meantime.
2. Creo truly que le gustará la catedral.
3. Hay que bear in mind que allí venían peregrinos from everywhere y que hacían el viaje on foot.
4. Perhaps Vd. have the desire to ver Santiago again.
5. In the first place, noticed las estatuas del Pórtico.
6. También el "botafumeiro" attracted my attention.
7. Los acólitos dressed in rojo pulled una cuerda y in that manner sacudían el incensario.

131

a principios de

8. At the beginning of la semana Pedro estaba back ~~*de vuelta*~~ en Segovia.

A los pocos días

9. A few days later terminaba el curso.

En vez de

10. Instead of estudiar él prefería divertirse viajando.

2. *Translate:*

In the afternoon he took walks. On seeing him they embraced + Kissed. Then let's go

Por la tarde daba paseos. Al verse se abrazaron y besaron. Entonces vamos

at the same time. People came from everywhere. What a beautiful girl!

ahora mismo. Acudía gente de todas partes. ¡Qué muchacha más bonita!

He imagines that he is in love. How glad I am to know you! There is no

Se figura que está enamorada. ¡Cuánto me alegro de conocerle! No habrá

time to answer your questions. He approached to greet him. along

tiempo de contestar a sus preguntas. Se acercó para saludarle. A lo largo

the way there were trees. Money doesn't interest me a great deal.

del camino había árboles. No me interesa gran cosa el dinero. Al poco

On one side there was a table. There he waited for him friend

rato le despertaron. A un lado había una mesa. Allí le esperaba su amigo.

according to him, the statue was very worn away

Según él, la estatua estaba muy gastada.

CHAPTER THIRTEEN

A. GRAMMAR AND IDIOM PRACTICE

Don José was still in   *enjoying*   *this delightful*

Aún estaba don José en Asturias gozando de aquel clima delicioso cuando
recibió *another letter* otra carta de Pedro. Era una carta bastante larga, escrita en Barcelona
con fecha del* *a date of* 15 de agosto, *he thereby* unas horas antes de salir él en avión *for* para Londres.
Decía que se había detenido *had stopped* dos días en Madrid — el primero y el dos de
agosto — para visitar el soberbio *magnificent* Museo del Prado. Después había ido a Toledo, *afterwards had gone* 5
ciudad que *apparently* por lo visto le había interesado* mucho *by being* por estar situada *on* en una
colina casi rodeada *hill* *almost completely surrounded* por completo por el río Tajo, por su aspecto *by* *appearance of a medieval city* de ciudad
medieval y, **sobre todo,** *and, especially* por las leyendas *that refer to it.* *Now we know* que a ella se refieren. (Ya sabemos
que Pedro era muy aficionado a* *fond* las leyendas.) *One of these tells that* Una de ellas cuenta que cuando
Alfonso VI conquistó *conquered* la ciudad a los moros, *from the Moors* en 1085, *his horse knelt* su caballo se arrodilló 10
al pasar *in passing in front of* en frente de una pequeña mezquita. *mosque.* *Surprised the king by such a miracle,* Sorprendido el rey de tal milagro,
he ordered that they enter to investigate, + there, mandó que entraran a investigar, y allí, en un lugar oculto *hidden place, they discovered* descubrieron una
imagen de Cristo *christ* y junto a ella *beside it,* una luz que *a light that had been burning since* ardía desde el tiempo de los
visigodos. *visigoths.* Como es natural, Pedro fué a ver *went* esta *this* hermosa joya *jewel* del arte árabe, *arabian art,*
today called *hermitage of the Light of Christ.* llamada hoy ermita del *Cristo de la Luz.* 15

Otra leyenda que Pedro había leído *had read* es *is that related by* la relatada por Zorrilla con el título *title*
de *A buen juez, mejor testigo.* *A good judge, better witness; He relates this* Refiere esta leyenda que una vez *once* un soldado *soldier* español
had sworn eternal fidelity to a youngster before había jurado fidelidad eterna a una joven ante la imagen de un Cristo crucificado.
El soldado se fué después *in* a las guerras *wars* que España sostenía *carried on thru all* por toda Europa y
when he returned, years later and now captain, he denied *he might have made the oath.* cuando regresó, años más tarde y ya capitán, negó que hubiera hecho jura- 20
they took declaration from mento. Tomaron declaración al *Cristo de la Vega* *Christ of the Meadow* y éste al tiempo que bajaba *he lowered*
the hand said *yes I swore this* *known today* la mano dijo: "Sí juro." Esta imagen es conocida hoy con el nombre de "El
the unnailed hand *hermitage is found* *seldom* Cristo de la mano desclavada," y la ermita donde se encuentra — raras veces* *rarely*
visited by *tourists* *on* *outskirts of* visitada por los turistas — está en las afueras de la ciudad.
Later *letter* *Another* *all* *I have followed your advise, I went* Luego continuaba la carta: "Para que Vd. vea que he seguido sus consejos fuí 25
also *its* *begun to be* también a Andalucía. Visité la mezquita de Córdoba, empezada a construir en
8th century and *had* *(400)* el siglo VIII y que en un tiempo* tuvo 1.200 columnas. *You were right,* Tenía Vd. razón, las
still remain *give its* *appearance of a forest of* 850 columnas que todavía quedan dan a su interior el aspecto de un bosque de **133**

A NEW
SHORTER
SPANISH
REVIEW
GRAMMAR

GRAMMAR
AND IDIOM
PRACTICE

palmeras. Después fuí a Sevilla para ver su hermosa Giralda. **Por cierto que**
no querían dejarme subir a la torre a menos que* entrase otra persona conmigo. ¡Como si yo tuviera cara de* hombre capaz de suicidarse! Afortunadamente llegaron otros turistas, y mientras la mujer les cobraba las entradas yo
5 entré por la puerta sin que ella lo notara. ¡Qué vista tan espléndida de la ciudad y del río Guadalquivir desde lo alto* de la torre!

Estas ciudades andaluzas tienen algo exótico que no sé describir bien. Algunas de las calles estrechas de Sevilla, cubiertas de* toldos que se extienden de un lado al otro de la calle para proteger del fuerte sol a los transeúntes, dan
10 la impresión de un bazar oriental. Por esta razón, a pesar del* intenso calor me hubiera gustado permanecer más tiempo allá. Su ambiente de alegría y de vida reposada y tranquila me hacen decir con los sevillanos: 'Quien no ha visto Sevilla no ha visto maravilla.'

Pasa de* la una y cuarto y tengo mucha hambre. En cuanto* termine de*
15 comer seguiré escribiéndole hasta que llegue la hora de* salir para el aeropuerto, a eso de* las cuatro de la tarde.''

B. IDIOMS AND PHRASES

con fecha de (l 15) *dated (the 15th)*	**desde lo alto** *from the top*
sobre todo *especially*	**cubiertas de** (toldos) *covered with*
era aficionado a *he was fond of*	(awnings)
raras veces *rarely, seldom*	**a pesar de** *in spite of*
en un tiempo *formerly*	**pasa de** (la una) *it's after* (one)
por cierto que *incidentally; to be sure*	**en cuanto** *as soon as*
a menos que *unless*	**terminar de** (comer) *to finish*
tener cara de (hombre) *to look like*	(eating)
(a man)	**a eso de** (las cuatro) *at about* (four)

C. GRAMMAR REVIEW

59. The Subjunctive in Adverbial Clauses.

Adverbial clauses are those introduced by conjunctions. The subjunctive mood is used in an adverbial clause when the action is represented as *not yet having taken place* (and therefore not a fact) at the time indicated by the verb.

Although it *may rain* tomorrow . . .	Aunque **llueva** mañana . . .
When you *come* tonight . . .	Cuando Vd. **venga** esta noche . . .

134

EL PRADO

THE FIRST PICTURE MUSEUM OF THE WORLD

Iberia

A NEW
SHORTER
SPANISH
REVIEW
GRAMMAR

GRAMMAR
REVIEW

If the action *has already taken place,* or *is accepted as a fact,* the indicative mood is used.

Although it *is raining* . . .	Aunque **llueve** . . .
When I *saw* you last night . . .	Cuando le **vi** a Vd. anoche . . .
When he *sees* me, he always speaks.	Cuando me **ve,** siempre me saluda.
When he *studies,* he learns.	Cuando **estudia,** aprende.

(1) Since they can never introduce a statement of fact, the following conjunctions are always followed by the subjunctive:

antes (de) que *before*	**para que** *in order that*
como si[1] *as if*	**sin que**[2] *without*

Lo leí antes de que Vd. **llegara.**   I read it before you *arrived.*
Lo escribió sin que yo le **ayudara.**   He wrote it without my *helping* him.
Me habla como si me **conociera.**   He speaks to me as if he *knew* me.

(2) The following conjunctions govern the subjunctive only when the action of the dependent verb *has not been completed,* or *is not stated as a fact:*

aunque *although*	**de manera que** *so that*	**en cuanto** *as soon as*
cuando *when*	**de modo que** *so that*	**hasta que** *until*
como (manner) *as*	**después (de) que** *after*	**mientras (que)** *while*[3]

En cuanto él lo **vea,** gritará.   As soon as he *sees* it, he will shout.
But: En cuanto lo **vió,** gritó.   As soon as he *saw* it, he shouted.

Quedaré hasta que Vd. lo **acabe.**   I'll stay until you *finish* it.
But: Quedé hasta que Vd. lo **acabó.**   I stayed until you *finished* it.

Some conjunctions have corresponding prepositional forms: **sin—sin que, antes de—antes de que,** etc. In such instances, when the subject of the independent and dependent verbs is the same, *the infinitive* is often used instead of the *conjunction with the subjunctive.*

---

[1] **Como si** is always followed by an imperfect or pluperfect subjunctive.

[2] Less common conjunctions of this type are:
a fin de que *in order that*   **a no ser que** *unless*
a menos que *unless*   **con tal que** *provided that*

[3] Less common conjunctions in this group are:
así que *as soon as*	**luego que** *as soon as*	**siempre que** *whenever*
bien que *although*	**si bien** *although*	**tan pronto como** *as soon as*

Antes de **salir (yo), (yo)** le pagué.   Before *leaving, I* paid him.
But: Antes que **yo saliese, él** me pagó.   Before *I left, he* paid me.

60. Cardinal Numerals. (See §77.)

Of the cardinal numerals, only **uno,** its compounds, and compounds of **ciento** are inflected. They regularly precede the noun they modify.

siete u[1] ocho árboles *7 or 8* trees   **cuatro** palabras *a few (four)* words
quinientas noches *500* nights   **setecientos** autores *700* authors

From 16 to <u>29</u> the numerals are <u>often written as one word,</u> with the graphic accent added to **dieciséis, veintiún, veintitrés,** and **veintiséis.**

dieciséis

veintiún (veinte y un) estados   *twenty-one* states
veintiuna (veinte y una) frases   *twenty-one* sentences

Note that **veintiún (veinte y un)** and **veintiuna (veinte y una)** are in the singular.

Estamos en la página **veintitrés.**   We are on page *twenty-three.*

Ciento becomes **cien** before a noun of either gender, and before **mil** and **millón.** Ciento (cien) and **mil** are seldom preceded by **un** or followed by **de; millón,** on the other hand, is considered to be a noun and is preceded by **un** and followed by **de.**

cien cambios *one hundred* changes   **cien** fuentes *one hundred* fountains
cien mil personas *100,000* persons   **cien** millones *100,000,000*
cien pesos *100* weights, pesos   **un millón de** gracias *a million* thanks

In oral counting and in dates above one thousand, Spanish does <u>not</u> count by hundreds as does English but by adding hundreds to (one) thousand.

mil setecientos *1700*   **mil novecientos sesenta** *1960*

Y appears only in the numbers 16–19, 21–29, etc. to 91–99.

diez y seis (dieciséis) *16*   *But:* **ciento veinte y ocho** *128*

---

[1] Before **o-** or **ho-, u** is used for **o.**

(1) The cardinal numerals are used to express the day of the month, except the *first*, **primero.** The article is regularly used in expressing dates, except when the date is in apposition with another expression of time, or follows the place name in the heading of a letter, or is used after the preposition **a.**

¿Cuál es la fecha (de hoy)?
¿Qué fecha es (tenemos) (hoy)?
¿Qué día del mes tenemos (hoy)?
¿A cuántos estamos (hoy)?

} *What is the date (today)?*

(Hoy) es **el dos** de junio.
(Hoy) estamos a **dos** de junio.

} (Today) is *the second* of June.

Mañana será **el primero** de mayo.
Hoy es jueves, **3** de agosto.
Madrid, **4** de febrero.

Tomorrow will be *the first* of May.
Today is Thursday, *the 3d* of August.
Madrid, *the 4th* of February.

(2) Cardinal numerals are used to express the hours of the day. (See §62.)

61. Ordinal Numerals. (See §78.)

Ordinal numerals may precede or follow the noun they modify. They follow the noun with titles, chapters of books, volumes, etc. Beginning with *eleventh*, the ordinal is replaced by the cardinal numeral. **Primero** and **tercero** drop their final **-o** before a masculine singular noun.

el capítulo **tercero** Chapter *III*
los **dos primeros**[1] coches
Carlos **Quinto** Charles *the Fifth*
la página **veintitrés** page *23*

el **tercer** capítulo the *third* chapter
the *first two* cars
Pío **Doce** Pius *the Twelfth*
el **primer** premio the *first* prize

The ordinal **primero** is used to express the first day of the month.

Hoy es el **primero** de marzo. Today is the *first* of March.

62. Hours of the Day.

To express the hour of the day, the verb **ser** is used with the feminine definite article (which agrees with **hora** or **horas** understood). **Media** *half*, is feminine, agreeing with **hora; cuarto** *quarter*, is a masculine noun. Time up

---

138 [1] Note that Spanish says *the two first*, not *the first two* as in English

NO
(p)
sept
don't pronounce the "p"

to the half hour is expressed by using **y**; after the half hour, the number of minutes is subtracted from the next hour by using **menos**.

¿Qué hora es (en su reloj)?	*What time is it* (by your watch)?
Es la una. *It is one o'clock.*	**Son las dos.** *It is two o'clock.*
Son las tres en punto.	*It is three o'clock* exactly.
Son las cuatro y pico.	*It is* a few minutes after *four.*
Eran las cinco y media. *It was 5:30.*.	**Eran las seis y cuarto.** *It was 6:15.*

Note that the imperfect, not the preterit, is used for time in the past.

Son las once menos diez.	*It is ten minutes to eleven.*
Llegaron **a las nueve.**	*They arrived at nine o'clock.*
Han dado **las diez.**	*It has struck ten.*
al mediodía; a media noche	*at noon; at midnight*

When a specific hour is mentioned, **de la mañana, de la tarde,** or **de la noche** is used rather than **por la mañana,** etc.

Son las siete **de la mañana.**	It is 7 *a.m.*
Eran las ocho **de la noche.**	It was 8 *p.m.*

But:

Trabajan **por la tarde.**	They work *in the afternoon.*

63. **Para** and **Por.**

(1) **Para** conveys the following ideas: (*a*) purpose, intent (*to, in order to* + infinitive), (*b*) destination, (*c*) use, purpose, suitability, (*d*) point of future time (usually *by*), (*e*) comparison, contrast, (*f*) with **estar,** *to be about to.*

(*a*)	Leemos **para** aprender.	We read (in order) *to* learn.
	Estudia **para** (ser) médico.	He is studying *to* be a doctor.
	¿Para qué?	*Why?* (i.e., *For* what purpose?)
(*b*)	Han embarcado **para** el Brasil.	They have embarked *for* Brazil.
(*c*)	un vaso **para** agua[1]	a water glass
(*d*)	Acábelo **para** el viernes.	Finish it *by* Friday.
(*e*)	**Para** su edad sabe demasiado.	*For* his age he knows too much.
(*f*)	Estamos **para** salir.	We are *about to* leave.

---

[1] Compare: un vaso **de** agua *a glass of water;* una copa **de** cristal *a crystal goblet.*

139

A NEW
SHORTER
SPANISH
REVIEW
GRAMMAR

GRAMMAR
REVIEW

(2) **Por** translates the following expressions: (*a*) *for* meaning *for the sake of, because of, in behalf of, on account of, in exchange for;* (*b*) *during;* (*c*) *through, along;* (*d*) *by* expressing agent with the passive voice, means, manner; (*e*) *to* (*in an effort to*) when the result is in doubt or when something is yet to be done; and (*f*) *to be in favor of* with **estar.**

(*a*) Me sacrifico **por** él.	I sacrifice myself *for* him.
Hágalo **por** mí.	Do it *for* me (*for my sake*).
¿**Por** qué?	*Why?* (i.e., *For* what reason?)
Muchos votaron **por** Eisenhower.	Many voted *for* Eisenhower.
No lo acabé **por** falta de tiempo.	I didn't finish it *for* lack of time.
Dió su vida **por** su país.	He gave his life *for* his country.
Dió dos pesos **por** el libro.	He gave two pesos *for* the book.
(*b*) Quedó allí **por** dos meses.	He stayed there *for* two months.
por la tarde	*in* (*during*) the afternoon
(*c*) Entró **por** la ventana.	He entered *through* the window.
Se paseó **por** la calle.	He strolled *along* the street.
(*d*) La carta fué escrita **por** él.	The letter was written *by* him.
por avión, **por** tren	*by* plane, *by* train
(*e*) Luchó **por** entrar.[1]	He struggled *to* enter.
El tema está **por** escribir.	The theme is (yet) *to* be written.
(*f*) Estoy **por** salir ahora.	I am *in favor of* leaving now.

D. VERB REVIEW

Caer *to fall;* **caerse** *to fall down;* **valer** *to be worth.*

Se cayó en la calle.	*He fell down* in the street.
Se me cayó el pañuelo.	*I dropped* my handkerchief.
Vale más que nos quedemos.	We *better* stay.

E. GRAMMAR EXERCISES

1. *Translate:*

1. I fall. *caigo*
2. She fell down. *se cayó*
3. Don't fall. *no te caigas*
4. Falling. *cayendo*
5. You have fallen. *ha caído*
6. They fell down. *se cayeron*
7. (That) he might fall. *que se caiga*
8. I am worth. *Yo valgo*
9. It will be worth more. *Valdramas*

[1] In **Luchó por entrar** the result is in doubt; in **Pagó para entrar** purpose only is involved and there is no doubt as to the outcome.

2. *Pronounce in Spanish:*
5, 15, 50, 500, 20, 31, 42, 53, 64, 75, 86, 97, 100, 103, 206, 408, 711, 900, 1959, 7,654,321.

3. *Give the correct form of the verb in parentheses:*

1. Lo terminé antes de que él (*volver*). *volviera*
2. Le daré el dinero en cuanto yo lo (*recibir*). *reciba*
3. Siempre le visito cuando (*venir*) a la ciudad. *viene*
4. Me trata como si me (*conocer*) toda la vida. *conociera*
5. Lo hice sin que él lo (*saber*). *supiera*
6. Aunque (*llover*) anoche, salí. *llovió*
7. Aunque (*llover*) esta noche, saldré. *llueva*
8. Hablé despacio para que ellos me (*comprender*). *comprendieron*
9. Volvió la espalda de modo que yo no (*poder*) verle la cara. *pudiera*
10. Me quedé hasta que Vd. (*llegar*). *llegó*
11. Me quedaré hasta que Vd. (*llegar*). *llegue*
12. Le visité ayer cuando (*pasar*) por su casa. *pasó*
13. Le visitaré cuando (*pasar*) por su casa. *pase*
14. Me llevó a la fuente para que (*beber*). *bebiera*

4. *Replace the dashes by* **para** *or* **por:**

1. La frase fué escrita en la pizarra _por_ el profesor _para_ los alumnos.
2. Nunca se molesta _por_ nadie.
3. ¿Hay cartas _para_ mí?
4. Lo haré _por_ Vd. (*for your sake*).
5. Estoy _para_ (*about to*) salir _por_ España.
6. Me dió cuatro pesetas _por_ el libro.
7. Estudiamos _para_ aprender.
8. Estaré de vuelta _para_ el martes.
9. Lo hicimos _por_ obligación y no _por_ amor.
10. Estuve allí _por_ dos horas.
11. Viajó _por_ (*through*) la Argentina.
12. La puerta fué cerrada _por_ el muchacho.
13. Lo enviaron _por_ avión.
14. Sabe mucho _para_ su edad. (*age*)
15. Ella habla _por_ (*for the sake of*) hablar.
16. Esta mesa sirve _para_ todo.
17. El periódico fué vendido _por_ el vendedor.
18. Tenemos clase _por_ la tarde.

19. El médico lleva tres pesos _por_ sus consultas.
20. Estudiaba _para_ abogado.
21. Pasamos _por_ aquí ayer.

5. *Translate:*

(*a*)

1. When it strikes twelve we shall occupy our seats.
2. He finished his work early in order that the young lady could take him to the station.
3. Before he left everyone came to say good-by.
4. He stayed in Oviedo for more than nine weeks.
5. By August 6th he was back in Madrid, after twenty-one days in the north.
6. Isn't today Wednesday, September 7th?
7. Although he was the only one that I knew, he refused to help me.
8. Finally he said that he would do it provided that I showed more interest.
9. Pedro was very serious for his age.
10. Before his vacation ended, he made up his mind to travel through the south and west of Spain by bus.

(*b*)

1. I stopped in Madrid (on) the first and second of the month to see the Prado Museum.
2. The mosque of Cordova was built by the Moors in the VIIIth century.
3. I paid fifty pesetas for a book about the mosque.
4. Pedro could not get into the Giralda without somebody accompanying him.
5. They treated him as if he were a crazy child.
6. But he was able to go up alone while the woman was talking.
7. As soon as I finish (**de**) eating (*inf.*), I'll continue writing.
8. Unless you hear from me again, please do not write.
9. I am leaving for the airport in a couple of hours.
10. I think that the plane leaves for London at about three o'clock.

F. EXERCISE ON IDIOMS AND PHRASES

Translate the words underlined:

1. As soon as I finish saldré para el aeropuerto.
2. Unless no salga el avión hoy.
3. Me gustó especially Toledo porque ya sabe Vd. que I'm fond of leyendas.
4. Una niña en la calle me dijo que yo looked like extranjero.
5. In spite of la hora (it was after la una) fuí a ver una ermita seldom visitada por los turistas.
6. From the top of la Giralda se ve muy bien la ciudad.
7. Formerly muchas calles de Sevilla estaban covered with toldos.
8. Vendrán a buscarme at about las dos y media.

PUBLISHED BY THE SPANISH STATE TOURIST DEPARTMENT. MADRID

SPAIN

CHAPTER FOURTEEN

A. GRAMMAR AND IDIOM PRACTICE

(*Continúa la carta de Pedro.*) "En Sevilla conocí a dos señores de las Islas
Canarias. Uno de ellos era un hombrón enorme que hablaba muy bien el
inglés; el otro era pequeñito y muy moreno. Pues bien, aquél me contó cosas
tan interesantes de la isla de Tenerife que casi me fuí con ellos en avión a
Santa Cruz. Me dijo, entre otras cosas, que había allí un árbol extraño llamado 5
drago cuya copa da la impresión de un paraguas gigantesco y cuya savia es de
un color tan rojo como el de la sangre. El segundo me habló con entusiasmo
del Teide, el pico más alto en tierra española (12,200 pies), llamado también
"Monte Pelado" por carecer de* vegetación en su cono volcánico. Cuando me
prometieron acompañarme a donde yo quisiera, estuve a punto de* abandonar 10
mi excursión por el resto de Europa. Pronto, sin embargo, me di cuenta de
que para llevar a cabo* este viaje ideal no sólo me faltaba* tiempo sino
dinero. ¡Qué lástima! ¿verdad?* Porque Vd. sabe bien que a mí me encantan
las montañas y que no hay nadie que me gane a subirlas. ¿Ha oído de algún
norteamericano que haya escalado el Teide? Creo que no. 15

Para no ser tentado de nuevo por los simpáticos canarios, aquella misma
noche* tomé el avión de Granada, ciudad donde pasé muchas horas visitando
la Alhambra. ¡Qué maravilloso edificio! Quien no haya visto este palacio-
fortaleza no comprenderá del todo las *Leyendas de la Alhambra* de Washington
Irving. La gente de Granada, sin embargo, no me parece tan alegre como la de 20
Sevilla.

El largo viaje de Granada a Valencia lo hice en autobús. Es una hazaña que
no le recomiendo al que quiera viajar cómodamente. Es un viaje de muchas
horas, por carreteras malas y polvorientas y, en verano, el calor es insoportable.
En este momento* me le imagino a Vd. pensando: '¿Por qué fué este 25
muchacho a Valencia?' La contestación es fácil. Desde que leímos aquella
novela de Blasco Ibáñez, *La barraca*, he tenido ganas de ver cómo funciona
el famoso Tribunal de las Aguas, que se reúne todos los jueves, al mediodía,* 145

A NEW
SHORTER
SPANISH
REVIEW
GRAMMAR

GRAMMAR
AND IDIOM
PRACTICE

delante de la Puerta de los Apóstoles de la catedral. Lo más interesante es que este tribunal — uno de los más antiguos de Europa — usa los mismos procedimientos de hace seis siglos.

Los siete 'jueces,' viejos campesinos de la Huerta, se sientan muy serios en sillas de cuero que llevan en el respaldo el nombre del distrito que cada uno representa. Ante ellos exponen sus quejas los querellantes, y allí mismo,* con rapidez extraordinaria, estos 'jueces' resuelven los conflictos que han surgido durante la semana con motivo de* la distribución y aprovechamiento de las aguas de riego. Los parientes, amigos y vecinos de querellantes y acusados escuchan la sentencia en medio de gran silencio, pues saben que no existe el derecho de apelación a tribunales superiores. La sentencia es por lo general* una multa, pero el que se niega a* pagarla recibe un castigo aún más temido: la pérdida del derecho a regar sus tierras por cierto tiempo. Lo que más me impresionó fué la simplicidad de los procedimientos. Allí no hay abogados, ni papeles, ni 'red tape.'

Es hora de* terminar. Acaban de avisarme que el coche sale para el aeropuerto dentro de* unos minutos. Le hablaré de todo cuando volvamos a vernos en la universidad. Hasta entonces.

Pedro"

B. IDIOMS AND PHRASES

carecer de (vegetación) *to lack* (vegetation)

a punto de *about to*

llevar a cabo *to carry out*

me faltaba (tiempo) *I lacked* (time)

no sólo (me faltaba tiempo) **sino** (dinero) *not only* (did I lack time) *but* (money)

¿verdad? *don't you think so?*

aquella misma noche *that very night*

en este momento *at this very moment*

he tenido ganas de (ver) *I have wanted to* (see)

al mediodía *at noon*

allí mismo *right there*

con motivo de *on account of*

por lo general *as a rule*

se niega a (pagar) *he refuses to* (pay)

es hora de (terminar) *it is time to* (end)

dentro de (unos minutos) *in* (a few minutes)

C. GRAMMAR REVIEW

64. The Subjunctive in Adjectival (Relative) Clauses.

An adjectival clause is introduced by a relative pronoun, usually **que**, and, like an adjective, it modifies a noun. The subjunctive is used in adjectival clauses when the antecedent of the clause is (*a*) negative, that is, non-existent, or (*b*) indefinite. When the antecedent is indefinite, the relative clause often describes qualities or characteristics sought; occasionally (*c*) the sentence is in the form of a question.

(*a*) No hay nada que me **asuste**.	There is nothing that *frightens* me.
But: Hay cosas que me **asustan**.	There are things that *frighten* me.
(*b*) Busco una criada que **cocine**.	I'm looking for a servant who *cooks*.
But: Tengo una criada que **cocina**.	I have a servant who *cooks*.
(*c*) ¿Hay algo que le **moleste**?	Is there something that *bothers* you?
But: Hay algo que le **molesta**.	There is something that *bothers* you.

65. Demonstrative Adjectives and Pronouns.

(1) Adjectives.

SINGULAR		PLURAL		
Masculine	*Feminine*	*Masculine*	*Feminine*	
este	esta	estos	estas	*this, these*
ese	esa	esos	esas	*that, those* (near you)
aquel	**aquella**	**aquellos**	**aquellas**	*that, those* (yonder)

There are two demonstratives to translate the English word *that*. **Ese** refers to something near or associated with the person addressed; **aquel** refers to something distant from both speaker and person addressed. Note the correlation: **este—yo—aquí; ese—usted—ahí; aquel—él—allí.**

este asunto *this* matter	**ese** error *that* error (of yours)
aquel fuego *that* fire	**aquella** cantidad *that* quantity
Yo tengo **este** libro (aquí).	I have *this* book (here).
Vd. tiene **ese** libro (ahí).	You have *that* book (there).
Él tiene **aquel** libro (allí).	He has *that* book (yonder).

A NEW
SHORTER
SPANISH
REVIEW
GRAMMAR

GRAMMAR
REVIEW

(2) Pronouns. The forms above may all be used as pronouns and with the same distinctions in meaning. They then acquire the graphic accent to distinguish them from the corresponding adjectives (**éste, ése, aquél,** etc.).

(*tres lápices:*) **Éste** es azul, **ése** es rojo, y **aquél** es amarillo.	(three pencils:) *This one* is blue, *that one* (near you) is red, and *that one* (yonder) is yellow.

Éste sometimes means *the latter* and **aquél** *the former.*

Pedro y Pablo son primos; **éste** es abogado, **aquél** es músico.	Peter and Paul are cousins; *the former* is a musician, *the latter* is a lawyer.

Note that in Spanish *latter* precedes *former* (contrary to English usage).

66. Neuter Demonstrative Pronouns.

There are three neuter forms of demonstrative pronouns: **esto, eso,** and **aquello,** which are used to refer to an idea, to a previous statement, or to an object whose gender is not known.

¿Qué es **esto?**	What is *this?*
¿Cuándo fué todo **eso?**	When did all *that* take place?
Aquello fué algo triste.	*That* (*affair*) was somewhat sad.

67. The Definite Article used Demonstratively.

The definite article replaces the demonstrative pronoun before **de** and before **que.**

El del sombrero es mi tío.	*That one with* the hat is my uncle.
Los parientes de José y **los de** María han llegado.	Joseph's relatives and Mary's (*those of Mary*) have arrived.
No recuerdo **lo del** accidente.	I don't remember (*that matter of*) the accident.
El que lo robó era ladrón.	*The one who* stole it was a thief.
La que nos gusta más es ésta.	*The one* we prefer is this (one).

68. Days of the Week, Months, and Seasons.

(1) The names of the days of the week are masculine and are not capitalized. The definite article is used with these names, except after **ser,** and corre-

sponds to English *on*. Only **sábado** and **domingo** add **-s** to form the plural (unaccented **-es** and **-is** have the same form for the singular and plural).

el lunes	*(on) Monday*	**el jueves**	*(on) Thursday*	**el sábado**	*(on) Saturday*
el martes	*(on) Tuesday*	**el viernes**	*(on) Friday*	**el domingo**	*(on) Sunday*
el miércoles	*(on) Wednesday*				

Llegará **el jueves**.	He will arrive *(next) Thursday*.
Llegó **el viernes**.	He arrived *(last) Friday*.
Van a misa **los domingos**.	They go to Mass *(on) Sundays*.
Hoy es **miércoles**.	Today is *Wednesday*.

(2) The names of the months are masculine and are regularly not capitalized. Only when they are modified are they accompanied by the definite article:

el diciembre pasado *last December.*

enero	*January*	**abril**	*April*	**julio**	*July*
febrero	*February*	**mayo**	*May*	**agosto**	*August*
marzo	*March*	**junio**	*June*	**septiembre**	*September*
octubre	*October*	**noviembre**	*November*	**diciembre**	*December*

(3) The names of the seasons are:

el invierno *winter*   **la primavera** *spring*   **el verano** *summer*   **el otoño** *fall*

As in English the article may be omitted: **en (el) invierno** *in (the) winter.*

69. Pero, Mas, and Sino.

Pero is the usual word for *but* (= *nevertheless*); **mas,** equivalent to **pero,** is a literary form. **Sino** has the force of *but on the contrary, but rather, but instead,* and is used only after a preceding negative, which it contradicts. No form of the verb, except the infinitive, may be used after **sino. Sino que** has the same use and meaning as **sino** when a clause follows.

Él se cayó al agua **pero** no se ahogó.	He fell into the water *but* didn't drown.
No deseaba trabajar **sino** jugar.	He didn't want to work *but* to play.
No es española **sino** francesa.	She isn't Spanish *but* French.

149

No estudió la lección **sino que**	He didn't study the lesson *but*
fué al cine.	went to the movies.
No perdió el dinero **sino que** lo gastó.	He didn't lose the money *but* spent it.

70. Diminutives and Augmentatives.

One of the characteristics of the Spanish language is the ease with which it adds suffixes to words to denote smallness, affection, large size, scorn, and the like.

The more common diminutive suffixes, denoting small size or affectionate interest, are: **-ito, -cito, -ecito, -illo, -cillo,** and **-ecillo.** A final vowel is dropped when the ending is added and some final consonants undergo a spelling-change.[1]

poco *little*		**poquito** *very little*	
pobre *poor*		**pobrecito** *poor fellow*	
mujer *woman*		**mujercita** *little woman, darling*	
voz *voice*		**vocecita** *thin little voice*	
viejo *old*		**viejecito** *nice (little) old man*	
cigarro *cigar*		**cigarrillo** *cigarette*	
autor *author*		**autorcillo** *inferior author*	
pan *(loaf of) bread*		**panecillo** *roll*	

The more frequent augmentative suffixes, denoting large size or scorn, are: **-ón** and **-azo.**

hombre *man*   **hombrón** *huge man*   **perro** *dog*   **perrazo** *large dog*

D. VERB REVIEW

Creer *to believe, think;* **leer** *to read.*

¡Ya lo creo! *I should say so!*   **Creo que sí (no).** *I think so (not).*

---

[1] There is no way of determining which suffix the Spaniard will use at any given moment; only observation will help the student.

E. GRAMMAR EXERCISES

1. *Translate:*

1. She believed (*pret.*). *ella creo*
2. He read (*pret.*). *el leo*
3. Believing. *creyendo*
4. Reading. *leyendo*
5. I have read. *he leído*
6. You have believed. *Vd. ha creído*
7. We read (*pret.*). *nosotros leímos*
8. They might believe. *ellos creyeran*
9. They believed. *ellos creyeron*
10. She might read. *ella leera*

2. *Translate, and give the infinitive of:*

1. supe *I found out saber*
2. anduvimos *we walked andar*
3. quisieron *they wanted querer*
4. juegue *I may play jugar*
5. haz *do hacer* — Command
6. oyese *I might hear oír* — subj.
7. dé *dar*
8. sentamos *we seated sentar*
9. sintamos *we may feel sentir*
10. dimos *I gave dar*
11. di *dar*
12. sepan *they may know saber*
13. ruegue *I may beg rogar*
14. saldremos *we shall leave salir*
15. cayeron *they fell caer*
16. oigan *they may hear oír*
17. leyendo *reading leer*
18. iban *they were going ir*
19. creyendo *believing creer*
20. veía *I was seeing ver*

3. *Translate the following words and explain the formation of each:*

1. librito *small book*
2. mujerona *large woman*
3. Luisita *little Louise*
4. jovencito *quite young man*
5. platillo *saucer*
6. pobrecito *poor man*
7. familión *large family*
8. pececito *small fish*
9. poquito *very little*
10. campanilla *small bell*
11. vocecita *thin little voice*
12. cuerpecito *small body*
13. viejecito *nice old man*
14. zapatilla *slipper*
15. Juanito *Johnny*
16. crucecita *small cross*
17. caballazo *large horse*
18. florecita *small flower*
19. diablillo *little devil*
20. mosquito *mosquito*
21. mocito *youngster*
22. sillón *arm chair*
23. manaza *large hand*
24. chiquillo *small child*
25. picarón *great road*

4. *Translate the italicized words:*

1. (*This*) caja es (*Mary's*). *Esta*
2. ¿Qué fué (*that*) ruido? *ese*
3. ¿Qué es (*that*) que Vd. tiene en la mano? *eso*
4. (*This one*) me gusta más; Vd. se puede llevar (*that one*). *Esta* *ese*
5. Carlos y María son hermanos; (*the latter*) es rubia, (*the former*) es moreno. *ésta* *aquél*
6. ¿Qué es (*that*)? (*This*) es un cuaderno. *eso* *esto*
7. Leeré (*these*) esta semana, (*those*) no los leeré nunca. *éstos* *ésos*
8. (*These*) plumas son azules, (*those*) son rojas. *Estas* *ésas*
9. ¿Por qué usa Vd. (*those*) dos apellidos? *esos*
10. ¿No cree Vd. que (*that*) sea posible? *eso*

A NEW
SHORTER
SPANISH
REVIEW
GRAMMAR

GRAMMAR
EXERCISES

5. *Give the proper form of the infinitive in parentheses:*

1. Venga lo que (*venir*) *venga*, sea lo que (*ser*) *sea*, cueste lo que (*costar*) *cueste*, no acepto.
2. No hay nadie en esta clase que lo (*saber*) *sepa*.
3. Busco un compañero que me (*ayudar*) *ayude*.
4. ¿Hay algo que Vd. no (*entender*) *entienda*?
5. Sálvese el que (*poder*) *pueda*.
6. Haré lo que Vd. me (*mandar*) *mande*.
7. No me importa lo que (*decir*) *digan* los demás mañana.
8. El que (*llegar*) *llega* primero recibirá el premio.
9. ¿Hay algún secreto que él no (*saber*) *sepa*?
10. Quiero una corbata que (*ser*) *sea* bonita.

6. *Translate:*

(a)

1. These two men were not from continental Spain but from the Canary Islands; they did not work but they traveled.
2. The former was a nice old man; the latter was big and strong.
3. The one with the beret spoke very loud.
4. Sundays they spent (them) strolling along the streets of Seville.
5. If they left Tuesday they would be back by Thursday.
6. They were looking for someone who would accompany them.
7. Do you know anyone who wants to go?
8. There was no one who wanted to make the long trip. I am sure of that.
9. My opinions and Don José's are quite different.
10. In winter the days are a *mucho* great deal shorter than in spring and autumn.

(b)

1. In Seville he met a very rich huge man, from the Canary Islands.
2. His companion, on the other hand, was very small.
3. The latter did not speak English, the former told him interesting things about the Island of Tenerife.
4. There is no one—said the former—who is better acquainted with the Island than I.
5. Do you know any American who has climbed (**al**) Teide?
6. Both men promised to take Pedro wherever (*subjunctive tense*) (**a donde**) he wished to go.
7. He who has not seen the Canary Islands has not seen a paradise.
8. I don't recommend the trip to Valencia to anyone who wishes to travel comfortably.

9. The people of Granada do not seem (*sing.*) to me as gay as those (that) of Sevilla.

10. In Valencia Pedro did not visit monuments but went to see how the Tribunal functioned.

F. EXERCISE ON IDIOMS AND PHRASES

Translate the words underlined:

1. At this very moment él se dió cuenta de que he lacked tiempo.
2. That very night Pedro estuvo about to carry out sus planes.
3. Not only did he want to visitar las Islas Canarias but de subir al Teide.
4. A veces Pedro estaba un poco loco, don't you think so?
5. Right there él y su amigo decidieron que it was time to separarse de los dos canarios.
6. El avión sale at noon y in veinte minutos podemos estar en el aeropuerto.
7. As a rule Pedro refused to dar propinas.
8. Decía que on account of el largo viaje no le quedaba mucho dinero.

TRANSLATE!

Do Sentences

CHAPTER FIFTEEN

A. GRAMMAR AND IDIOM PRACTICE

Lo primero que hizo Pedro al regresar a la universidad en septiembre fué visitar a don José, a quien **dió cuenta de** cuanto había hecho desde que salió de España. Se disculpó de* no haber escrito más cartas por faltarle el tiempo y por no estar seguro de su dirección en Madrid.

5 — Bueno, no importa — le dijo el profesor. — Lo importante es que Vd. ha terminado el viaje sin novedad. Ahora quisiera pedirle un favor. ¿Tendría inconveniente en* hablar un día a los estudiantes de español sobre su viaje a España?

— ¡Oh, no señor! — se apresuró a* contestar. — No soy orador y, además, 10 Vd. sabe muy bien que no puedo expresarme en español. Lo que podría hacer, si Vd. insiste, es enseñarles mis diapositivas en color y hacer algunos comentarios en inglés.

— **Está bien. Vaya** pensando sobre esto y ya le avisaré el día de la reunión. Probablemente dentro de dos o tres semanas.

15 Vinieron bastantes estudiantes a escuchar a Pedro. Los que le conocían sabían que no tenía pelos en la lengua y que **al menos** hablaría con franqueza. Otros habían oído decir a don José que valía la pena ir a escucharle, pues tenía cosas interesantes que contar.

Pedro tardó unos minutos en llegar. Por fin apareció con una caja debajo 20 del* brazo, un proyector y una pantalla. Sin decir una palabra abrió la caja y empezó a sacar de ella varios objetos que puso encima de* una mesita: una boina vasca, dos piezas de Talavera, una pulsera de labor toledana y una navaja de Albacete que llamó mucho la atención. Era una navaja enorme, con una hoja curvada de más de doce pulgadas y una inscripción que decía: "Si esta 25 víbora te pica, no hay remedio en la botica."

Pedro empezó su charla explicando que primero diría unas palabras sobre la España pintoresca, la que ven todos los turistas, y que después trataría de interpretar lo que había visto. Dijo que volvía enamorado de* aquellas ciudades

viejas, con calles tan estrechas que **algunas veces** tiene uno que arrimarse a
las paredes para dejar pasar un borrico cargado de botijos; de la gente, amable
y atenta, siempre deseosa de complacer y ayudar al extranjero. Habló luego de
los bailes flamencos y de las corridas de toros, las cuales le parecieron
monótonas y cansadas. Concluyó esta parte de su charla afirmando que Granada 5
era la ciudad que más le había gustado y que estaba de acuerdo con* los
granadinos que dicen: "Quien no ha visto Granada, no ha visto nada."

— Ahora debo confesar — añadió con cierto aire de superioridad — que
poco de lo moderno en España me ha impresionado grandemente. Sus grandes
ciudades no pueden compararse con las nuestras: tienen más torres de iglesias 10
que chimeneas de fábricas; los taxis son del siglo pasado; las calles siempre
llenas de gente que pasea sin prisa en vez de trabajar; los trenes lentos y sucios.
Y, con permiso de los profesores presentes, tengo que admitir que no he visto
una mujer bonita en todo el país.

Los comentarios de Pedro a las diapositivas que proyectó fueron aún más 15
desconcertantes. Tanto así que un profesor español que hasta aquel momento le
había escuchado sin despegar los labios, **al cabo** no pudo contenerse más y
dijo:

— Se puede ver, señor Burk, que Vd. ha entrado en España, pero España
no ha entrado en Vd. Todo lo que dice no son más que generalidades, típicas 20
del turista que no sabe la lengua y es incapaz de enterarse de* nada. Claro está
que* Vd. tiene derecho a* opinar, pero no lo tiene para decir tonterías en
público. ¿De dónde ha sacado Vd. que esas casuchas que nos enseñó son
viviendas para la clase media? ¿A quién se lo preguntó Vd.? A nadie, estoy
seguro. Se trata* **por lo tanto** de conclusiones gratuitas sin valor alguno . . . 25
Y si Vd. no ha visto mujeres hermosas en España es porque no tiene ojos en
la cara.

— ¡Pobre de mí! — exclamó Pedro al ver salir al profesor Salinas. — Vd.
tiene la culpa, don José, por haberme metido en estas cosas.

— La verdad es — dijo don José — que Vd. ha cambiado un poco de ideas 30
desde que nos vimos en Segovia. ¿No es eso?*

B. IDIOMS AND PHRASES

dió cuenta de (cuanto había hecho)
   he reported on (all he had done)
se disculpó de (no haber escrito) *he*
   apologized for (not having written)
¿tendría inconveniente en (hablar)?
   would you have any objection to
   (talking)?
se apresuró a (contestar) *he hastened*
   to (answer)
está bien *all right*
vaya (pensando) *be* (thinking)
al menos *at least*
debajo de *under*
encima de *on top of*
enamorado de *in love with*

algunas veces *sometimes*
estaba de acuerdo con *he agreed*
   with
al cabo *finally*
(incapaz de) **enterarse de** (nada)
   (unable to) *find out* (anything)
claro está que *of course*
tiene derecho a (opinar) *you have*
   a right to (think)
se trata de (conclusiones) *it is a*
   question of (conclusions)
por lo tanto *therefore*
tiene la culpa *you are to blame*
¿no es eso? *is that not so?*

C. GRAMMAR REVIEW

71. Relative Pronouns, Adjectives, and Adverbs.

(1) **Que** *who, whom, that, which; when,* is invariable and is never omitted. As
a pronoun it is used as (*a*) subject or (*b*) object of a verb, and refers to
both persons and things. However, after a preposition (*c*) **que** usually
refers only to things. As a relative adverb (*d*) **que** means *when.*

(*a*) la mujer **que** vive aquí   the woman *who* lives here
     la caja **que** está llena   the box *that* is full
(*b*) el hombre **que** vi   the man (*whom*) I saw
     la casa **que** compró Vd.   the house (*that*) you bought
(*c*) el asunto de **que** hablé   the matter of *which* I spoke
     el interés con **que** escuchó   the interest with *which* he listened
(*d*) el año **que** nació   the year (*when*) he was born

(2) **Quien** (*pl.* **quienes**) *who, whom* refers to persons, not to things. It is
used principally (*a*) after prepositions and (*b*) to express *he who, one who,*
who.

(*a*) el tío de **quien** hablé   the uncle of *whom* I spoke
     el mozo con **quien** hablaba[1]   the waiter with *whom* I was speaking
     ¿A **quién** enamoró?   To *whom* did he make love?
(*b*) **Quien** busca halla.   *He who* seeks finds.

[1] **Que** may replace **quien** after **de** and **con.**

*a, de, en, + con, you use "que"
for others you use "el que" etc.*

(3) **El que (el cual), la que (la cual), los que (los cuales), las que
(las cuales)** *the one that* or *who, he who, one who, who, that, which* show
whether the antecedent is singular or plural, masculine or feminine, and
are therefore used to avoid confusion when there are two antecedents.

They are also used to replace **que** or **quien** after prepositions of more
than one syllable, after compound prepositions, and after prepositions such
as **para, por,** and **sin,** since these may combine with **que** to form
conjunctions.

Vi a la hija del médico, **la cual** (**la que**) es muy linda.	I saw the doctor's daughter, *who* is very pretty.
sus amigos entre **los cuales (los que)** me pongo	his friends among *whom* I place myself
dos árboles cerca de **los cuales (los que)** hay una casa	two trees near *which* is a house
la ventana por **la cual** entró	the window through *which* he entered
mi abrigo sin **el que** no salgo	my overcoat without *which* I don't go out

Lo cual and **lo que** *which* are neuter forms which refer to an idea or
statement already expressed.

Llegó a tiempo, **lo cual (lo que)** me gustó.	He arrived on time, *which (fact)* pleased me.

Lo que also means *what(= that which).*

Lo que dijo me sorprendió.	*What* he said surprised me.
Lo cual may not be used here.	

*lo que – that which
(whether literally or not)*

(4) **Cuyo (cuya, cuyos, cuyas)** *whose, of whom, which,* a relative adjective,
must immediately precede the noun it modifies. (Do not confuse it with the
interrogative **¿de quién?** *whose?*)

*Don't use cuyo in
a question.*

mi tía, **cuyo** hijo se graduó	my aunt, *whose* son graduated

(5) **Cuanto (cuanta, cuantos, cuantas)** *all the* . . . *that, as much as, as
many as; all that, all those who,* etc., is a relative adjective or pronoun.

cuanto tiempo tengo	*all the* time *that* I have
Le di **cuanto** tenía.	I gave you *all that* I had.
cuantos amigos me conocen	*all the* friends *that* know me
cuantos me ven	*all those who* see me

(6) **Donde** *where, a place (where)* is a relative adverb.

el pueblo **donde** nació	the town *where* he was born
Buscó **donde** estacionarse.	He looked for *a place* to park.

72. Uses of the Infinitive.

In Spanish the infinitive is used:

(1) As a noun; it is sometimes accompanied by the definite article.

el poder power   **el pesar** grief   **el parecer** opinion

El saber no ocupa lugar.	*Knowledge* is no hindrance.
Necesito[1] **leer** mucho.	I need *to read* a great deal.
Es fácil **verle.**	It is easy *to see* him.

(2) Instead of the subjunctive, after verbs of command, permission, and causa-tion, usually when the subject of the infinitive in English is a personal pronoun. (Cf. §58.) Sometimes the infinitive is passive in meaning.

Nos mandó **callar.**	He ordered us *to be silent.*
Le permitió **salir** de noche.	He let her *go out* at night.
Me hizo **perder** el tren.	He made me *miss* my train.
Haga Vd. **escribir** las frases.	Have the sentences *written.*

(3) After verbs of perception (**ver, oír,**), instead of the present participle. (Cf. §47.2.)

Los vimos **bailar.**	We saw them *dance* (dancing).
Se las oímos **cantar.**	We heard her *sing* (singing) them.

Note that the infinitive follows the main verb immediately. When there are two pronoun objects they both usually precede the main verb.

(4) In exclamations, and in impersonal commands instead of the subjunctive.

¿Cómo? ¡**Mandarnos** marchar!	What? *Order us* to leave!
No **fijar** carteles.	*Post* no bills.

(5) As the object of a preposition:

(*a*) Where English regularly uses the present participle.

antes de **comer** before *eating*	al **llegar** on *arriving*
después de **dormir** after *sleeping*	sin **pensar** without *thinking*

---

158 [1] For list of common verbs that are followed by the infinitive without a preposition, see §79.

(b) After another verb.[1] The use or non-use of a preposition depends on the verb that governs the infinitive. Verbs of motion, beginning, learning, teaching, helping, and others require **a** before a dependent infinitive.

Corrió a cerrar la puerta.	*He ran to* close the door.
Empezaba a aprender a nadar.	*He was beginning to learn to* swim.
Le **enseñó a** patinar.	*He taught* him *to* skate.
Me **ayudó a** bajar del autobús.	*He helped* me *to* get off the bus.
Volvieron a sentarse.	They sat down *again.*

Some verbs require **de:**

Acabamos de terminarlo.	*We have just* finished it.
Dejaron de escuchar.	*They stopped* listening.
Ha cesado de llover.	*It has stopped* raining.

Some verbs take **en** or **por:**

Se empeñó en salir.	*He insisted on* going out.
Tardan en comprender.	*They are slow in* understanding.
Estoy por comprarlo.	*I am in favor of* buying it.

Para is used to express purpose. It may replace **a** with verbs of motion when there is stress on the purpose.

Comen **para** vivir.	They eat *to* live.
Corren a la ventana **para** cerrarla.	They run to the window *to* close it.

(c) After adjectives, past participles, and adverbs.

Es **capaz de** hacerlo en una hora.	He is *able to* do it in an hour.
Estaba **dispuesto a** aceptar.	He was *ready to* accept.
Hace **bien en** prestar atención.	He does *well in* paying attention.

(d) After nouns

Tiene **deseos de** acabar el examen.	He is *eager to* finish the test.
Tenemos **derecho a** votar.	We have a *right to* vote.
Les dieron **permiso para** ir al cine.	They gave them *permission to* go to the movies.

---

[1] For a list of other common verbs followed by various prepositions before complementary infinitives, see §79.   **159**

A NEW
SHORTER
SPANISH
REVIEW
GRAMMAR

GRAMMAR
REVIEW

73. Absolute Use of the Past Participle.

The past participle may be used in the absolute construction, that is, it may stand apart syntactically from the rest of the sentence. It agrees in gender and number with the noun or pronoun it modifies, which regularly follows.

Terminado el acto, salieron.	The function *ended*, they left.
Dicho esto, se marcharon.	*After* this *was said*, they left.

74. Irregular Past Participles.[1]

abrir: **abierto**	*opened, open*	morir: **muerto**	*dead, died*
cubrir: **cubierto**	*covered*	poner: **puesto**	*placed, set*
decir: **dicho**	*said, told*	romper: **roto**	*broken; torn*
escribir: **escrito**	*written*	ver: **visto**	*seen*
hacer: **hecho**	*made, done*	volver: **vuelto**	*returned*

When the stem of a verb ends in a strong vowel (**a, e, o**), the **i** of **-ido** acquires the graphic accent to prevent the two vowels from forming a diphthong which would obscure the participial ending.

caer: **caído**	*fallen*	oír: **oído**	*heard*
leer: **leído**	*read*	traer: **traído**	*brought; worn*

Some past participles possess additional meanings when used as adjectives.

acostado	*lying (down)*	**conocido**	*well-known, familiar*
agradecido	*grateful*	**divertido**	*amusing, entertaining*
apoyado	*leaning*	**dormido**	*asleep, sleeping*
atrevido	*daring*	**parado**	*standing still*
bendito	*holy, blessed*	**querido**	*dear, beloved*
callado	*silent*	**resuelto**	*bold, resolute*
cansado	*tired; tiresome*	**sentado**	*sitting down, seated*

D. VERB REVIEW

Conducir[2] *to conduct, lead; drive;* **traer** *to bring; wear.*

Conduje mi propio coche.	*I drove* my own car.
No **traje** mi traje de baño.	*I didn't bring* my bathing suit.

---

[1] See §80 for additional irregular past participles.
[2] Has a spelling-change also; see Verb Chart. Conjugated like **conducir; reducir** *to reduce,* **traducir** *to translate,* and others ending in **-ucir.**

E. GRAMMAR EXERCISES

1. *Translate:*

(a)

1. He drove. *él condujo*
2. We may conduct. *conduzcamos*
3. I lead. *yo conduzco*

4. They might lead. *condujeron*
5. I bring. *traigo*
6. Bring it to us. *tráiganolo usted*

7. You have brought. *usted a traído*
8. We might bring. *nosotros trajéramos*
9. Bringing. *trayendo*

(b)

1. el ser humano *the human being*
2. el parecer mío *my opinion*

3. el poder de Dios *the power of God*
4. Querer es poder. *Where there is a will, there is a way.*

(c) *Give the past participle of:*

1. abrir *abierto*
2. ver *visto*
3. romper *roto*

4. leer *leído*
5. volver *vuelto*
6. escribir *escrito*

7. traer *traído*

2. *Some past participles are used as nouns; (a) give the masculine singular past participle of the following verbs, and translate each as a noun:*

1. decir *dicho*
2. hacer *hecho*
3. imponer *impuesto*
4. morir *muerto*

5. pecar *pecado*
6. poner *puesto*
7. oír *oído*
8. pedir *pedido*

9. resultar *resultado*
10. significar *significado*
11. sentir *sentido*

(b) *Do the same with the feminine singular past participle of:*

1. cubrir *cubierta*
2. comer *comida*
3. caer *caída*
4. entrar *entrada*
5. decir *dicha*

6. ir *ida*
7. correr *corrida*
8. llegar *llegada*
9. medir *medida*
10. mirar *mirada*

11. despedir *despedida*
12. salir *salida*
13. subir *subida*
14. volver *vuelta*

3. *Translate the words in parentheses:*

1. No se permite (*smoking*) *fumar* aquí.
2. Le oí (*expressing*) *expresar* sus vanas ideas.
3. Al (*stopping*) *detenerse*, vió al gato (*sleeping*) *dormir* detrás de la puerta.
4. A pesar de (*trying*) *tratar*lo, no lo logramos.
5. Antes de (*reading*) *leer*lo, ella ya sabía el contenido.
6. Les vimos (*constructing*) *construir* una hermosa casa.
7. Después de (*eating*) *comer* la carne, se sintió enfermo.
8. A la sombra del árbol vimos (*sleeping*) *dormir* (*dog*) al perro.

161

A NEW
SHORTER
SPANISH
REVIEW
GRAMMAR

GRAMMAR
EXERCISES

9. Por *haber* (*having*) llegado temprano tuvimos la oportunidad de (*listening* *escuchar* *to*)le.

10. Acertó sin *saber* (*knowing*)lo.

OK 11. El camino va *subir* (*climbing*) la montaña.

OK 12. Los vi *correr* (*running*) hacia la tienda.

OK 13. *Hablando* (*Talking*) tan alto, la gente no puede oír *tocando* (*ringing*) la campana.

14. *Diciendo* (*Saying*) que sí, aceptó la invitación.

15. Ella siguió *jugando* (*playing*) toda la mañana.

4. *Translate the italicized words:*

1. La música de *que* (*which*) hablamos es muy linda.
2. *Quien* (*What*) Vd. quiere es imposible.
3. (*He who*) espera a veces desespera.
4. El sujeto con *quien* (*whom*) ella bailaba vive abajo.
5. Una señorita, *quien* (*whose*) nombre no recuerdo, preguntó por Vd.
6. Ella nunca se olvidará del día *que* (*when*) nací.
7. Visitamos las casas de nuestros amigos, *las cuales* (*which*) están bien construidas.
8. La mujer a *quien* (*whom*) Vd. se dirigió es la dueña.
9. *Cuanto* (*All that*) él es, se lo debe a su madre.
10. El libro *cuyo* (*of which*) precio era tan alto, no se vendió.
11. El asunto a *que* (*which*) Vd. se refiere salió bien.
12. La prima de Juan, *la* (*who*) acaba de llegar, es de Cangas.
13. La chica *la que* (*whom*) Vd. vió anoche es parienta mía.
14. *Lo que* (*What*) yo poseo está a su entera disposición.
15. Al fin perdió su puesto, *lo que* (*which*) no me sorprendió.
16. El piso *que* (*that*) busco debe ser grande y cómodo.
17. El artista de *quien* (*whom*) Vd. hablaba pinta bien.
18. Ésta es la puerta por *la cual* (*which*) entró.
19. Tengo *lo que* (*what*) necesito.
20. *Quien* (*Who*) calla otorga.
21. Hoy llegó temprano, *lo* (*which*) me extrañó.

5. *Translate:*

(*a*)

1. The lady, whose group went to Spain, was Mrs. Romero.
2. Her sister, who was a blonde, also formed part of the group.
3. She is the one who interested me most in the trip.
4. When he returned to America he spoke of all that he had seen and done.
5. He still remembered the names of the people with whom he had traveled.

6. He declared that he had enjoyed his visit, which (fact) pleased Don José.
7. What he said about bullfights and about death, however, annoyed a Spaniard who was present.
8. What? Be in Spain and not see beautiful women!
9. Of course, I have seen many travel who seem not [to] have eyes in their heads (face).
10. It is difficult today to find a place (where) to park.

(b)

1. Would you have [any] objection to (en) talking to the other students?
2. Those who knew Pedro came to hear him.
3. Some had heard Don José say that his talk would be brief.
4. He was late in arriving, which surprised (a) everybody.
5. From a box he took out several objects, which he placed on the table.
6. He spoke of picturesque Spain, the one that all tourists love.
7. You don't have [any] right to say such things about my country—shouted a Spanish professor, who until that moment had been listening very attentively.
8. What? Speak in public in order to say only foolish things!
9. You are capable of saying that in Spain women wear wide skirts under which they carry a knife with which they kill their lovers!
10. Poor (de) me!—said Pedro on seeing the professor leave. — Seeing is believing!
11. The meeting ended, Don José thanked Pedro for his talk.

F. EXERCISE ON IDIOMS AND PHRASES

1. *Translate the words underlined:*

   1. I have no objection to hablar, he hastened to answer.
   2. Si Vd. quiere I'll report on todos los incidentes del viaje.
   3. Of course usted have no right to abusar de nuestra paciencia.
   4. Therefore le ruego que be pensando en lo que va a decir.
   5. It's a question of entretener a los estudiantes at least por media hora.
   6. All right. I agree with you.
   7. Si no les gusta mi charla, you'll be to blame.
   8. Llegó con una caja under el brazo y la puso on top of la mesa.
   9. Dijo que estaba in love with el español pero apologized for no poder expresarse bien en esta lengua.
   10. Confesó que sometimes no había podido find out todo lo que hablaba la gente.

2. *Translate:*

Al cabo no pudo contenerse más. No se meta usted en tales asuntos. ¿De dónde ha sacado usted eso? No despegó los labios en toda la noche. A veces no dice más que tonterías. No ha vuelto por aquí desde que llegó. La conocí el año pasado. Hoy carece de todo. Se reúnen todos los jueves. No lo comprendo del todo. Se arrodilló ante la imagen. Entró sin que le vieran. Es mejor andar sin prisa. Viajó por todo el mundo. Dicen que no tiene pelos en la lengua.

APPENDIX

AND

CUESTIONARIOS

APPENDIX

75. Pronouns.

SUBJECT	OBJECT		
	Unstressed (USED WITH VERBS)		Stressed (WITH PREPOSITIONS)
	Indirect	*Direct*	
SINGULAR			
yo I **tú** you **usted** you **él** he, it **ella** she, it	**me** to me, myself **te** to you, yourself **le** to you **le** to him, it **le, la**² to her, it **se** to { yourself himself herself itself	**me** me, myself **te** you, yourself { **le, lo** *m.* you { **la** *f.* you **le, lo**¹ him, it **la** her, it **se** { yourself himself herself itself	**mí** me, myself **ti** you, yourself **usted** you **él** him, it **ella** her, it **sí** { yourself himself herself itself
PLURAL			
nosotros, -as we **vosotros, -as** you **ustedes** you **ellos** they **ellas** they	**nos** to { us ourselves **os** to { you yourselves **les** to you **les** to them **les, las**² to them **se** to { ·yourselves themselves	**nos** { us ourselves **os** { you yourselves { **les, los** *m.* you { **las** *f.* you **los,**³ **les**⁴ them **las** them **se** { yourselves themselves	**nosotros, -as** us ourselves } **vosotros, -as** you yourselves } **ustedes** you **ellos** they **ellas** they **sí** { yourselves themselves

---

¹ Referring to things, **lo** is more frequent than **le**.

² **La** and **las** are not very common as indirect objects.   ³ Persons or things.   ⁴ Normally persons only.

76. Additional Radical-Changing Verbs of Class I.

acertar (a) to hit the mark; do the
  right thing; happen
atender to attend (to), pay attention
atravesar to cross, pass over
cocer[1] to cook; *esp.* boil, stew
colgar[1] to hang (up)
confesar to confess
demostrar to show, demonstrate
devolver to give back, return
encerrar to shut (up), lock
envolver to wrap (up)

errar[2] to err
helar to freeze
manifestar to reveal; express
oler[2] to smell
resolver to decide; solve
soltar to let go (of); release
temblar to tremble
tender (a) to extend; tend
torcer[1] to twist; turn
tropezar[1] **(con)** to run (into)
volar to fly

77. Cardinal Numerals.

0. **cero**	17. **diez y siete**	80. **ochenta**
1. **un(o), una**	**(diecisiete)**	90. **noventa**
2. **dos**	18. **diez y ocho**	100. **ciento, cien**
3. **tres**	**(dieciocho)**	101. **ciento un(o)**
4. **cuatro**	19. **diez y nueve**	200. **doscientos,-as**
5. **cinco**	**(diecinueve)**	300. **trescientos,-as**
6. **seis**	20. **veinte**	400. **cuatrocientos,-as**
7. **siete**	21. **veinte y un(o)**	500. **quinientos,-as**
8. **ocho**	**(veintiún(o))**	600. **seiscientos,-as**
9. **nueve**	22. **veinte y dos**	700. **setecientos,-as**
10. **diez**	**(veintidós)**	800. **ochocientos,-as**
11. **once**	30. **treinta**	900. **novecientos,-as**
12. **doce**	31. **treinta y un(o)**	1000. **mil**
13. **trece**	32. **treinta y dos**	2000. **dos mil**
14. **catorce**	40. **cuarenta**	1,000,000. **un millón (de)**
15. **quince**	50. **cincuenta**	2,000,000. **dos millones (de)**
16. **diez y seis**	60. **sesenta**	
(dieciséis)	70. **setenta**	

---

[1] Has a spelling-change; see Verb Chart.
[2] Since Spanish orthography does not permit the diphthongs **ue** or **ie** to begin a word, the forms where **ue** or **ie** would stand at the beginning of a word are spelled respectively **hue** and **ye: huelo**, etc., **yerro**, etc.

78. Ordinal Numerals.

1st. **primer(o)**   5th. **quinto**   8th. **octavo**
2d. **segundo**   6th. **sexto**   9th. **noveno (nono)**
3d. **tercer(o)**   7th. **séptimo**   10th. **décimo**
4th. **cuarto**

79. Infinitives with and without a Preposition.

Common verbs that are followed

(1) *Directly by the infinitive:*

bastar to be enough
conseguir (i) to succeed in
convenir to be proper, be well; suit
creer to believe, think
deber should, ought; must
decidir to decide
desear to wish, desire
esperar to hope, expect
gustar to please, like
hacer to make, cause, have
intentar to try
lograr to succeed in
necesitar to need
oír to hear

olvidar to forget
parecer to seem
pensar (ie) to intend
poder to be able, can; may
preferir (ie, i) to prefer
pretender to try
procurar to try
prometer to promise
proponerse to propose
querer to wish, want, will
saber to know how, can
soler (ue) to be accustomed
temer to fear, be afraid
ver to see

(2) *By* **a:**

acercarse a to approach
acostumbrarse a to get used to
alcanzar a to manage to
aprender a to learn to
apresurarse a to hurry to
asistir a to attend
asomarse a to peer out
atreverse a to dare to
ayudar a to help to
comenzar a to begin to
decidirse a make up one's mind to
detenerse a to stop to

dirigirse a to speak to; make one's way to
disponerse a to get ready to
echar a to start to
empezar a to begin to
enseñar a to teach to
invitar a to invite to
ir a to go to
llegar a to come to
negarse a to refuse to
obligar a to force to
pararse a to stop to

parecerse a to look like
ponerse a to start to
retirarse a to retire to
salir a to go out to

sentarse a to sit down to
venir a to come to
volver a to (do) again

(3) *By* de:

acordarse de to remember to
alegrarse de to be glad to
carecer de to lack
deber de must
dejar de to stop; fail to
despedirse de to say good-by to
enamorarse de to fall in love with
encargarse de to take charge of
enterarse de to find out
gozar de to enjoy

gustar de to enjoy
haber de to be to
olvidarse de to forget to
pensar de to think of
quejarse de to complain of
reírse de to laugh at
salir de to leave
servir de to serve as
tratar de to try to
tratarse de to be a question of

(4) *By* en:

complacerse en to take pleasure in
consentir en to consent to
convenir en to agree to
convertirse en to change into
entrar en to enter

fijarse en to notice
insistir en to insist on
pensar en to think of
quedar en to agree to

(5) *By* con:

casarse con to marry
contar con to rely on
encontrarse con to meet

soñar con to dream of
tropezar con to run into

(6) **Que** translates *to* after expressions of quantity:

algo que hacer *something to* do
demasiado que hacer *too much to* do
mucho que hacer *much to* do

nada que hacer *nothing to* do
nada que ver con *nothing to* do with
poco que hacer *little to* do

80. Additional Irregular Past Participles.

bendecir—**bendito** blessed, holy

componer—**compuesto** composed, compound

descubrir—**descubierto** discovered

devolver—**devuelto** returned

disponer—**dispuesto** disposed

envolver—**envuelto** wrapped (up)

exponer—**expuesto** exposed, expressed

freír—**frito** fried

imponer—**impuesto** imposed

imprimir—**impreso** (imprimido) printed

oponer—**opuesto** opposed; opposite

prender—**preso** (prendido) seized

resolver—**resuelto** decided; solved

satisfacer—**satisfecho** satisfied, pleased

suponer—**supuesto** supposed

CUESTIONARIOS

I

1. ¿Qué clase de muchacho era Pedro Burk?
2. ¿Cuál era su deporte favorito?
3. ¿Por qué no hablaba él español en la clase?
4. ¿Qué preguntó Pedro un día al profesor?
5. ¿Cree el profesor que los norteamericanos pueden aprender lenguas extranjeras?
6. ¿Qué debía hacer Pedro para perder el miedo de hablar español?
7. ¿Qué le habían prometido a Pedro sus padres?
8. ¿Qué tendría que hacer Pedro el año que viene?
9. ¿Cuándo esperaba él contestación a su carta?
10. ¿Cuándo pensaba volver a ver a D. José?
11. ¿Qué debe hacer uno para aprender a hablar una lengua?
12. ¿En qué año de estudios estaba Pedro en la universidad?
13. ¿Es Vd. un estudiante de segundo o de tercer año?
14. ¿Pronuncia Vd. bien el español?
15. ¿Cree Vd. que es importante pronunciar bien una lengua extranjera?

II

1. ¿Cuándo volvió Pedro a hablar con el profesor?
2. ¿Qué le preguntó D. José?
3. ¿Por qué ha tenido suerte Pedro?
4. ¿Tenía más clases Pedro aquel día?
5. ¿Dónde hablaban Pedro y el profesor?
6. ¿Qué pensaba hacer Pedro aquel verano?
7. ¿Por qué quería él ir a España?
8. ¿En qué lugares hay Cursos de Verano en España?

9. ¿Cuál era la ventaja de ir a Segovia?
10. ¿Qué clase de ciudad es Segovia?
11. ¿Dónde marcó D. José los lugares que tenían Cursos de Verano?
12. ¿Qué haría Pedro después de estudiar en España?
13. ¿Cree Vd. que Pedro aprenderá mucho en España?
14. ¿Le gustaría a Vd. ir a España para estudiar español?
15. ¿Quién dió dinero a Pedro para ir a Europa?

III

1. ¿Por qué volvió D. José a su casa?
2. ¿Qué hora era cuando regresó a su casa?
3. ¿Qué notó su esposa al verle?
4. ¿Qué le preguntó ella al verle?
5. ¿Cómo estaba la sopa?
6. ¿En qué era algo raro Pedro, según el profesor?
7. ¿Qué había dicho D. José de los españoles?
8. ¿Quién fué a despedirse del profesor?
9. ¿Cuándo se verían de nuevo Pedro y el profesor?
10. ¿Dónde estarían ellos entonces?
11. ¿Qué le dará Pedro al profesor en España?
12. ¿A dónde iba D. José aquel verano?
13. ¿Cómo hicieron el viaje Pedro y D. José?
14. ¿Dónde desembarcó Pedro?
15. ¿A quién llamó Pedro por teléfono en Madrid?
16. ¿Qué tres palabras entendió la criada?
17. ¿Por qué no vió Pedro al profesor?

IV

1. ¿Qué se quitó D. José al llegar a su casa?
2. ¿Dónde se sentó después?
3. ¿Por qué creía D. José que Pedro estaba enfadado con él?
4. ¿Por qué pensaba escribirle una carta?
5. ¿Qué iba a decirle en la carta para animarle?
6. ¿Quién vino a su cuarto?
7. ¿De quién era la carta que trajo la criada?
8. ¿En qué lengua estaba escrita la carta?
9. ¿Qué dice Pedro de Segovia en la carta?
10. ¿Por dónde había dado él muchos paseos?
11. ¿Qué había admirado Pedro en Segovia?
12. ¿Con quién daba paseos la mayoría de las veces?
13. ¿Cómo era el castillo de Turégano?
14. ¿Qué cosas encantan a Pedro?
15. ¿Qué decía Pedro de la vida en Segovia?
16. ¿Cómo eran sus compañeros?

171

17. ¿Por qué no hablaba mucho con ellos?
18. ¿Tenían ellos más edad que Pedro o menos?
19. ¿Por qué le gustaría a Pedro ver al profesor?
20. ¿Cree Vd. que Pedro está contento?

V

1. ¿Qué se preguntaba D. José una y otra vez?
2. ¿Por qué estaba él preocupado?
3. ¿Cuándo pensaba D. José pasar por Segovia?
4. ¿Quién esperaba al profesor en la estación?
5. ¿De dónde acababa de regresar Pedro?
6. ¿Por qué fué Pedro a Pamplona?
7. ¿Cuánto tiempo duró este viaje?
8. ¿Cuándo se celebran las fiestas de San Fermín?
9. ¿Qué se celebra durante estas fiestas?
10. ¿Por qué soltó Pedro una carcajada?
11. ¿Qué hizo uno de los toros?
12. ¿Qué hizo el dependiente al ver al toro?
13. ¿Qué hizo el parroquiano?
14. ¿Qué hizo el toro después de un rato?
15. ¿Por qué no atacó el toro al hombre en el café?
16. ¿Qué debe hacer uno si se encuentra con un toro?
17. ¿Qué hizo el profesor al llegar al hotel?
18. ¿Por qué tenía hambre D. José?
19. ¿A qué invitó D. José a Pedro?
20. ¿Por qué aceptó Pedro si ya había cenado?

VI

1. ¿Qué vino le gustaba a Pedro?
2. ¿Qué cualidades tiene este vino?
3. ¿Qué es el gazpacho?
4. ¿Qué ingredientes debe tener el gazpacho para estar bien hecho?
5. ¿Qué monumento imponente hay en Segovia?
6. ¿Qué hacía todos los días una joven segoviana?
7. ¿Qué prometió ella al Diablo?
8. ¿Qué le prometió el Diablo a ella?
9. ¿Cuánto tardó el diablo en construir el acueducto?
10. ¿Por qué se desmayó la muchacha?
11. ¿Comió Pedro el gazpacho? ¿Qué más tomó?
12. ¿Por qué no tenía reloj D. José?
13. ¿Qué hora era cuando terminaron de comer?
14. ¿Cuándo se acuesta la gente en España?
15. ¿Qué propuso el profesor al salir del comedor?
16. ¿Qué dice Pedro de la vida de Segovia por la noche?

17. ¿Se acostaba Pedro temprano o tarde?
18. ¿A qué hora se acuesta Vd. generalmente?

VII

1. ¿Cómo era la noche?
2. ¿Desde dónde contemplaron la llanura castellana?
3. ¿Dónde tomaron un refresco Pedro y el profesor?
4. ¿Dónde vivían los estudiantes extranjeros?
5. ¿Cuándo tenía clases Pedro?
6. ¿Qué haría D. José aquella mañana?
7. ¿De qué edificios sacaría él fotografías?
8. ¿Cómo era el cuarto de Pedro en la Residencia?
9. ¿Qué se veía desde el balcón de su cuarto?
10. ¿Por qué no tenía Pedro un compañero de cuarto?
11. ¿Qué dijo Carlos V de la lengua castellana?
12. ¿Qué confesó Pedro a D. José?
13. ¿Con quién se sentaron en el comedor?
14. ¿Qué lengua hablaban los estudiantes en el comedor?
15. ¿En qué consistía la comida?
16. ¿Qué tuvieron de postre?
17. ¿Por qué no aprendía mucho Pedro?
18. ¿Qué hacía él durante las horas de clase?
19. ¿Qué hacían la mayoría de los profesores?
20. ¿Por qué estaba desilusionado D. José?

VIII

1. ¿Quién era la directora del grupo?
2. ¿Qué decía de ella un amigo de Pedro?
3. ¿Dónde tenían lugar las clases?
4. ¿Cuántas personas formaban parte del grupo?
5. ¿Tenían todos la misma edad y la misma preparación?
6. ¿Dónde vivía la familia de California?
7. ¿Cuántos había en esta familia?
8. ¿Quién era el único que hablaba español? ¿Por qué?
9. ¿Cuántos años tenían los hijos de esta familia?
10. ¿Quiénes eran los otros compañeros de Pedro?
11. ¿Estaban todos interesados en aprender español?
12. ¿Quiénes eran los mejores amigos de Pedro?
13. ¿Qué hizo el profesor al llegar al hotel?
14. ¿Qué olvidaba D. José en el cuarto?
15. ¿Qué hizo Pedro mientras D. José pagaba la cuenta?
16. ¿Para quién era el paquete que llevaba D. José?
17. ¿Por qué dió las gracias Pedro al profesor?
18. ¿Por qué es notable la ciudad de Ávila?

19. ¿Por qué es famoso El Escorial?
20. ¿En qué ocasión se puso enfermo Pedro?

IX

1. ¿Por qué pudieron hablar un rato más Pedro y D. José?
2. ¿Dónde se encontraban ellos?
3. ¿Qué impresiones tenía Pedro de España?
4. ¿Por qué le impresionó la meseta castellana?
5. ¿Es España un país agrícola o industrial?
6. ¿Viven en el campo los campesinos españoles?
7. ¿Cómo son los campesinos que Pedro había visto?
8. ¿Cómo es el cielo de Segovia?
9. ¿Cómo es el clima de esta región?
10. ¿Con qué otro clima lo comparaba Pedro?
11. ¿Cuántas semanas le quedaban a Pedro en Segovia?
12. ¿A dónde pensaba ir Pedro la semana próxima?
13. ¿Por qué quería Pedro separarse del grupo?
14. ¿Cuándo se reuniría de nuevo con el grupo?
15. ¿Por qué no pudieron seguir hablando?
16. ¿Por qué no se verían de nuevo en España D. José y Pedro?
17. ¿Cuándo volverían a verse ambos?
18. ¿Cuál fué el último consejo que el profesor dió a Pedro?
19. ¿Dónde pasaría D. José bastante tiempo?
20. ¿Qué vió el profesor por la ventanilla del tren?

X

1. ¿Por qué iba lleno de gente el expreso de Madrid?
2. ¿Qué hizo un mozo con la maleta del profesor?
3. ¿Quién estaba sentado junto a la ventanilla?
4. ¿Qué hizo D. José después de sentarse en su asiento?
5. ¿De qué estaba él arrepentido?
6. ¿Por qué se quitó D. José la chaqueta?
7. ¿Por cuánto tiempo durmió él?
8. ¿Qué le despertó?
9. ¿Por qué querían algunos pasajeros tener las ventanas cerradas?
10. ¿Por qué querían otros tenerlas abiertas?
11. ¿Qué dijo a D. José su compañero de viaje?
12. ¿Cómo se llamaba este señor?
13. ¿Qué libro estaba leyendo?
14. ¿Por qué no entendía todas las palabras del libro?
15. ¿Qué cree Noriega de la lengua que se habla en los Estados Unidos?
16. ¿Por qué no encontraba las palabras en el diccionario que tenía?
17. ¿Qué le ofreció Noriega a D. José?

18. ¿Qué clase de hombre era Carlos Noriega?

19. ¿Qué esperaba él hacer algún día?
20. ¿Dónde estaba situado el bar?

XI

1. ¿Qué explicó el profesor a su nuevo amigo?
2. ¿Qué dijo D. José de Nueva York?
3. ¿Por qué quería el señor Noriega visitar Nueva York?
4. ¿Qué representa Nueva York para muchos extranjeros?
5. ¿Por qué había disminuido la marcha el tren?
6. ¿Qué vió el profesor desde el tren?
7. ¿Qué exclamó D. José al ver el castillo de la Mota?
8. ¿Quién murió en este castillo?
9. ¿Cuánto tiempo paraba el tren en Medina del Campo?
10. ¿Por dónde dieron un paseo los nuevos amigos?
11. ¿Sobre qué continuó haciendo preguntas el Sr. Noriega?
12. ¿Qué tres cosas quería saber él?
13. ¿Qué preguntas quería hacer D. José al Sr. Noriega?
14. ¿Por qué no podría éste contestarlas?
15. ¿Dónde podrían ellos hablar de todo?
16. ¿Por qué no aceptó D. José la invitación de su amigo?
17. ¿A qué hora llegó el tren a Oviedo?
18. ¿Quiénes esperaban al profesor en la estación?
19. ¿Cómo se llamaba la hija más pequeña de su amigo?
20. ¿Por qué no había querido acostarse la niña?

XII

1. ¿A dónde tiene que ir el amigo de D. José?
2. ¿Cuándo llegó la carta de Pedro?
3. ¿Desde dónde escribía Pedro la carta?
4. ¿Por qué había cambiado de planes?
5. ¿Por qué tenía Pedro deseos de visitar Santiago de Compostela?
6. ¿Por qué fué importante esta ciudad en la Edad Media?
7. ¿Qué se descubrió allí a principios del siglo IX?
8. ¿Qué hay hoy en el lugar donde se descubrió el sepulcro?
9. ¿Qué parte de la catedral le impresionó más a Pedro?
10. ¿Dónde puso Pedro los cinco dedos de la mano derecha?
11. ¿Qué había detrás del altar mayor?
12. ¿Qué hacen muchos peregrinos al ver esta estatua?
13. ¿Qué hacían siete acólitos vestidos de rojo?
14. ¿Cómo se llama el gran incensario de la catedral?
15. ¿De dónde venían antiguamente los peregrinos?
16. ¿Por qué era necesario derramar mucho incienso?
17. ¿De quién es la estatua arrodillada que hay a la entrada?
18. ¿Por qué está la estatua tan gastada?

19. ¿Con qué objeto acercó Pedro su cabeza a la estatua?
20. ¿De qué no está seguro Pedro?

XIII

1. ¿Cómo es el clima de Asturias en verano?
2. ¿Qué fecha tenía la carta de Pedro?
3. ¿Por qué se había detenido Pedro en Madrid?
4. ¿Por qué le había interesado mucho Toledo?
5. ¿Quién conquistó esta ciudad a los moros? ¿En qué año?
6. ¿Qué hizo el caballo del rey al pasar en frente de la mezquita?
7. ¿Qué descubrieron dentro de la mezquita?
8. ¿Cómo se llama hoy esta mezquita?
9. ¿Cómo se titula otra leyenda que Pedro había leído?
10. ¿Qué había jurado un soldado español?
11. ¿A dónde fué el soldado después?
12. ¿Qué negó él cuando regresó a Toledo?
13. ¿Quién había sido testigo de su juramento?
14. ¿Con qué nombre es conocida la imagen de este Cristo?
15. ¿Qué dice Pedro del interior de la mezquita de Córdoba?
16. ¿Por qué no querían dejarle subir a la Giralda?
17. ¿Qué se veía desde lo alto de la Giralda?
18. ¿Por qué tienen toldos en verano algunas calles de Sevilla?
19. ¿Qué dicen los sevillanos de su ciudad?
20. ¿Por qué tiene que interrumpir Pedro su carta?

XIV

1. ¿A quién conoció Pedro en Sevilla?
2. ¿Qué impresión produce el árbol llamado drago?
3. ¿Dónde se puede ver este árbol?
4. ¿Cómo es la savia de este árbol?
5. ¿Qué es el Teide?
6. ¿Por qué es llamado también Monte Pelado?
7. ¿Por qué no fué Pedro a las Islas Canarias?
8. ¿Por qué se marchó Pedro de Sevilla aquella misma tarde?
9. ¿Cómo pasó Pedro muchas horas en Granada?
10. ¿Quién escribió las *Leyendas de la Alhambra?*
11. ¿Cómo hizo Pedro el viaje de Granada a Valencia?
12. ¿Por qué no fué éste un viaje muy cómodo?
13. ¿Con qué objeto fué Pedro a Valencia?
14. ¿Dónde se reúne el Tribunal de las Aguas?
15. ¿Quiénes son los "jueces" de este tribunal?
16. ¿Dónde se sientan estos "jueces" y qué representa cada uno?
17. ¿Qué conflictos resuelven ellos?
18. ¿En qué consisten por lo general las sentencias?

19. ¿Qué pierden los sentenciados si no pagan la multa?
20. ¿Por qué es interesante este tribunal?

XV

1. ¿Por qué no escribió Pedro más cartas al profesor?
2. ¿Qué contó Pedro a D. José al volver a la universidad?
3. ¿Qué favor le pidió el profesor a Pedro?
4. ¿Por qué no quería hablar Pedro de su viaje a España?
5. ¿Cuándo tendría lugar la primera reunión del Club Español?
6. ¿Por qué vinieron bastantes estudiantes a escuchar a Pedro?
7. ¿Qué traía Pedro debajo del brazo?
8. ¿Qué sacó Pedro de la caja?
9. ¿Cuál de los objetos llamó mucho la atención?
10. ¿Cómo era la hoja de la navaja?
11. ¿Qué inscripción tenía la navaja en el mango?
12. ¿Qué dijo Pedro de las corridas de toros?
13. ¿Qué ciudad dijo que le había gustado más?
14. ¿Qué dicen de su ciudad los granadinos?
15. ¿Qué dijo Pedro de las grandes ciudades españolas?
16. ¿Había visto Pedro muchas mujeres bonitas en España?
17. ¿Qué le dijo a Pedro un profesor que le escuchaba?
18. Según este profesor, ¿por qué no vió Pedro mujeres bonitas?
19. ¿Quién era este profesor?
20. ¿Cree Vd. que Pedro había cambiado de ideas?

SPANISH-ENGLISH VOCABULARY

All words used in the text are included in the Vocabularies, except certain proper names which have the same form in English. Nouns that denote male beings, and those that end in **-o** are masculine; nouns that denote female beings, and those ending in **-a, -ión, -d,** and **-umbre** are usually feminine. The gender of other nouns (and exceptions to the rules above) is indicated. Radical-changing verbs are marked (**ie, ue, i**). A dash indicates that the key word is repeated. Adjectives that are regularly declined are given only in the masculine singular form. Adverbs ending in **-mente** are not separately entered. The preposition that a verb governs is indicated in parentheses.

In definitions, words given in parentheses are explanatory and need not be used in translation. The basic meaning of each word is normally given first.

Idioms which contain a noun are entered under the first noun. Idioms which contain an adjective, but not a noun, are entered under the adjective, and so on, in order, under an adverb, a pronoun, or a verb. Expressions included in parentheses in idioms and in their translations are intended only to clarify the usage and do not form a part of the idiom. Under each entry word, the idioms are arranged in alphabetical order, but article and object pronouns are disregarded in the alphabetizing.

A

a to; at, in, into, on, by, with, etc.; from; *not translated when used to indicate the direct object;*
  ¿a dónde? where?
  a los (pocos días) de (a few days) after
  a los (pocos minutos) after (a few minutes)
  al (poco rato) (shortly) afterward
abajo down, below; downstairs
abandonar to desert, leave, give up
abierto *p.p. of* **abrir:** open, opened
abogado lawyer
abrazar to embrace
abrazo embrace
  dar un — to embrace

abrigo (evening) wrap; coat
abril (el) April
abrir to open; *refl.* open
absoluto absolute
abuelo grandfather; *pl.* grandparents
abundancia abundance
abundante abundant
aburrido bored
abusar (de) to abuse
acabar to end, finish
  acabar de + *inf.* to have just + *p.p.*
  acabó de (comer) he finished (eating)
acaso perhaps
accidente (el) accident
acción action, act

aceite (el) oil, olive oil
aceptar to accept
acercar to draw up, bring near
  acercarse (a) to approach
acertar (ie) to guess right
  acertar (a) to happen
acólito acolyte, assistant
acompañar to go with, come with
aconsejar to advise
acordarse (ue) (de) to remember
acostado lying (down)
acostar (ue) to put to bed; *refl.* go to bed
acostumbrado accustomed; usual
acostumbrar to accustom; be accustomed
acto act; function
actriz (la) actress
actual present (*of time*)
acudir to come (*in answer to a call*)
acueducto aqueduct
acuerdo agreement
  estar de acuerdo to agree
acusado (person) accused
Adela Adele
adelantar to advance, progress
además besides
¡adiós! good-by!
admirar to admire, wonder at
admitir to admit
adquirir (ie, i) to acquire, gain
advertir (ie, i) to warn, tell; notice
aeropuerto airport
afeitarse to shave
aficionado (a) fond (of)
afirmar to state, declare
afortunado fortunate
afueras suburbs, outskirts
agitado agitated, restless
aglomeración gathering, crowding
agosto August
agradable pleasant
agradecer to be thankful for
agradecido grateful, thankful
agrícola agricultural
agua (el, *but fem.*) water

aguardar to wait; wait for
¡ah! ah! oh!
ahí there (*near the person addressed*)
ahogarse to choke; drown
ahora now
  ahora mismo right now
  hasta ahora so far
  por ahora for the present
aire (el) air
ajo garlic
al = a + el;
  al (terminar) when I (finish), on (finishing)
ala (el, *but fem.*) wing
Albacete *city and province in southeastern
  Spain*
Alberto Albert
alcanzar to overtake, catch up with
alcázar (el) fortress; royal palace
alcoba bedroom
alegrarse (de) to be glad (to)
alegre merry, gay
alegría joy, gladness
alemán German; **el alemán** German (*the
  language*); German
Alfonso VI (1072–1109), *king of Castile and
  Leon*
algo something, anything; somewhat, a little
  algo de (nuevo) something (new)
alguien someone, somebody
algún *used for* **alguno** *before a masc. sing.
  noun*
alguno some, any; a few
alguno someone, anyone, some, any
Alhambra, la *Moorish castle in Granada*
alma (el, *but fem.*) soul; heart
almacén (el) store; warehouse
almorzar (ue) to have, eat, luncheon
almuerzo luncheon, lunch
altar (el) altar
  altar mayor main altar
alto high; tall; upper (*story*)
  desde lo alto from the top
altura height, altitude
alumno pupil

179

allá   there; yonder
allí   there
  allí mismo   right there
  por allí   over there, around there
ama (el, *but fem.*)   housekeeper
amable   kind, lovable
amar   to love
amarillo   yellow
ambiente (el)   atmosphere; surroundings
ambos   both
América   America
americano   American; el — American (*the language*); American, North American
amigo   friend
amistad   friendship
amistoso   friendly
amo   master; owner
amor (el)   love
ancho   broad, wide
Andalucía   Andalusia (*region in southern Spain*)
andaluz   Andalusian
andar   to go, walk
andén (el)   platform
ángel (el)   angel
animación   animation; movement
animal (el)   animal; brute
animar   to encourage; animate
anoche   last night
anochecer   to get dark
ante   before, in the presence of
antes   before, first, sooner; formerly
  antes de   before
  antes de que   before
  cuanto antes   as soon as possible
  lo antes posible   as soon as possible
antiguamente   formerly
antiguo   old, ancient; *before the noun modified* former
antiquísimo   very old
anunciar   to announce
añadir   to add
180   **año**   year

¿cuántos años tiene Vd.?   how old are you?
de tercer año   third-year, junior
tiene (diecisiete) años   he is (seventeen) years old
aparecer   to appear
  se le apareció   he appeared before her
apelación   appeal
apellido   (family) name
apenas   hardly, scarcely
aplicado   industrious
apóstol (el)   apostle
apoyado   leaning
aprender (a)   to learn
apresurarse (a)   to hurry, hasten
aprovechamiento   use; exploitation
aprovecharse (de)   to take advantage (of)
aquel, -ella   that; those
aquél, -élla, -ello   that one; he; the former; that; those
aquí   here
  por aquí   this way, round here
árabe   Arab, Arabian, Arabic
árbol (el)   tree
arcada   archway, exterior portico or gallery
arder   to burn, blaze
arma (el, *but fem.*)   arm, weapon
armario   wardrobe; closet
arpa (el, *but fem.*) harp
arreglar   to arrange
arreglo   arrangement
arrepentido   repentant, repented
arrepentirse (ie, i) (de)   to repent
arriba   up, above; upstairs
arrimarse (a)   to lean against
arrodillado   in a kneeling position
arrodillarse   to kneel
arte (el, *but both masc. and fem.*)   art
artista (el *or* la)   artist
artístico   artistic
asegurar   to assure; assert
así   so, thus, like this (that)
  así es la vida   such is life
  así que   as soon as

asiento seat, chair
asignatura subject (*of study*)
asistir (a) to attend
asociación association
asomarse (a) to peer out
aspecto aspect; air, appearance
Asturias *former kingdom, now a province, in northern Spain*
asunto affair, matter
asustar to frighten, scare
atacar to attack
atención attention
    llamar la — to attract one's attention
    prestar — to pay attention
atender (ie) to attend (to)
atento attentive
átomo atom
atractivo charm, attractiveness
atravesar (ie) to cross
atreverse (a) to dare
atrevido daring, bold
aumentar to increase
aun, aún even, still, yet
aunque though, although, even if
ausencia absence
auto car, auto
autobús (el) bus
automático automatic
autor (el) author
autorcillo inferior author
ave (el, *but fem.*) bird; fowl
avenida avenue
aventura adventure; chance
Ávila *city and province in west central Spain*
avión (el) plane; **en —** by plane
avisar inform, let (*someone*) know, notify about
ayer yesterday
ayudar (a) to help
azúcar (el) sugar
azul blue

B

bailar to dance
baile (el) dance

bajar to go down, come down; get off; lower
bajo low; short
balcón (el) window; balcony
banquillo stool
bañar to bathe; *also refl.*
baño bath
bar (el) bar
Barcelona *seaport and province in northeastern Spain*
barco boat
barraca cabin, hut
base (la) base; basis
    hecha a base de (patatas) prepared mainly with (potatoes)
bastante enough, quite some, quite a bit, quite, rather, quite a few
bastar to be enough
batalla battle
baúl (el) trunk
bazar (el) bazaar, market place
beber to drink
bello beautiful
bendecir to bless
bendito blessed, holy
bendito *p.p. of* **bendecir**
besar to kiss
besito little kiss
beso kiss
bestia beast, animal
Biblia Bible
biblioteca library
bien well; clearly, perfectly
    bien que although
    está bien all right
    hacer bien to do the right thing
    pero bien well
    si bien although
billete (el) ticket
blanco white
Blasco Ibáñez, Vicente (1867–1928), *Spanish novelist*
boca mouth
boina beret; round woolen cap
bolsa purse

181

bolsillo pocket

bondad goodness, kindness

bonísimo very good

bonito pretty

borrar to erase

borrico donkey

bosque (el) woods, forest

botica drugstore

botijo earthen jug with spout

bóveda arch, vault

bravo wild, savage; brave

brazo arm

breve brief, short

brillante brilliant

broma joke; **en —** as a joke

Bruselas Brussels, *capital of Belgium*

buen *used for* **bueno** *before a masc. sing. noun*

bueno good; well; all right

 ¡bueno! fine! all right!

Burgos *city and province in north central Spain*

burlarse (de) to make fun (of)

burro donkey

buscar to look for; get; call for

C

caballazo large (clumsy) horse

caballero knight; gentleman

caballo horse; **montar a —** to ride (horse-back)

caber to be contained

cabeza head

cabo end; **al cabo** finally

 llevar a cabo to carry out

cabra goat

cada each, every

 cada cual, cada uno each one

caer to fall

 caerse to fall down

 se me cayó (el pañuelo) I dropped (my handkerchief)

café (el) coffee; restaurant

caída fall

caja box, case

cajón (el) drawer

calidad quality

caliente hot, warm

calma calm, quiet

calor (el) heat

 hacer calor to be hot (*weather*)

 tener calor to be warm (*persons*)

callado silent, taciturn

callar to be silent, keep still; *also refl.*

calle (la) street

cama bed

camarero waiter

cambiar (de) to change

cambio exchange, change

caminar to travel, walk

camino road; way

campana bell, (*church*) bell

campanilla hand bell

campeador (el) champion, mighty in battle

campesino farmer, peasant

campo field; country

Canarias, las (Islas) Canary Islands

canario inhabitant of the Canary Islands

cansado weary, tired; tiresome

cansar to tire, weary

cantar to sing

cantidad quantity

capa cape, cloak

capaz able (to), capable (of)

capital (la) capital (*of a country or state*)

capital (el) capital (*money*)

capitán (el) captain

capítulo chapter

cara face

 tener cara de (hombre) to look like (a man)

carácter (el) character

carcajada outburst of laughter

 soltar una — to burst out laughing

cardinal cardinal

carecer (de) to be lacking, be wanting

cargado loaded

cargo charge; office

cariño affection

Carlos Charles; **Carlos V** (1517–1556), *crowned king of Spain in 1517 and Emperor of the Holy Roman Empire in 1519*
carne (la) meat; flesh
carretera highroad, highway
carta letter
cartel (el) poster
casa house
  a casa home
  en casa at home
  en casa de (su amigo) at (his friend's)
casar to marry
  casarse con to marry, get married
casi almost
caso case
  hacer caso de to pay attention to
castellano Castilian, Spanish (*the language*)
castigar to punish
castigo punishment
castillo castle
casucha hut, hovel
catedral (la) cathedral
católico Catholic
catorce fourteen
causa cause; **a — de** because of
causar to cause; produce
celebrar to celebrate; be glad of; **—se** to take place
célebre celebrated
cenar to eat, have supper
central central, middle
céntrico central, in the center of the city
centro center; downtown
cerca near; **— de** near, nearly
cero zero
cerrar (ie) to shut, close
Cervantes, Miguel de (1547–1616), *Spain's greatest writer*
cesar (de) to cease, stop
Cid, el the Cid (1040?–1099), *national hero of Spain*
ciego blind
cielo sky; heaven
cien *used for* **ciento** *before the word modified*

ciento *one* hundred, *a* hundred
cierto certain, sure; a certain
  por cierto que incidentally, by the way
cigarrillo cigarette
cigarro cigar
cinco five
cincuenta fifty
cine (el) movies
ciudad city
ciudadanía citizenship
claro clear, bright; light
  claro (está) (que) of course
clase (la) class, kind; classroom
clima (el) climate
club (el) club
cobrar to collect, gather
cocer (ue) to cook; boil, stew
cocinar to cook
coche (el) carriage, cab; car
coger to take, pick (up); gather
colgar (ue) to hang, hang up
colina hill
colocar to place, put
Colón, Cristóbal Christopher Columbus (1451–1506)
color (el) color
  (raza) de — colored (race)
  ¿de qué — es? what color is it?
columna column
combatir to fight, combat; oppose
comedia comedy; play
comedor (el) dining room
comentario commentary
comenzar (ie) (a) to begin
comer to eat (dinner), dine
cometa (el) comet
comida meal; dinner; food
como as, like, such as; **— si** as if
¿cómo? how? what?
  ¿a cómo (se vende este paño)? what (is the price of this cloth)?
  ¿cómo era (el castillo)? what was (the castle) like?
cómodo comfortable

183

compañero companion, comrade
— **de cuarto** roommate
— **de viaje** traveling companion
compañía company; **en — de** with
malas —s bad company
comparar (a) to compare
complacer to please
complejo complex
completo complete
por completo completely
componer to compose
Compostela, *see* **Santiago**
compra purchase; shopping
ir de compras to go shopping
comprar to buy
comprender to understand
compuesto composed; compound
compuesto *p.p. of* **componer**
común common, usual
con with; by
con (franqueza) (frank)ly
conceder to grant
concluir to conclude; finish
conclusión conclusion
condición condition
conducir to lead; drive (*a car*)
conferencia lecture
confesar (ie) to confess
confianza confidence
confiar to confide; trust
conflicto conflict, dispute
conmigo with me
cono cone
conocer to be acquainted with, know; *in the
preterit often* met
conocimiento acquaintance; knowledge;
often pl.
conquistar to conquer; win
conseguir (i) to attain, get; succeed in
consejo counsel, piece of advice; *pl.* advice
consentir (ie, i) (en) to consent
conservar to keep, preserve
184 **considerar** to consider

consigo with himself, herself, yourself, themselves
consistir (en) to consist (of)
constante constant
constituir to constitute
construir to build
consulta consultation; doctor's office
consultar to consult
contar (ue) to count; tell
contar con to count on
contemplar to contemplate
contener to contain; hold back, restrain
contenido contents
contento satisfied, contented
contestación answer
contestar (a) to answer
contigo with you
continuar to keep on, continue
contra against
contrario contrary
al — on the contrary
de lo — otherwise
contraste (el) contrast
controlado controlled
convencer to convince
convencerse (de) to be convinced
convenir to be proper, be well
convenir en to agree
conversación conversation
conversar to converse
convertir (ie, i) to convert; change; *refl.*
become converted, be changed
copa (stem) glass, goblet
copa top (*of a tree*)
corazón (el) heart
corbata necktie
Córdoba Cordova (*city and province of
southern Spain*)
correr to run
corresponder to correspond
corrida bullfight
corriente (la) current (*of a stream*)
cortaplumas (el) penknife

cortar to cut, cut off
corte (el) cut
corte (la) court
cortés polite, courteous
cortesía politeness, courtesy
corto short
cosa thing
  cosa de about
  (no) . . .gran cosa (not) . . . very much
  otra cosa anything else
costar (ue) to cost
costumbre habit, custom
creador (el) creator
crecer to increase
creer to believe, think
criada maid, servant
criado servant
criar to bring up, raise; *refl.* grow up
cristal (el) glass; (long) pane (of glass)
Cristo Christ
criticar to criticize
crucecita small cross
crucificado crucified
cruz (la) cross
cruzar to cross
cuaderno notebook
cuadro picture
cual (such) as
  el cual who, which
  lo cual that which, what
¿cuál? which? which one? what?
cualidad quality
cualquier *used for* **cualquiera** *before a noun*
cualquiera any (*at all*), anyone
cuando when
  de vez en cuando from time to time
¿cuándo? when?
cuanto as much as, as many as, all that
  — antes as soon as possible
  en — as soon as
  en — a as for
cuanto as much as, as far as
¿cuánto? how much? how many? how long?

¿a — (se vende)? what (is the price)?
¿a —s estamos del mes? what day of the month is it?
¡cuánto (me alegro)! how (glad I am)!
cuarenta forty
cuarto fourth
cuarto quarter; room
cuatro four
cubierta deck
cubierto *p.p. of* **cubrir**
cubrir to cover
cuenta account; bill
  dar — de to report on
  darse — de to realize
  por — propia on one's own account, paying one's own expenses
  tener en — to take into consideration, bear in mind
cuento (short) story, tale
cuerda rope
cuero leather; hide
cuerpecito little body
cuerpo body
cuidado care, worry
  con — carefully
  perder — not to worry
cuidar to take care (of)
culpa blame, fault; guilt
  tener la culpa to be to blame
cumplimiento fulfillment; compliment
cumplir to fulfill, keep (*one's word*)
cura (el) (parish) priest
cura cure
curar to cure
curiosidad curiosity
curso course (*of study*)
curvado curved
cuyo whose, of whom, of which

CH

chaqueta coat, jacket
charla chat, talk
charlar to chat, talk

chico small boy, youngster
chillido scream
chimenea smokestack
chiquillo small child
chiste (el) joke
chocolate (el) chocolate

D

D. *abbreviation of* don
dar to give; hit, strike; take (*steps*)
  dar (las buenas tardes) to wish (good afternoon)
  dar a to face, open on
  dar con to find
de of; from; about; by; with; as; *after a superlative* in; *after a comparative* than;
  de (postre) as (dessert)
debajo under; — de under
deber to owe; ought, should; must, must have, can(not)
deber (el) duty
débil weak
decidir to decide
  decidirse (a) to make up one's mind
décimo tenth
decir to say, tell
  es decir that is to say
declaración declaration, statement; deposition
declarar to declare
dedicar to dedicate; devote
dedo finger; toe
defecto defect
dejar to leave; let, allow
  dejar de to stop, fail
  dejemos esto let's drop this matter
del = de + el
  del que, de lo que, *etc.* than
delante in front, ahead
  delante de in front of
delicado delicate; fancy
delicioso delightful; delicious
demás (the) rest
demasiado too much, too many; too

demostrar (ue) to show
denso dense
dentro inside; — de inside of
dependiente (el) clerk
deporte (el) sport
derecho right; straight
derramar to scatter; pour
desaparecer to disappear
desayuno breakfast
descansar to rest
descanso rest, quiet
desclavado unnailed
desconcertante disconcerting
desconocido unknown, unfamiliar
describir to describe
descubierto *p.p. of* descubrir
descubrir to discover
desde from (*in position*); since (*in time*)
  desde que since (*in time*)
desear to wish, desire
desembarcar to disembark, land
deseo wish, desire
  sentir —s de to be anxious to
  tener —s de to wish to
deseoso desirous; anxious
desesperar to be desperate
desgracia misfortune
  por desgracia unfortunately
desilusión disappointment
desilusionado disappointed
desmayarse to faint
despacio slowly
despedida farewell
despedir (i) to dismiss, discharge
  despedirse (de) to say good-by (to)
despegar to separate; open
despertador (el) alarm clock
despertar (ie) to wake up; *also refl.*
después after, afterwards, later
  — de after
  — de que after (conj.)
destruir to destroy
detener to hold back, stop
  detenerse (a) to stop (off)

determinar to determine; decide
detrás behind, in back
  detrás de behind, in back of
devolver (ue) to return, give back
devuelto *p.p. of* **devolver**
día (el) day
  de día in the daytime
  ocho días a week
  por día per day, a day
  todo el día the whole day
  todos los días every day
diablillo little devil
diablo devil
diapositiva slide
diario daily; daily paper
diccionario dictionary
diciembre (el) December
dicha happiness
dicho *p.p. of* **decir**
dicho saying, proverb
diez ten
diferencia difference
diferente different
difícil difficult, hard
dificultad difficulty
dinero money
Dios (el) God
  ¡Dios mío! Good Heavens!
dirección direction; address
directora lady director
dirigir to direct
  dirigirse a to head for, go to; address,
    turn to
discípulo pupil
disculpar to excuse
  disculparse de to apologize for
discurso speech
disfrutar (de) to enjoy
disminuir to diminish
disponer to dispose, arrange
  disponerse (a) to get ready
disposición disposition; disposal
  estoy a su disposición I am at your dis-
    posal

dispuesto ready
dispuesto *p.p. of* **disponer**
distancia distance
distinguir to distinguish
distinto distinct, different
distracción amusement; distraction
distribución distribution, apportionment
distrito district
divertido amusing, entertaining
divertir (ie, i) to divert, amuse; *refl.* to have
    a good time
divisa foreign exchange
doce twelve
dólar (el) dollar
doler (ue) to ache, hurt
  me duele (el cuerpo) (my body) aches
dolor (el) pain, ache; sorrow
  dolor de (cabeza) (head)ache
domingo Sunday
Domingo Dominic
don Don (*a title used before the Christian
    names of men, often meaning* "Master")
donde where, in which, to which
¿dónde? where?
  ¿a dónde? where . . . to?
  ¿de dónde? where . . . from?
  ¿por dónde? where?
Don Quijote: *El Ingenioso Hidalgo Don
    Quijote de la Mancha* the masterpiece
    (novel) of Cervantes
doña Doña (*a title used before the Christian
    names of women, meaning* "Mistress")
dormido asleep
dormir (ue, u) to sleep
  dormirse to fall asleep
dos two
  los dos both
drago dragon tree
duda doubt; difficult point
  sin duda doubtless
dudar to doubt
dueño master; owner
dulce sweet; soft; fresh; *pl.* candy
durante during

187

durar to last
duro hard; stern; tough

E

e *used before words beginning with* **i-** *and* **hi-**
and
echar to throw; pour
  echarse (a) to start
edad age
  tener más (menos) edad to be older
(younger)
Edad Media Middle Ages
edificar to build
edificio building
efecto effect
  en efecto as a matter of fact
ejemplo example
  por ejemplo for instance
ejército army
el the
el *used before phrases with* **de** *and before a*
relative the one, he, those
  el que he who, the one that, those who,
the ones that; who, which, that
él he, him, it
elegancia elegance
elegir (i) to elect, choose
elevar to elevate, raise
ella she, her, it
ellas they, them
ello it
ellos they, them
embarcar to embark, set sail
embargo: sin embargo however
empeñarse (en) to insist
empezar (ie) (a) to begin
emplear to employ, use
en in; at; into, on, upon
enamorado (de) in love (with)
enamorar to enamor, make love to
encantador charming
encantar to charm

encanto charm
encargado in charge
encargarse (de) to take charge
encender (ie) to light, turn on
encerrar (ie) to shut in, lock up
encierro enclosure; driving of bulls into a
pen before a bullfight
encima on top, above
  encima de on top of, on
encontrar (ue) to find
  encontrarse (aburrido) to be (bored)
  encontrarse con to meet
enemigo enemy
enero January
enfadado angry
enfermo ill, sick
engañar to deceive; *refl.* be mistaken
enorme huge
enseñar (a) to teach; show
entender (ie) to understand
enterar to inform
  enterarse de to find out
entero whole, entire
entonces then, at that time
entrada entrance, admission (fee)
entrar (en) to go in, come in
  es bueno de entrar y malo de salir it's
easy to take but hard to fight off
entre between; among
entregar to deliver, hand (over)
entretener to entertain
entusiasmo enthusiasm
enviar to send; ship
envolver (ne) to wrap up
envuelto *p.p. of* **envolver**
época period, epoch
equipo team
ermita hermitage
errar (ye) to err, be mistaken
error(el) error
esbelto tall; slender
escalar to scale, climb
escalera stairway, stairs

188

escapada escapade, quick trip
  hacer una — to skip away
escapar to escape
  escaparse to escape, run away
escoger to choose
escolar school, scholastic
esconder to hide; *also refl.*
Escorial, El *town and famous monastery near Madrid*
escribir to write
escrito *p.p. of* **escribir**
escuchar to listen, listen to
escuela school; **a la —** to school
escultor (el) sculptor
ese that, those
ése that one, that fellow
esfuerzo effort
eso that
  a eso de las (cuatro) at about (four) o'clock
  ¿no es eso? isn't that so?
  por eso that's why
espalda shoulder, back; *pl.* back
espantar to frighten; astonish
España Spain
español, -la Spanish; **el —** Spanish (*the language*); Spaniard
especial special
especie (la) species; kind, sort
espectáculo spectacle, show
espejo mirror
esperanza hope
esperar to hope; wait for; meet
espiar to spy
espíritu spirit
espléndido splendid
esposa wife
esposo husband
estación station; season
estacionarse to park
estado state;
  los Estados Unidos the United States
estar to be

¿está (don José)? is (Don José) at home?
estamos a (dos) it is (the second)
estar para to be about to
estar por to be in favor of
estatua statue
este this, these
este (el) east
éste this one; the latter; these
estilo style
  por el estilo of that sort
estilográfico: (pluma) estilográfica fountain pen
estimar to esteem, respect
estirar to stretch
esto this
estrechar to tighten; clasp, shake (*hands*)
estrecho narrow; tight
estudiante(el) student
estudiantil student, of a student
estudiar to study
estudio study; studio
etc. = etcétera and so forth
eterno everlasting, eternal
Europa Europe
evitar to avoid; spare
examen(el) examination; **salir bien del —** to pass the examination; **sufrir un —** to take an examination
excelente excellent
exclamación exclamation
exclamar to exclaim
excursión excursion, trip, tour
exigir to require, demand
existir to exist; be
exótico exotic
explicar to explain
explosión explosion
exponer to expose
expresar to express
expresión expression
expreso express
expuesto *p.p. of* **exponer**
extender (ie) to extend; *refl.* spread out

extenso extensive; long
extranjero foreign; foreigner
  al extranjero abroad
extrañar to wonder (at), be surprised (at)
  me extrañó it surprised me
extraño queer, strange; stranger
extraordinario extraordinary

F

fábrica factory
fácil easy
falta lack, want; failure
  le hace falta (algo) he needs (something)
faltar to lack, be lacking; fail
  faltar a la clase to miss class
  me faltaba (tiempo) I lacked (time)
familia family
familión(el) large family
famoso famous
favor(el) favor
  hágame el favor de (avisar) please (let
  me know)
  por favor please
favorable favorable
favorito favorite
fe(la) faith
febrero February
fecha date
  con fecha de dated
felicidad happiness
feliz happy
feo ugly, homely
fiar to trust
  fiarse de to trust
fidelidad fidelity
fiero fierce, wild
fiesta holiday; festival
figura figure; shape
figurar to figure; imagine
  figurarse to imagine, fancy
fijar to fix
  fijarse en to notice
filete(el) filet

fin(el) end; purpose
  a fin de in order to
  a fin de que in order to
  al fin finally
  en fin in short, in a word
  fin de semana week end
  por fin finally
final(el) end
fingir to pretend
flamenco: baile — Andalusian dance to the
  accompaniment of gypsy music
flor(la) flower
florecita little flower
folleto pamphlet, booklet
formar to form
fortaleza fortress; fortitude
fortuna fortune; wealth
fósforo match
fotografía photograph; **sacar —s** to take
  pictures
francés, -esa French; **el francés** French
  (*the language*); Frenchman
franqueza frankness; freedom
frase(la) phrase; sentence
frecuencia frequency
freír to fry
frente(el) front
  en frente de in front of
frente(la) forehead; face
fresco fresh; cool
frío cold;
  hacer frío to be cold (*weather*)
  tener frío to be cold (*persons*)
frito *p.p. of* **freír**
fuego fire
fuente (la) fountain; spring
fuera outside, out
  fuera de outside of
fuerte strong; loud
fuerza force; strength
fumar to smoke
funcionar to work, operate
fútbol(el) football

gabán(el) overcoat
gaceta gazette
gallinero hencoop
gana appetite, craving
  tener ganas de to feel like
ganar gain; earn (*a living*)
  ganar a to surpass in, beat in
gastado worn away
gastar to waste; spend (*money*)
gato cat
gazpacho *cold soup made of bread crumbs,*
  oil, vinegar, tomatoes, onions, and garlic
general general
  en — as a rule
  por lo — generally
generalidad generality
generalmente usually
genio genius; disposition; temper
gente(la) people, folks
gigantesco gigantic
Giralda, la *famous Moorish tower in Seville*
gloria glory; Heaven
gobierno government
golf(el) golf
golpe(el) blow
gordo fat; big
gozar (de) to enjoy
gracia grace; *pl.* thanks
  dar las gracias a to thank
graduarse to be graduated
gran *used for* **grande** *before a sing. noun*
granadino citizen of Granada
grande large, big; great, grand
grandeza greatness, grandeur
Granja, la *site of one of the royal palaces,*
  in the province of Segovia
gratuito gratuitous, unwarranted
grave serious
gritar to shout, cry out
grito shout, cry
grupo group
Guadalquivir, el *river in southern Spain*

guante(el) glove
guardar to guard, keep, put away
guerra war
guía(el) guide
guía guidebook
guiar to guide; drive
gustar to please, be pleasing
  me gusta (el café) I like (coffee)
  nos gusta más we prefer
  gustar de to enjoy
gusto pleasure
  con mucho gusto gladly, certainly

Habana, la Havana
haber to have
  haber de to be to
habilidad ability, skill
habitación room
habla(el, *but fem.*) speech
  de — española Spanish-speaking
hablar to speak, talk
hacer to make; do; have, cause; pay
  hace (ocho días) (a week) ago
  hace (ocho días) que (está aquí) (he
    has been here) for (a week)
  (le) hace (borrar lo escrito) he has
    (him erase what is written)
  hacerse (amigos) to become (friends)
hacia toward
hacienda estate, property, farm
hacha(el, *but fem.*) axe
hallar to find
hambre(el, *but fem.*) hunger
  tener hambre to be hungry
hampa(el, *but fem.*) vagrancy; rowdies
hasta up to, as far as; till, until
  hasta que until, till
hay *impersonal form of* **haber** there is, there
  are
  hay que (estudiar) it is necessary (to
    study)

no hay que (olvidar) one should not (forget)

hazaña feat, exploit

hecho *p.p. of* **hacer**

hecho act, deed; fact

helar (ie) to freeze

herida wound

herir (ie, i) to wound, strike

hermana sister

hermano brother; *pl.* brother and sister

hermoso beautiful, handsome, fine

hielo ice

hija daughter; girl

hijo son; boy; *pl.* children

historia history; story

histórico historical

hoja leaf; sheet; blade

hombre(el) man

hombrón(el) large man

hora hour, time (*of day*)

  a estas horas at this late hour

  ¿a qué hora (se acuestan)? when (do they go to bed)?

  es (la) hora de (salir) it is time (to leave)

  ¿qué hora es? what time is it?

  ¿qué hora tiene Vd.? what time is it?

hotel(el) hotel

hoy today

huerta (vegetable) garden

Huerta, la *irrigated region near Valencia*

huevo egg

huir to flee, run away

  huir de to avoid

humano human

humor(el) humor

huracán(el) hurricane

I

ida going

idea idea

ideal ideal

idioma(el) language

iglesia church; **a la —** to church

imagen(la) image; picture

imaginar to imagine; *also refl.*

imitar to imitate

impedir (i) to prevent, hinder, keep from

imponente imposing

imponer to impose; inflict

importancia importance

importante important

importar to be important, matter

  no importa never mind

imposible impossible

impresión impression

impresionar to impress

impreso *p.p. of* **imprimir**

imprimir to print

improvisado improvised; temporary

impuesto *p.p. of* **imponer**

impuesto tax, impost, duty

incapaz incapable, unable

incensario incense burner

incidente(el) incident

incienso incense

incomparable incomparable

inconveniente(el) objection

indicar to show; inform of

industrial industrial

infeliz unhappy; unlucky

inferioridad inferiority

influencia influence

Inglaterra England

inglés, —esa English; **el —** English (*the language*), Englishman

ingrediente(el) ingredient

inmóvil motionless

inscripción inscription

insistir (en) to insist (on)

insoportable unbearable

instante(el) instant, moment

  al instante at once

instrumento instrument, tool

inteligente intelligent

intensidad intensity

intenso intense

intentar to attempt, try

interés(el) interest; concern

interesado interested
  los interesados those interested
interesante interesting
interesantísimo very interesting
interesar to interest, be interesting
interior (el) interior; inside
interpretar to interpret
interrumpir to interrupt
íntimo intimate, familiar
inútil useless
investigar to investigate
invierno winter
invitación invitation
invitar (a) to invite
ir (a) to go; *refl.* go away, go off
  va (cantando) he is (singing)
  vamos come on, let's go
  vamos a (hablar) let's (speak)
  vamos a ver let's see
  vaya (pensando) be (thinking)
Isabel Isabel, Elizabeth; **— la Católica**
  (1479–1504), *queen of Castile*
isla island
Italia Italy
italiano Italian; **el —** Italian (*the language*); Italian
izquierdo left
  a la izquierda to the left

J

Jaca *city in the province of Huesca, in northeastern Spain*
Jaime James
jamás never, not . . . ever
jardín(el) garden
jerga jargon
Jorge George
José Joseph
joven young; young man, young woman
jovencito quite young (man)
joya jewel
Juan John
Juanito Johnny
juego game; set

jueves(el) Thursday
juez (el) judge
jugar (ue) (a) to play; gamble
  jugar a(l golf) to play (golf)
julio July
junio June
junto joined; *pl.* together
  junto a close to, beside
juramento oath
jurar to swear
justicia justice
juzgar to judge

K

kilómetro kilometer (*about 0.62 miles*)

L

la the
  a la (española) in the (Spanish) fashion
  a la una at one o'clock
la *used before phrases with* **de** *and before a
relative* the one;
  la que she who, the one that
la her, to her; it; you, to you
labio lip
  sin despegar los labios without saying a
word
labor (la) labor; farming; embroidery; de-
sign, workmanship
lado side
  al lado de beside
ladrillo brick
ladrón(el) thief, robber
lana wool
lápiz(el) pencil
largo long
  a lo largo de along; **de largo** in length,
long
las the
  a las (dos) at (two) o'clock
  son las (tres) it is (three) o'clock
las *used before* **de** *and before a relative* those
  las que those who, those that
las them, to them; you, to you

lástima pity; **es —** it's too bad
lavar to wash; *also refl.*
le him, you; to him, to her, to you
lección lesson
leche (la) milk
leer to read
legendario legendary
legumbre vegetable
lejos far, far away
  a lo — in the distance
  — de far from
lengua tongue; language
lento slow
león (el) lion
les them, you; to them, to you
letra letter (*of the alphabet*); handwriting
levantar to raise, lift; *refl.* rise, get up, stand
  up
ley (la) law
leyenda legend
librarse to escape
libre free
librito small book
libro book
lindo dainty, pretty
lo the; what is
lo *used before phrases with* **de** *and before
  relatives* that
  lo de (anoche) that affair of (last night)
  lo que that which, what
lo him, you; it; so
loco crazy
lodo mud, mire
lograr to obtain; win; succeed in
Londres London
Lorenzo Lawrence
los the
los *used before phrases with* **de** *and before
  relatives* the ones, those;
  los que those who, those which
los them, you
lucha struggle, fight
194 **luchar** to struggle, fight

luego in a minute, presently; then, next
  luego que as soon as
lugar place, spot
  en (primer) lugar in the (first) place
  en su lugar if I were you
  tener lugar to take place
Luis Louis
Luisa Louise
Luisita little Louise
luna moon
  hay luna the moon is shining
lunes (el) Monday
luz (la) light

LL

llamar to call; knock; attract
  se llama (Carlos) his name is (Charles)
llanura plain
llave (la) key; valve
llegada arrival
llegar (a) to arrive, reach
llenar to fill
lleno full
llevar to take, carry; wear; charge; *refl.* carry
  off
llorar to weep, cry
llover (ue) to rain
lluvia rain

M

madera wood
madre (la) mother
Madrid Madrid, *capital of Spain*
maestra teacher
maestro master; teacher
magnífico splendid, magnificent
mal badly
mal (el) evil, ill
mal *used for* **malo** *before masc. nouns*
maleta suitcase
malo bad, wicked; wrong
mamá mamma
manaza large hand

mandar to send; order

manera manner, way; **a — de** like

  de esta — in this way

  de — que so that

mango handle

manifestar (ie) to reveal; express

mano (la) hand; paw

mantener to maintain, keep

manzana apple

mañana morning

  a la — siguiente the next morning

  (las dos) de la — (two o'clock) in the
    morning

  por la — in the morning

mañana tomorrow

mapa (el) map

mar (el *and* la) sea

maravilla marvel, wonder

maravilloso marvelous

marcar to mark

marcha march; step; speed

marchar to march; go

  marcharse de to go away, leave

María Mary

marido husband

marina navy

martes (el) Tuesday

marzo March

mas but

más more, most; longer

  (un rato) más (a while) longer

  (¡qué cosa) más (rara)! (what a strange
    thing)!

  nos gusta más we prefer

  más bien rather

  más que nada more than anything

  no (entendí) más que (tres) (I under-
    stood) only (three)

  ¿qué más? what else?

matar to kill

Matilde Matilda

mayo May

mayor greater, greatest; older, oldest

mayoría majority

  a la — nos impide la falta the lack
    prevents most of us

  la — de (las veces) most (times)

me me; to me; myself

medicina medicine

médico doctor

medida measure

medieval medieval

Medina del Campo *city in the province of
    Valladolid, in north central Spain*

medio half, a half; middle

  media hora half an hour, a half hour

  las (dos) y media half past (two)

medio middle; mean

  en medio de in the middle (midst) of

mediodía (el) noon; **al —** at noon

medir (i) to measure

Méjico = México Mexico

mejor better, best

mejora improvement

melocotón (el) peach

menor less, least; younger, youngest

menos less, least; fewer

  al menos at least

  a lo menos at least

  a menos que unless

  no puede menos de (mirar) he can't
    help (looking)

  por lo menos at least

mentir (ie, i) to lie

mentira lie, falsehood

menudo tiny; **a —** often

mercado market

merced mercy, favor; grace

merecer to deserve

mes (el) month

mesa table; (flat-topped) desk

meseta mesa, plateau

mesita small table

meter to put in, put inside; get mixed up;

  meterse to meddle

mezquita mosque

mi   my
mí   me, myself
miedo   fear; **muerto de —**   scared to death
   tener miedo   to be afraid
mientras (que)   while
   mientras tanto   in the meanwhile
miércoles (el)   Wednesday
miga   bread crumb
mil   (a) thousand; many
milagro   miracle
   hacer un milagro   to perform a miracle
millar (el)   thousand
millón (el)   million
minuto   minute
mío   my, mine, of mine; **el mío**   mine
mirada   glance, look
mirar   to look, look at
misa   Mass (*church service*)
miseria   misery; poverty
Misisipí, el   the Mississippi
mismo   self, very; same
mitad   half; middle
mocito   youngster
moderación   moderation
moderno   modern
modo   manner, way
   de ese modo in that way
   de modo que   so that, and so
   de ningún modo   by no means
   de todos modos   at any rate
molestar   to disturb, bother
   no se moleste por mí   don't bother on my
      account
momento   moment, minute
   en este momento   at this minute
monarca (el)   monarch
monasterio   monastery
moneda   coin; money
monótono   monotonous
montado   riding, mounted (*on horseback*)
montaña   mountain
montar   to mount, ride
Monte Pelado   "Baldy"
monumento   monument

moreno   brown; dark (*of complexion*); brunet
morir (ue, u)   to die; *also refl.*
moro   Moor
mortal   mortal, fatal, deadly
mosquito   mosquito
mostrador (el)   counter (*in a shop*)
mostrar (ue)   to show
motivo   ground, cause, reason
   con motivo de   on account of
mover (ue)   to move; *also refl.*
mozo   lad, youth, young fellow; servant,
      waiter, porter
muchacha   girl
muchacho   boy; *pl.* children
muchedumbre   crowd
muchísimo   very much
mucho   much, a lot of, a good deal; long (*of
      time*); greatly, very much, hard; *pl.* many
mudo   dumb, silent
muerto   *p.p. of* **morir**
muerto   dead person
mujer (la)   woman; wife
mujercita   small woman
mujerona   large woman
mula   mule
multa   fine
multitud   multitude, crowd
mundo   world
   de todo el mundo   from everywhere
   por todo el mundo   everywhere
   todo el mundo   everybody
   ver mundo   to travel to see the world
muralla   wall
muro   wall
museo   museum
   Museo del Prado   Prado Museum
      (Madrid)
música   music
músico   musician
muy   very
   muy (gastado)   very much (worn away)

N

nacer   to be born

196

nacimiento birth

nada nothing, not . . . anything; not at all;
  más que nada more than anything

nadar to swim

nadie nobody, not . . . anybody, no one;
  más (alto) que nadie (tall)er than anyone

natural natural; native

navaja razor; (jack)knife

Navarra Navarre (*province and former kingdom in northern Spain*)

necesario necessary

necesitar to need

negar (ie) to deny
  negarse a to refuse

negocio business affair; deal; *pl.* business

negro black

nevar (ie) to snow

ni nor, not . . . or, and not
  ni (bueno) ni (malo) neither (good) nor
  (bad)
  ni siquera not even

niebla fog, mist
  hay niebla it is foggy

nieve (la) snow

ningún *used for* **ninguno** *before a masc.
noun*

ninguno no, not . . . any, no one, none

niña little girl, child

niñita little girl, child

niño child, little boy; *pl.* children

no no, not
  ¿no? aren't they?

noble noble

noche (la) night
  a media noche at midnight
  (las nueve) de la noche (nine o'clock) at
  night
  de noche at night, in the nighttime
  esta noche tonight
  por la noche in the evening, at night

nombrar to name, appoint

nombre (el) name; noun

nono ninth

norte (el) north

Norteamérica North America

norteamericano North American

nos us, to us, ourselves

nosotros we, us, ourselves

nota note; mark

notabilísimo very remarkable

notable remarkable, notable

notar to note, notice

noticia (piece of) news, information; *pl.*
  news

novecientos nine hundred

novedad novelty; trouble
  sin novedad without incident

novela novel

noventa ninety

noviembre (el) November

novio lover, fiancé

nube (la) cloud

nuestro our, of ours; **el —** ours

Nueva York New York

nueve nine

nuevo new
  de nuevo again

Nuevo México New Mexico

número number

numeroso numerous

nunca never, not . . . ever
  (mejor) que nunca (better) than ever

O

o or

obedecer to obey

objeto object; purpose

obligación obligation

obligar (a) to oblige, force

obra work

observador (el) observer

observar to observe; watch

obstante: no — nevertheless, however

obtener to obtain, get, secure

ocasión opportunity, occasion

octubre (el) October

oculto hidden, secret

ocupar to occupy

ocurrir to occur; take place; **ocurrirse** occur (to one)

ochenta eighty

ocho eight

oeste (el) west

oficial (el) officer

oficina office

ofrecer to offer

¡oh! oh!

oído hearing; (inner) ear

oír to hear;
 ¡oiga! listen!
 oye decir que (ha llegado) he hears that
  (he has arrived);
 oye hablar de (ella) he hears of (her)

ojo eye;
 cuestan un ojo de la cara they are terribly expensive

oler (hue) to smell

olor (el) smell, fragrance

olvidar to forget; leave (*forgotten*); *also refl.;*
 se me olvidó (el reloj) I forgot (left)
  (my watch);
 olvidarse de to forget

once eleven

opinar to have an opinion

opinión opinion

oponer to oppose; *refl.* object

oportunidad opportunity

opuesto *p.p. of* **oponer**

orador (el) orator

orden (el) order, rank

orden (la) order, command

organizado organized

órgano organ

oriental oriental

origen (el) origin

oro gold

os you, to you, yourselves

otoño autumn, fall

otorgar to consent

otro other, another; another one;
 otras tantas mías just as many of mine

Oviedo *city in the province of Oviedo (Asturias), northern Spain*

P

Pablo Paul

paciencia patience

padre (el) father; *pl.* parents

pagar to pay, pay for

página page

país (el) country

paisaje (el) landscape

palabra word

palacio palace

Palma de Mallorca *city on the island of Majorca (Balearic Islands)*

palmera palm tree

Pamplona *city in the province of Navarre*

pan (el) bread; living

panecillo roll

pantalla screen

paño cloth

pañuelo handkerchief

papá (el) papa, dad

papel (el) paper; role

paquete (el) package

par (el) pair; couple

para for, in order to, to
 para que in order that, so that

parado standing still

paraguas (el) umbrella

parar to stop; *also refl.*

parecer to seem, appear;
 parece (otro) he looks like (another person)
 me parece I think
 ¿qué le parece? what do you think?
 parecerse a to look like

parecer (el) opinion

pared (la) wall

parienta relative

pariente (el) relative

parroquiano customer

parte (la) part;
  a otras partes to other places
  de todas partes from everywhere
  formar parte de to be a member of
  la mayor parte de (ellos) most of (them)
  por otra parte on the other hand
partida departure; game
partir (de) to depart
pasado past, last
pasajero passenger
pasar to pass, go; spend (*time*); happen; *also refl.*
  pasa de (la una) it is after (one o'clock)
  ¿qué te pasa? what is the matter with you?
  ¡que lo pase bien! good luck!
pasear to go for a walk *or* ride;
  pasearse to take a walk *or* ride; travel for amusement
paseo walk; ride; drive
  dar un paseo to take a walk
paso step, pace; pass; passage
  dar un paso to take a step
patata potato
patinar to skate
paz (la) peace
pecado sin
pecar to sin
pececito small fish
pedazo piece
pedido request; order
pedir (i) to ask, ask for
Pedro Peter
pegar to paste, stick; hit, beat
peligro danger
pelo hair
  no tener pelos en la lengua to be outspoken
pelota ball
pena pain, penalty; trouble
  vale la pena it is worth while
péndulo pendulum
pensar (ie) to think, have an opinion; consider; intend

piensa (ir) he intends (to go)
piensa en (ir) he thinks about (going)
¿qué piensan de (España) what do they think of (Spain)?
peor worse, worst
Pepe Joe
pequeñito very small
pequeño small, little
perder (ie) to lose; waste (*time*); miss
  perderse to get lost
pérdida loss
perdonar to forgive, pardon
peregrinación pilgrimage
peregrino pilgrim
perezoso lazy
perfección perfection
periódico newspaper
permanecer to remain
permiso permission
permitir to allow, permit
pero but
perrazo large dog
perro dog
persona person
Perú, el Peru
pesar (el) grief
  a pesar de in spite of
peseta peseta
peso weight; peso (*Spanish American* "dollar")
piano piano
picar to sting, prick; bite
picarón (el) great rogue
pico beak; peak; odd
  (la una) y pico a little after (one o'clock)
pie (el) foot
  a pie on foot
  se pone de pie he stands up
piedra stone
pierna leg
pieza piece; room; play
  — de Talavera Talavera ware (fine pottery)
pintar to paint
pintor (el) painter

199

pintoresco picturesque
Pío Pius
piso story; floor
pizarra blackboard
placer to please
plan (el) plan
planear to plan
planeta (el) planet
planta plant
plata silver
platillo saucer
plato dish
playa beach
plaza (city) square
pluma feather; pen
población population; town
pobre poor; ¡— **de mí!** poor me!
pobrecito poor fellow
poco little, a little; *pl.* few
  poco a poco little by little
  un poco a little
  un poco de (agua) a little (water)
poder to be able; can, could, may, might, be possible
poder (el) power
poesía poetry; poem
poeta (el) poet
polvo dust; powder
  hay polvo it is dusty
polvoriento dusty
poner to put, set, put on; send
  poner un telegrama to send a telegram
  ponerse to become; set (*of the sun*)
  ponerse a to start
poquito very little
por through, along, by, on account of, because of; as; in, at, etc.
  ¿por qué? why?
porque because, for
por qué (el) reason
pórtico entrance, doorway, portico
portugués, -esa Portuguese
  el — Portuguese (*the language*); Portuguese

200

poseer to possess, own
posible possible
  lo antes posible as soon as possible
postre (el) dessert
  de postre as dessert
precio price
preciso necessary
preferencia preference
preferir (ie, i) to prefer
pregunta question
  hacer una pregunta to ask a question
preguntar to ask (*a question*)
  — por to ask for, inquire about
  preguntarse to wonder
premio prize; reward
prender to seize, arrest
prensa press
preocuparse to worry
  no se preocupe por mí don't worry about me
preparación preparation
preparar to prepare
presenciar to witness
presentar to present; introduce
  presentarse to appear
presente present
presidente (el) president
preso *p.p. of* **prender**
prestar to lend; pay (*attention*)
primavera spring (*the season*)
primer *used for* **primero** *before masc. nouns*
primero first
primitivo primitive
primo cousin
principal principal, main
principio beginning
  a —s de toward the beginning of
  al — at first
prisa haste
  con mucha prisa very hurriedly
  de prisa fast, quickly
  sin prisa unhurriedly
  tener prisa to be in a hurry

probable   probable

probar (ue)   to prove; test, try out; taste, sample

procedimiento   process; procedure

procurar   to try

producir   to produce

profesor (el)   teacher; professor

promesa   promise

prometer   to promise

pronto   soon; **de —**   all of a sudden

   tan pronto como   as soon as

pronunciar   to pronounce

propina   tip

propio   own; proper

proponer   to propose; *also refl.*

propósito   purpose, intention

   a propósito   by the way

proteger   to protect

provincia   province

provincial   provincial

próximo   next, nearest

proyectar   to project; plan

proyector (el)   projector

prueba   proof

público   public

pueblo   people; village

puente (el)   bridge

puerta   door; gate

pues   then; well, well then; since

   pues bien   well then, very well

puesto   *p.p. of* **poner**

puesto   position, post; place

pulgada   inch

pulsera   bracelet; wrist watch

punto   point; moment

   a punto de   on the point of

   en punto   exactly

   hasta cierto punto   to a certain extent

pupitre (el)   school desk

puro   pure; sheer

Q

que   who, whom, which, that; when

(mucho) que (hacer)   (much) to (do)

que   that; *after a comparative* than

   (creo) que (sí)   (I think so)

¿qué?   what? what a!

   ¿para qué?   what for?

   ¿por qué?   why?

   ¿qué hay?   what goes on? what's up?

   ¿qué será de él?   what will become of him?

   ¿qué tal le gusta?   how do you like?

   ¿qué tienes?   what is the matter with you?

¿qué?   how?

quedar   to remain, be left; *with participles* be; *refl.* stay

   me quedan (cosas) que (hacer)   I have (things) left (to do)

queja   complaint

   exponer quejas   to submit complaints

quejarse (de)   to complain

querellante (el)   plaintiff

querer   to want, wish; care for (*a person*); be willing; try

   no quiso (ir)   he refused (to go)

   querer decir   to mean

querido   dear, beloved

queso   cheese

quien   who, whom, he who, etc.

¿quién?   who? whom?   **¿de quién?**   whose

quince   fifteen

quinientos   five hundred

quinto   fifth

quitar   to take off, take away

   quitarse   to take off

quizás (quizá)   maybe, perhaps

R

radio (la *and* el)   radio

rapidez (la)   rapidity

rápido   rapid, rapidly

raro   rare; strange, curious, odd

rascacielos (el)   skyscraper

rato   while, (short) time

   al poco rato   soon

raza   race

razón (la)   reason
   no le falta razón   he is right
   tener razón   to be right
real   royal; real
realizar   to fulfill, carry out
recibir   to receive
recién   recently
   recién (llegado)   (one who has) recently
   (arrived)
recoger   to pick up
recomendar (ie)   to recommend
reconocer   to recognize
recordar (ue)   to recall; remind
redondo   round
referir (ie, i)   to refer; relate, tell; **referirse**
   to refer
refrescante   refreshing
refresco   cold drink; refreshment
regalar   to give (*a present*)
regalo   present, gift
regar (ie)   to irrigate, water
región   region, district
regla   rule; ruler
regresar   to return (*home*)
regreso   return
   a mi regreso   on my return
reina   queen
reinar   to reign
reír (i)   to laugh
   reírse de   to laugh at
relación   relation; story, account
relatar   to relate, tell
reloj (el)   clock; watch
remedio   remedy
rendir (i)   to subdue; yield
   rendirse   to surrender
reñir (i)   to quarrel; scold
repente: de —   all of a sudden
repetir (i)   to repeat
reposado   restful, quiet, peaceful
representar   to represent; perform (*a play*)
res (la)   head of cattle, beast, animal
reservado   reserved
residencia   residence (hall for students)

resolver (ue)   to decide; settle; solve (*a
   problem*)
respaldo   back (*of a seat*)
respectivo   respective
responder   to reply
responsabilidad   responsibility
responsable   responsible
resto   rest, remainder; remnant
resuelto   *p.p. of* **resolver**
resuelto   determined
resultado   result
resultar   to result; prove to be, turn out to be
retirar   to withdraw; *refl.* retire
retrasado   late
reunión   meeting
reunir   to gather
   reunirse   to meet
   reunirse con   to join
revista   review; magazine
rey (el)   king
rico   rich
riego   irrigation
río   river
robar   to rob, steal
rodear   to surround
rogar (ue)   to ask, request
rojo   red
Roma   Rome
románico   Romanesque
romano   Roman
romper   to break
ropa   clothes
roto   *p.p. of* **romper**
roto   torn
rubí (el)   ruby
rubio   blond, golden-haired
ruido   noise, sound
ruina   ruin
ruso   Russian; **el ruso**   Russian (*the language*); Russian

S

sábado   Saturday
saber   to know; know how; find out, learn

sabe (tocar el piano) he knows how (to play the piano)

sabe a (tabaco) it tastes of (tobacco)

saber (el) learning, knowledge

sabroso delicious, tasty

sacar to take out, draw out; get

¿de dónde ha sacado eso? where did you get that idea?

sacrificar to sacrifice

sacudir to shake, shake off

sal (la) salt; wit

sala living room; parlor; hall

salida way out, exit; departure

salida del sol sunrise

salir to go out, come out

sale de(l país) he leaves (the country)

saltar to jump, leap

salud health

saludar to greet, bow to

salvar to save; *refl.* escape

san *used for* **santo** *as a title before the Christian names of saints* St.

sangre (la) blood

sano healthy, sound; wholesome

Santa Cruz *capital of the largest of the Canary Islands*

Santander *seaport and province in northern Spain*

Santiago St. James; **— de Compostela** *city in northwestern Spain*

santo holy, saintly; saint

satisfacer to satisfy

satisfecho *p.p. of* **satisfacer**

satisfecho contented, satisfied

savia sap

sayal (el) sackcloth robe

se *used for* **le** *or* **les** *before* **le, la, lo,** etc.; to him, to her, to you, to them

se himself, to himself, herself, yourself, themselves; one

se each other, to each other, one another

seco dry; thin

secreto secret

sed thirst; **tener sed** to be thirsty

seda silk

Segovia *city and province in west central Spain*

segoviano inhabitant of Segovia

seguida: en seguida at once

seguir (i) to follow; go on, keep on

sigue (comiendo) he keeps on *or* keep on (eating)

según according to; according to what, as

segundo second; second-class

seguro sure; safe, secure

estoy seguro de que (vendrá) I'm sure (he will come)

seis six

selección choice

semana week

hasta la — que viene see you next week

sensato sensible

sentado sitting

sentar (ie) to seat; *refl.* sit down

(las comidas no me) sientan (bien) (the meals don't) agree (with me)

sentencia sentence (*in court*)

sentenciado person who has been sentenced

sentido sense; meaning

sentir (ie, i) to feel; feel sorry, regret

se siente (contento) he feels (satisfied)

señal (la) sign

señalar to point out; name, mark

señor (el) gentleman; lord; sir; Mr.; *pl.* ladies and gentlemen; Mr. and Mrs.

señora lady; wife; madam; Mrs.

señorita young lady; Miss

separar to separate

separarse de to part, leave

septiembre (el) September

séptimo seventh

sepulcro grave, tomb

ser to be;

a no ser que unless

es que (no la conoce) the fact is (he doesn't know her)

somos (diez) there are (ten) of us

ser (el) being; person
sereno calm, serene
serie (la) series
serio serious; reliable
servicio service
servir (i) to serve, be of service
   sirve de (guía) he serves as (a guide)
sesenta sixty
setecientos seven hundred
setenta seventy
Sevilla Seville (*city and province in southern
   Spain*)
sevillano inhabitant of Seville
sexto sixth
si if, whether
sí yes, certainly, indeed
   (creo) que sí (I think) so
sí himself, herself, yourself, themselves
sí each other, one another
siempre always, ever
   para — forever
   — que whenever
siesta afternoon nap
siete seven
siglo century
significado meaning
significar to mean
siguiente following, next
silencio silence
silueta silhouette
silla chair
sillón (el) armchair
símbolo symbol
simpático congenial, nice
simplicidad simplicity
sin without
   sin (duda) doubt(less)
   sin que without
sinceridad sincerity
sincero sincere
sino but; except; **sino que** but
siquiera even, at least
sitio site, place, spot
204 **situación** situation

situado situated, located
soberbio superb, magnificent
sobre on, upon, over, above; about
sobrino nephew
sol (el) sun; sunlight
   hace sol, hay sol it is sunny
soldado soldier
soler (ue) to be accustomed
solo alone, only, single
sólo only
   no sólo (tiempo) sino (dinero) not only
   (time) but (money)
soltar (ue) to let go, let loose
solterona old maid
sombra shade, shadow
   a la sombra in the shade
sombrero hat
sometido (a) under the control (of)
sonar (ue) to sound; ring
sonreír (i) to smile; *also refl.*
sonrisa smile
soñar (ue) (con) to dream (of)
sopa soup
sorprender to surprise
sorpresa surprise
sostener to support, hold up; carry on
Sr. = Señor
su his, her, its, your, their
suave soft, gentle
subida ascent
subir to go up, come up, climb; put on
   (*train*)
   sube a (la Giralda) he goes up (la Giralda)
   sube a(l tren) he gets on (the train)
suceder to happen
sucio dirty
Sudamérica South America
sudoroso sweating, sweaty
suelo ground; floor
sueño sleep; dream
   tener sueño to be sleepy
suerte (la) lot; luck, fortune
   ¡mucha suerte! good luck!
   tener suerte to be lucky

sufrir to suffer

suicidarse to commit suicide

sujeto subject; fellow

superior superior; upper
  escuela superior high school

superioridad superiority

suponer to suppose

supuesto *p.p. of* suponer
  por supuesto of course

surgir to rise, arise

suyo his, of his, her, of hers, your, their;
  el — his, hers, yours, theirs

T

tabaco tobacco

Tajo, el Tagus (*river in central Spain and
  Portugal*)

tal such, such as
  con tal (de) que provided that

Talavera: — de la Reina *city in the province of Toledo, famous for its pottery*

tamaño size

también too, also

tampoco not . . . either

tan so, as; such a;
  ¡qué (vista) tan (espléndida)! what a
    (splendid view)!
  tan (alto) como as (tall) as

Tancredo, don *name given to contestant who
  performs in the bull ring the stunt of standing motionless before the bull; he usually
  escapes unscathed*

tanto so much, as much; *pl.* so many
  mientras — meanwhile
  por lo — therefore
  tanto (dinero) como as much (money) as

tardar to delay, be late; take (*time*)
  tarda en (servir) he is slow in (serving)

tarde late

tarde (la) afternoon
  ¡buenas tardes! good afternoon!
  (las dos) de la tarde (two o'clock) in the
    afternoon

por la tarde in the afternoon

tarjeta card

taxi (el) taxi

taza cup

te you, to you, yourself

teatro theater

Teide, el Mt. Teyde *on the Island of Tenerife;
  el. 12,220 ft.*

telefonear to telephone

teléfono telephone
  llamar por teléfono to phone

telegrama (el) telegram, wire

tema (el) theme

temblar (ie) to tremble

temer to fear

temprano early

tender (ie) to hold out, extend

tener to have, possess; hold
  tiene (las manos blancas) her (hands)
    are (white)
  tiene escrita (la carta) he has (the letter)
    written
  tiene que (escribir) he has to (write)
  tiene (algo) que (escribir) he has (some-
    thing) to (write)
  tuve (una carta) I received (a letter)

Tenerife *largest of the Canary Islands*

tenis (el) tennis

tentar to tempt

tercer *used for* tercero *before a masc. noun*

tercero third

terminar (de) to end, finish

tesis (la) thesis

testigo witness

ti you

tía aunt

tiempo time; weather; a — in time, on
  time; al — que as; ¿(por) cuánto — ?
  how long?; en un — formerly; hace
  buen — it is fair weather; hace —
  some time ago: más — longer

tienda tent; shop, store

tierra earth, land

tímido timid, shy

tío uncle
típico typical
tirar to throw; pull; shoot
   tira de (la cuerda) he pulls (the rope)
titular to entitle
título title
tocar to touch; play
todavía still, yet; **— no** not yet
todo all, every
   todo el (día) the whole (day)
   todos los (días) every (day)
todo all, everything
   del todo wholly; (not) . . . at all
   sobre todo especially
   todos all, everyone
toldo awning
toledano of Toledo
Toledo *city and province in central Spain*
tomar to take; drink; eat
Tomás Thomas
tomate (el) tomato
tontería foolishness, nonsense
tonto foolish, silly; fool
torcer (ue) to twist; turn
torero bullfighter
toro bull; *pl.* bullfight
torre (la) tower
tortilla omelet
trabajar to work; till
trabajo work; **cuesta —** it's hard
traducir to translate
traer to bring; wear (*clothes*)
traje (el) suit; clothes
  traje de baño bathing suit
tranquilo calm, quiet
transeúnte (el) passer-by
transmitir to transmit
tratar to treat
   trata de (hablar) he tries to (speak)
   se trata de (escuchar) it is a question of
    (listening)
trece thirteen
treinta thirty
tren (el) train

tres three
tribunal (el) tribunal, court
triste sad; sorry
tropezar (ie) to stumble (into)
tu your
tú you
Turégano *village in the province of Segovia*
turista (el *and* la) tourist
tuyo your, of yours; **el —** yours

U

u *used before words beginning with* **o-** *and*
   ho- or
último last (*in a series*)
  por — finally
   últimos de (julio) toward the end of
   (July)
un, una a, an; *pl.* some, a few
   unos (zapatos) a pair of (shoes)
   unos cuantos a few
un *used for* **uno** "one" *before a masc. noun*
único only, sole, unique
unir to unite; *refl.* join
universidad university
universitario of a university;
   jóvenes —s university students
uno one
uno one; someone
   uno a otro each other
usar to use; wear (out)
uso use
usted you
útil useful
utilizar to use

V

vacaciones vacation
vagón (el) coach
Valdepeñas *town in central Spain, province*
   of Ciudad Real, famous for its wines
Valencia *seaport and province in eastern Spain*
valer to be worth
  vale más it is better
valiente brave

valor (el) value; courage
vano vain; useless
  en vano in vain; needlessly
vapor (el) steam; steamship
varios several
vasco Basque
vaso glass (*for drinking*)
Vd. = usted you
vecino neighbor; citizen (*of a town*)
vega meadow, plain
vegetación vegetation
veinte twenty
vencer to conquer, defeat
vendedor (el) seller
vender to sell
venir to come; arrive
  (el año) que viene next (year)
  se viene he comes along
  viene a (visitar) he comes to (visit)
ventaja advantage
ventana window
ventanilla small window (*of a train*)
ventilado ventilated
ver to see
  ¡a ver! let's see!
  se ve (satisfecho) he is (satisfied)
  se ve que (no entiende) it is clear that
    (he doesn't understand)
  (nada que) ver con (nothing to) do with
veranear to spend the summer
verano summer
veras: de veras really
verdad truth; **es —** it is true
  ¿verdad? isn't it? aren't you? etc.
verdadero true; real
verde green
verdura verdure; *pl.* vegetables
vestido dress; costume; clothes
vestir (i) to dress; *also refl.*
  se viste de (rojo) he wears (red)
vez (la) time (*in a series*); turn; **a la vez** at
  the same time; **a veces** at times;
    algunas veces sometimes; **de vez en
    cuando** from time to time; **dos veces**

twice; **en vez de** instead of; **muchas
veces** often; **otra vez** again; **pocas
veces** rarely; **raras veces** seldom,
rarely; **tal vez** perhaps; **una vez** once;
una y otra vez again and again; **varias
veces** several times
viajar to travel
viaje (el) trip, journey
  hace un viaje he takes a trip
víbora viper
viceversa vice versa
víctima victim
vida life
  (saber) qué es de su vida (to find out)
    how he is getting along
  (sin) vida life(less)
viejecito nice old man
viejo old
viento wind; **hace —** it is windy
viernes (el) Friday
vinagre (el) vinegar
vino wine
violín (el) violin
virgen (la) virgin
virtud virtue
visigodo Visigoth
visita visit, call
  hace una — he pays a visit
visitar to visit, make a call
vista sight; view
  a la vista de in sight of
  ¡hasta la vista! see you later!
visto *p.p. of* **ver**
  por lo visto apparently
viuda widow
vivienda dwelling, house
vivir to live; dwell
  ¡viva! hurrah! long live!
vivo alive; lively, vivid
vocal vocal
vocecita small, thin voice
volar (ue) to fly
volcánico volcanic
voluntad will

volver (ue) to return; come back; *refl.* turn around, turn
    se vuelve (cansado) he becomes (tired)
    vuelve a (leerlo) (he reads it) again
    vuelve en sí he comes to
vosotros you
votar to vote
voz (la) voice
    en voz alta out loud, in a loud voice
vuelta return; turn
    dar la — to turn back
    dar una — to take a walk
    de — back
vuelto *p.p. of* **volver**

vuestro your, of yours
    el — yours

Y

y and
ya already; now; later
    ¡ya lo creo! I should say so!
    ya no no longer
yo I

Z

zapatilla slipper
zapato shoe
Zorrilla, José (1817–1893), *lyric and dramatic poet*

ENGLISH-SPANISH VOCABULARY

A

a, an un, una; *often not translated*
able: be — poder
about de, sobre; (*before numerals*) unos, cosa de; **at —** (*of hour of the day*) a eso de; **be — to** estar para; **think —** pensar (ie) en
accident accidente *m.*
accompany acompañar
according to según
account: on — of a causa de, por
ache doler (ue); **my body ached** me dolía el cuerpo
acquainted: be — with conocer
addition: in — to además de
address (*n.*) señas; (*v.*) dirigirse a
admire admirar
advantage: take — of aprovecharse de
advice consejo(s)
afraid: be — tener miedo
after (*prep.*) después de; (*conj.*) después de que; **it is — one o'clock** pasa de la una, (*also in time*) y

afternoon tarde *f.;* **in the —** por la tarde; **(two o'clock) in the —** (las dos) de la tarde
afterwards después, más tarde; **shortly —** al poco rato, poco después
again otra vez, de nuevo; **(I'll see you) —** volveré a (verle)
age edad *f.*
ago: (some time) — hace (tiempo)
agree estar de acuerdo; (*food*) sentar (ie) bien
airport aeropuerto
all (*adj.*) todo, -a; **— (night)** toda la (noche); **— (tourists)** todos los (turistas); (*pron.*) todo; todos, -as; todo el mundo; **— that** todo lo que, cuanto, -a; (*adv.*) **not at —** no . . . nada; de ningún modo
all of a sudden de repente
all right está bien
allow permitir, dejar
almost casi
alone solo

along por
already ya
also también
although aunque
always siempre
America América
American americano
among entre
and y; (*before* i- *or* hi-) e
angry enojado
annoy molestar, fastidiar
another otro (*not used with* un)
answer contestar (a), responder (a)
any cualquier(a); (*after a negative*) ninguno;
  often omitted
anyone cualquier(a); alguien (*after a negative*) nadie
anything algo; **— (new)** algo de (nuevo);
  not . . . — nada
apologize for disculparse de
apparently por lo visto
appear parecer, aparecer
approach acercarse (a)
aqueduct acueducto
Argentina la Argentina
arm brazo
around: — here por aquí
arrange disponer
arrive (at or **in)** llegar (a)
as como; **— (dry) —** tan (seco) como; **— if**
  como si; **— many —** tantos como; **—
  much . . . —** tanto . . . como; **— soon
  — possible** cuanto antes, lo antes
  posible
ask (*inquire*) preguntar (a); **— a question**
  hacer una pregunta; (*request*) pedir (i);
  — for pedir (i)
asleep: fall — dormirse (ue, u)
assure asegurar
Asturias Asturias
at (*time*) a; (*place*) en; (*after* llamar, llegar,
  sentar) a
attack atacar
attend asistir (a)

attention atención *f.;* **attract —** llamar
  la atención; **pay —** prestar atención,
  hacer caso de (a)
attentively atentamente
attract, *see* **attention**
August agosto
aunt tía
autumn otoño
away: right — ahora mismo; **go —** irse

B

back: (to be) — (estar) de vuelta; **turn —**
  dar la vuelta
bad malo
badly mal
be ser, estar; **aren't they?** ¿no es verdad?
  they are to — han de (estar, ser); **is he
  in? is he at home?** ¿está?; **it was after
  one o'clock** pasaba de la una; (*with
  participles and adjectives* quedar; *with
  present participles* ir
bear: — in mind tener en cuenta
beautiful hermoso
because porque
become ponerse; (*by one's efforts*) hacerse;
  what will — of him? ¿qué será de él?
bed cama; **go to —** acostarse (ue)
before (*adv.*) antes; (*prep.*) antes de; (*conj.*)
  antes de que
begin empezar (ie) (a)
beginning principio; **at the — of** a principios de
behind detrás de
believe creer
beret boina
best mejor; **which dessert did you like
  —?** ¿qué postre le gustó más?
better mejor
between entre
big grande
bill cuenta
black negro
blame culpa; **be to —** tener la culpa
blond rubio

boat barco; **by —** en barco
body cuerpo
book libro
bore aburrir; **to get bored** aburrirse
both ambos, los dos
bottle botella
box caja
boy muchacho, niño, joven
break romper
brief breve
bring traer
brother hermano; **— and sister** hermanos
build construir
bull toro
bullfight corrida (de toros); toros
burst: **— out laughing** soltar (ue) una carcajada
bus autobús *m.*; **by —** en autobús
but pero; (*after a negative*) sino, sino que
buy comprar
by por; de; (*time*) para; *not translated with pres. part.*

C

café café *m.*
call llamar
camera cámara (fotográfica)
can poder; (= *know how*) saber; *sometimes expressed by future of verb*
Canada Canadá *m.*
Canary Islands Islas Canarias
capable capaz
capital capital *f.*
captain capitán *m.*
car coche *m.*; auto; **by —** en auto
care cuidado
carefully con cuidado
carry llevar; **— out** llevar a cabo
Castile Castilla
castle castillo
cathedral catedral *f.*
century siglo
certain cierto; **a —** cierto
210 Cervantes Cervantes

chair silla
change cambiar (de)
charge: be in **—** of estar encargado de
child niño; **children** hijos, niños
choose elegir (i)
church iglesia; **leave —** salir de la iglesia
cigarette cigarrillo
city ciudad *f.*
class clase *f.*; **in —** en la clase
classmate compañero de clase
clearly claramente
climate clima *m.*
climb subir (a)
close cerrar (ie)
close to cerca de
clothes ropa; vestidos
coffee café *m.*
cold frío
colleague colega *m.*
come venir (a); **— down** bajar; **— in** entrar (en); **— out** salir; **— to** volver (ue) en sí; **— up** subir; **— upon** encontrarse (ue) con; **— with** acompañar
comfortable cómodo
companion compañero; **traveling —** compañero de viaje
complain quejarse (de)
completely del todo, por completo
conduct conducir
construct construir
continental continental
continue continuar; seguir
contrary: on the **—** al contrario
contrast contraste *m.*
conversation conversación *f.*
Cordova Córdoba
cost costar (ue)
could poder (podía, podría, etc.)
country (*as opposed to city*) campo; (*nation*) país *m.*
couple par *m.*
course: of **—** por supuesto; claro (está)
course (*of study*) curso; (*subject*) asignatura
courtesy cortesía

covered with cubierto de
crazy loco
cry llorar
cup taza
custom costumbre *f.*
cut cortar

D

dance bailar
dare atreverse (a)
daughter hija
day día *m.;* **a few days later** a los pocos días; **on the following —** al día siguiente
daytime: in the — de día; durante el día
deal: a great — mucho
death muerte *f.*
decide decidir
declare declarar
deny negar (ie)
desire (*n.*) deseo; (*v.*) desear; **have the — to** sentir deseos de
desk mesa
dessert postre *m.;* **for —** de postre
destroy destruir
devil diablo
dictionary diccionario
difference diferencia
different diferente
difficult difícil
dine comer
dining room comedor *m.*
dinner comida
disappear desaparecer
distance distancia; **at a very short —** a muy poca distancia
do hacer; *not translated as an auxiliary*
Don don, D.
door puerta
doubt (*n.*) duda; (*v.*) dudar
doubtless sin duda
down: go — bajar
dream of soñar (ue) con
dress vestir(se) (i)
dressed in vestido de

drink beber; tomar; **— up** beberse
drive conducir; guiar
dry seco
during durante

E

each cada; **— one** cada cual; cada uno; **— other** (*expressed by reciprocal pronoun*); uno a otro
early temprano
earn ganar
east este *m.*
easy fácil
eat comer; **— dinner** comer; **— up** comerse
effort esfuerzo
eight ocho
eighth octavo
either (*after a negative*) tampoco
end (*n.*) fin *m.;* (*v.*) terminar; acabar; **at the — of** a últimos de
England Inglaterra
English inglés *adj. and m.*
enjoy gozar (de)
enough bastante; **be —** bastar
enter entrar (en)
Escorial el Escorial
especially sobre todo
Europe Europa
even aun; **not —** ni siquiera
evening noche *f.*
ever: than — que nunca
every: — (month) todos los (meses)
everybody todos; todo el mundo
everyone todos; todo el mundo
everything todo
everywhere: from — de todo el mundo, de todas partes
evidently por lo visto
excellent excelente
except excepto
exclaim exclamar
expect pensar (ie)
expensive caro; **be terribly —** costar (ue) un ojo de la cara

211

explain explicar
express expresar
eye ojo

F

face cara
fact: in — en efecto; es que; **the — is** es que
fail (to appear at) faltar a
fall caer; **— asleep** dormirse (ue, u); **— down** caerse
family familia
famous famoso
far lejos; **— from** lejos de; **so —** hasta ahora
father padre *m.*
fear (*n.*) miedo; (*v.*) temer; tener miedo
feel sentir (ie, i); **— well** sentirse bien
few pocos; **a —** unos cuantos; **in a — minutes** a los pocos minutos
fewer menos
field campo
fifteen, fifteenth quince
fifty cincuenta
finally por fin; por último
find encontrar (ue); hallar; **— out** saber; enterarse de
fine excelente
finger dedo
finish terminar; acabar
first primero; **at —** al principio
five cinco
floor piso; suelo
flower flor *f.*
following siguiente
fond: be — of ser aficionado a
food comida
foolish things tonterías
foot pie *m.;* **on —** a pie
for para; por; durante; **— his age** para su edad; **— his part** por su parte
foreign extranjero
foreigner extranjero
forget olvidar; **I forgot** se me olvidó

form formar
former: the — aquél
formerly antes; en un tiempo
four cuatro
French francés, -esa; (*language*) el francés
friend amigo
friendly amistoso
from de; desde; (*after verbs indicating separation*) a
front: in — of delante de
full lleno
function funcionar

G

gay alegre
George Jorge
gentleman caballero, señor
get buscar, sacar; **— into** entrar en; **— lost** perderse (ie); **— off** bajar; **— on** subir a; **— ready** disponerse (a); **— up** levantarse
Giralda la Giralda
girl muchacha
give dar
glad: be — to alegrarse de
gladly: very — con mucho gusto
go ir (a); **— away** irse (de); marcharse (de); **— down** bajar; **— out** salir (de); **— to** dirigirse a; **— to bed** acostarse (ue); **— up** subir (a); **let's —** vamos, vámonos
golf golf *m.*
good bueno; **serve — meals** servir (i) bien; **taste —** saber bien; tener buen gusto
Good Heavens! ¡Dios mío!
good-by: say — despedirse (i) (de)
grade nota; calificación *f.*
Granada Granada
great gran; **a — deal** mucho
greater, greatest mayor
greatly: — (admired) muy (admirado)
greet saludar

group grupo
grow up criarse

H

half medio; **— an hour** media hora
hand mano *f.*; **on the other —** por otra
parte
handkerchief pañuelo
happen suceder; pasar
happy feliz
hard duro
hasten apresurarse (a)
hat sombrero
hate aborrecer, odiar
have tener; haber; **he has a headache** le
duele la cabeza; **— just** acabar de; **— a
good time** divertirse (ie, i); **— to** tener
que; **— (nothing) to (do)** no tener
(nada) que (hacer)
he él; **— who** el que; quien
head cabeza
headache dolor (*m.*) de cabeza; **he has a —**
le duele la cabeza
health salud *f.*
hear oír
Heavens: Good —! ¡Dios mío!
help ayudar (a)
her (*adj.*) su; (*as dir. obj.*) la; (*as ind. obj.*)
le; (*as obj. of a prep.*) ella
here aquí; **around —** por aquí; **come —**
ven(ga) aquí
hers (*adj.*) suyo; (*pron.*) el suyo; **of —** suyo
highly: — (respected) muy (respetado)
him (*as dir. obj.*) le, lo; (*as ind. obj.*) le; (*as
obj. of a prep.*) él; **with —** consigo; con
él
himself (*as obj. of a verb*) se; (*as obj. of
prep.*) sí
his (*adj.*) su, suyo; (*pron.*) el suyo; **of —**
suyo
hold: to be held tener lugar
home a casa; **at —** en casa
hope esperar
hotel hotel *m.*

hour hora; **at this late —** a estas horas
house casa
how? ¿cómo? ¿qué tal?; **— long?** ¿cuánto
tiempo?; **— many?** ¿cuántos?; **— much**
¿cuánto?; **— (happy)!** ¡qué (feliz)!
however sin embargo; no obstante
huge enorme; **— man** hombrón *m.*
humor humor *m.*
hundred ciento; **a —** ciento; **one —** ciento
hungry: be — tener hambre *f.*
hurry: be in a — tener prisa; **in a —** de
prisa
husband marido

I

I yo
if si
immediately en seguida
importance importancia
important importante
impossible imposible
in en; (*after a superlative*) de; **— the morning (afternoon,** etc.) por la mañana
(tarde, etc.); **(at two o'clock) — the
afternoon** (a las dos) de la tarde;
— (twenty minutes) dentro de (veinte
minutos)
inform informar
instant instante *m.*; momento
instead of en vez de
intelligent inteligente
intend pensar (ie)
interest (*n.*) interés *m.*; (*v.*) interesar
interesting interesante
into en
introduce presentar
invite invitar (a); **I was invited** se me invitó
island isla
it (*as dir. obj.*) lo, la; (*as obj. of a prep.*) él,
ella; *usually not expressed as a subject*
Italian italiano; (*language*) el italiano

J

join reunirse (con)

213

joke broma; **as a —** en broma
jokingly en broma
just: have — acabar de

K

keep guardar; **— on (eating)** seguir (i) (comiendo); **— still** callarse
kill matar
knife cuchillo
knock llamar
know (*be acquainted with*) conocer; (*have exact information*) saber; **— how** saber

L

lack faltar; **he lacks (time)** le falta (tiempo)
lady señora; **young —** señorita
landscape paisaje *m.*
language lengua; idioma *m.*
large grande
last (*adj.*) (*in a series*) último; **— (year)** el (año) pasado; (*v.*) durar
late tarde; **at this — hour** a estas horas; **be — in** tardar en
later más tarde; **a few days —** a los pocos días
latter: the — éste
laugh reír (i); **— at** reírse de
lawyer abogado
lead conducir
learn (*by study*) aprender (a)
least; at — a lo menos, al menos, por lo menos
leather cuero
leave (*exit from*) salir (de); marcharse (de); (*leave behind; postpone*) dejar
left: I have (many things) — (to do) me quedan (muchas cosas) que (hacer)
lend prestar
less menos
lesson lección *f.*
let dejar; permitir
let's: (*expressed by first person pl. of pres. subjunctive*); **— go!** ¡vamos!; **— see!** ¡a ver! ¡vamos a ver!

214

letter carta
life vida
light encender (ie)
like como; **he likes (the city)** le gusta (la ciudad); **I would —** quisiera, me gustaría; **I would — (to see)** quisiera (ver), me gustaría (ver); **if you —** si le gusta; **which dessert did you — best?** ¿qué postre le gustó más?
listen (to) escuchar
little (*small*) pequeño; poco; **a —** un poco; **— by —** poco a poco
live vivir
lock cerrar (ie)
London Londres
long largo; **(a kilometer) —** (un kilómetro) de largo; **for a — time** por mucho tiempo; **how —?** ¿cuánto tiempo?; **be — in** tardar en; **so —!** ¡hasta la vista!
longer: (to stay) — (quedar) más tiempo; **no —** ya no
look mirar; **— at** mirar; **— for** buscar; **— like** parecerse a; tener cara de
lose perder (ie); **to get lost** perderse (ie)
loud fuerte; **in a — voice** en voz alta
Louisiana la Luisiana
love (*n.*) amor *m.;* (*v.*) querer; amar; **in — with** enamorado de
lover novio; amante *m.*
lucky: be (very) — tener (mucha) suerte *f.*
lunch (*n.*) almuerzo; (*v.*) **have (eat) —** almorzar (ue)

M

Madrid Madrid
maid criada
make hacer; **— up one's mind** decidirse (a)
man hombre *m.;* **huge —** hombrón; **nice old —** viejecito; **young —** mozo; joven *m.*
manner manera; modo; **in (that) —** de (esa) manera, de (ese) modo
many muchos; **as — ... as** tantos ... como

marry casarse (con)

Mary María

matter (*n.*) asunto; (*v.*) importar; **what is the — with you?** ¿qué tiene Vd.?

me (*as dir. or ind. obj.*) me; (*as obj. of a prep.*) mí; **poor —!** ¡pobre de mí! **with —** conmigo

meal comida; **serve good meals** servir (i) bien

meantime: in the — mientras tanto

meet (*make the acquaintance of*) conocer; (*run into*) encontrarse (ue) con; (*at the station*) esperar

meeting acto

mention mencionar

middle: in the — of en medio de

midnight media noche; **at —** a media noche; a las doce de la noche

milk leche *f.*

mind mente *f.;* **bear in —** tener en cuenta; **make up one's —** decidirse (a)

mine (*adj.*) mío; (*pron.*) el mío; **of —** mío

minute minuto; **in a few minutes** a los pocos minutos

Miss señorita

miss echar de menos

moment momento; **at this very —** en este momento

Monday lunes *m.*

money dinero

month mes *m.*

monument monumento

Moor moro

more más

moreover además

morning mañana; **at three o'clock in the —** a las tres de la mañana; **in the —** por la mañana

mosque mezquita

most más; **— of** la mayoría de; la mayor parte de

mother madre *f.*

mountain montaña

Mrs. señora

much mucho; **as — as** tanto como; **how —?** ¿cuánto? **so —** tanto; **very —** mucho, muchísimo

museum museo

must (*compulsion*) tener que; (*inference*) deber; *also expressed by the future;* **one —** hay que

my mi; (*in direct address*) mío

N

name nombre *m.;* **his — is (Charles)** se llama (Carlos)

Navarre Navarra

near cerca de

nearly casi

necessary preciso; **it is —** hay que

need necesitar; **he needs (something)** le hace falta (algo)

neither . . . nor ni . . . ni

never nunca

nevertheless sin embargo

new nuevo

New Mexico Nuevo México

news noticia(s); **what is the —?** ¿qué hay de nuevo?

newspaper periódico

next (*adv.*) luego, después; (*adj.*) próximo; **— (week)** (la semana) que viene; (*prep.*) **— to** cerca de

nice: — old man viejecito

night noche *f.;* **at —** de noche; por la noche; **at six o'clock at —** a las seis de la noche; **that very —** aquella misma noche

nine nueve

no (*adj.*) ninguno; *often not translated;* (*adv.*) no

no longer ya no

no one nadie; ninguno

nobody nadie

nominate nombrar

noon mediodía *m.;* **at —** al mediodía

nor ni

north norte *m.*

North American norteamericano
not no; **— at all** no . . . nada
not even ni siquiera
not only . . . but no sólo . . . sino
nothing nada
notice fijarse en; notar
novel novela
now ahora; ya
number número

O

object objeto
objection inconveniente *m.*
occasionally de vez en cuando
occupy ocupar
occur ocurrir; **it occurred to her (to shut it)** se le ocurrió (cerrarla)
o'clock: at one — a la una; **it is three —** son las tres
of de
offer ofrecer
office oficina, despacho
often a menudo; muchas veces
oh! ¡ah!
old viejo; antiguo; **nice — man** viejecito
older (*of offspring*) mayor; **oldest** mayor
on en; sobre; **— (arriving)** al (llegar)
once una vez; **at —** en seguida
one uno; *also expressed by indef. reflexive* se; **— another** se; uno a otro; **— must** hay que; **— should not** no hay que; **no —** nadie, ninguno; **the — that (who)** el que; **the — with** el de
only (*adj.*) único; (*adv.*) sólo, no más que (*even before numerals*); **not — . . . but** no sólo . . . sino
open abrir
opinion opinión *f.*; parecer *m.*
opportunity oportunidad *f.*
or o
order (*n.*) orden *f.*; (*v.*) mandar; (*a meal*) pedir; **in — that** para que; **in — to** para

origin origen *m.*
other otro; **each —** se; uno a otro
ought deber
our nuestro
ours (*adj.*) nuestro; (*pron.*) el nuestro; **of —** nuestro
outside of fuera de
overcoat abrigo; gabán *m.*
Oviedo Oviedo
owe deber
own propio

P

package paquete *m.*
pain dolor *m.*
pair par *m.*; **a — of (shoes)** unos (zapatos)
palace palacio
Pamplona Pamplona
paper papel *m.*; (*newspaper*) periódico
paradise paraíso
pardon perdonar; **— me** perdone, dispense
parents padres *m. pl.*
park estacionarse
part parte *f.*; **for his —** por su parte
patient: be — tener paciencia
pay (for) pagar; **— attention** prestar atención; **— a visit** hacer una visita
pen pluma
people gente *f.*; personas; *also expressed by indef. reflexive* se; **many —** muchas personas; mucha gente; **young —** jóvenes *m. pl.*
perhaps acaso, quizás, tal vez
permit permitir
person persona
Peru el Perú
peseta peseta
phone llamar por teléfono
pick up recoger
picture fotografía; **take a —** sacar una fotografía
picturesque pintoresco
pity lástima; **it is a —** es lástima

place (*n.*) lugar *m.*; **a — to park** donde estacionarse; **in the first —** en primer lugar; **take —** tener lugar; celebrarse; (*v.*) colocar; poner

plan plan *m.*; proyecto

plane avión *m.*; **by —** en avión

plate plato

play jugar (ue); **— (tennis)** jugar a(l tenis)

pleasant agradable

please gustar (a); por favor; **— (let me know)** hága usted el favor de (avisarme)

pleasure placer *m.*; gusto

poor pobre; **— me!** ¡pobre de mí!

possible posible; **as soon as —** cuanto antes; lo antes posible

Prado Museum Museo del Prado

prefer preferir (ie, i); gustar más (a uno)

preoccupied preocupado

preparation preparación *f.*

present (*n.*) regalo; (*adj.*) presente; **for the —** por ahora; (*v.*) presentar

pretty bonito

probable probable; **probably** *expressed by future of verb*

professor profesor *m.*

promise prometer

pronounce pronunciar

provided that con tal (de) que

public público

pull tirar (de)

put colocar, poner; **— on** ponerse

Q

queer raro, extraño

question pregunta; **ask a —** hacer una pregunta, preguntar; **be a — of** tratarse de

quite bastante

R

rain llover (ue)

raise levantar

rapidly rápido

rather más bien; bastante

reach llegar (a)

read leer

ready: get — to disponerse a

realize darse cuenta de

really de veras

reason razón *f.*; motivo; **for this —** por esto

recall recordar (ue)

receive recibir

recommend recomendar (ie)

refuse negarse (ie) (a)

region región *f.*

regret sentir (ie, i)

reign reino

remain quedar, quedarse

remember acordarse (ue) (de)

repeat repetir (i)

reply responder

report on dar cuenta de

request pedir (i)

respect respetar

rest: the — los demás

restaurant restaurante *m.*

return (*n.*) vuelta; **on my —** a mi vuelta; (*v.*) volver (ue)

rich rico

right derecho; **all —** está bien; **be —** tener razón; **— away, — now** ahora mismo; **— there** allí mismo

ring tocar

Romanesque románico

room cuarto; habitación *f.*

roommate compañero de cuarto

rule: as a — en general, por lo general

run correr

S

sad triste

same mismo; **at the — time** a la vez, al mismo tiempo

Santiago Santiago

satisfied satisfecho; contento

Saturday sábado

say decir; — **good-by to** despedirse (i) de; **it is said** se dice; **that is to —** es decir

 school escuela; **to —** a la escuela

scold reñir (i)

seat asiento

second segundo

see ver; **let's —!** ¡a ver! ¡vamos a ver!

seem parecer

Segovia Segovia

seldom raras veces

sell vender

send enviar; mandar; — **a telegram** poner un telegrama

September septiembre *m.*

serious serio; grave

seriously en serio

servant criado, criada

serve servir (i)

set (*of the sun*) ponerse

seven siete

seventh séptimo

several varios

Seville Sevilla

she ella

shine: the sun is shining hace (hay) sol

shoe zapato

short (*in space*) corto; (*in time*) breve; **at a — distance** a poca distancia; **in —** en fin

shortly afterwards al poco rato, poco después

should deber; *expressed in main clauses by* ra *form of past subjunctive of* deber; *sign of conditional tense;* **one — not** no hay que

shout gritar

 show mostrar (ue); enseñar

shut cerrar (ie)

shy tímido

silver plata

since (*time*) desde que

sing cantar

single: (not) a — instant (no) . . . ni siquiera un instante, ni un solo instante

sir señor

sister hermana

sit down sentarse (ie)

sixth sexto

skirt falda

sleep dormir (ue, u); **sleeping, asleep** dormido

slowly despacio

small pequeño; **very —** pequeñito

smoke fumar

so así; tan; lo; **— . . . as** tan . . . como; **— far** hasta ahora; **— long!** ¡hasta la vista!; **— that** para que; de modo que; **I think —** creo que sí

some alguno; algunos, unos, unos cuantos; **— time ago** hace tiempo

somebody alguien

someone alguien

something algo

sometimes algunas veces

somewhat algo

 son hijo

soon pronto; **as — as possible** cuanto antes, lo antes posible

sorry: be — sentir (ie, i)

sort: of that — por el estilo

soup sopa

south sur *m.*

southwest suroeste *m.*

Spain España

Spaniard español *m.*

Spanish español *adj. and m.*

speak hablar

spend (*money*) gastar; (*time*) pasar(se)

spite: in — of a pesar de

spring primavera

stand up levantarse

state estado

station estación *f.*

stay quedarse

still todavía; **keep —** callarse

stop (*come to rest*) detenerse; parar(se)

strange raro

stranger extraño, extranjero

street calle *f.*
strike dar; **it strikes twelve** dan las doce
stroll (*n.*) paseo; **take a —** dar un paseo;
  (*v.*) pasearse
strong fuerte
student alumno; estudiante *m.*
study estudiar
subject (*of study*) asignatura
such (a) tal
sudden: all of a — de pronto
suddenly de repente
suffer sufrir
suitcase maleta
summer verano
sun sol *m.*
Sunday domingo
sure seguro; **I am sure that** estoy seguro
  de que
surprise sorprender
sweet dulce

T

table mesa
take tomar; (*lead, carry*) llevar; (*drink*) tomar;
  — a picture sacar una fotografía; **— a
  stroll** dar un paseo; **— a trip** hacer
  un viaje; **— advantage of** aprovecharse
  de; **— off** quitar, quitarse; **— out** sacar;
  — place tener lugar; **— walks** dar
  paseos
talk (*n.*) charla; (*v.*) hablar
tall alto
taste (*n.*) gusto; (*v.*) estar; **— good** saber
  bien; tener buen gusto
teach enseñar
teacher profesor *m.*; profesora
tear romper
Teide el Teide
telegram telegrama *m.*; **send a —** poner
  un telegrama
telephone (*n.*) teléfono; (*v.*) telefonear;
  llamar por teléfono
tell decir; contar (ue); **she was told** se le
  dijo

ten diez
Tenerife Tenerife
tennis tenis *m.*
term trimestre *m.*, semestre *m.*
terribly: be — expensive costar (ue) un
  ojo de la cara
than que; (*before a numeral*) de
thank dar las gracias (por); **— you** muchas
  gracias
that (*demonstr. adj.*) ese, esa; aquel, aquella;
  (*pron.*) eso; aquello; **— is, — is to say**
  es decir; **— one** ése, ésa; aquél, aquélla;
  — of el de; **— which** lo que; **that's
  why** por eso
that (*rel. pron.*) que; (*conj.*) que; **so —** para
  que; de modo que
the el (la, los, las), lo
their su
theirs (*adj.*) suyo; (*pron.*) el suyo; **of —** suyo
them (*as dir. obj.*) los, las; (*as ind. obj.*) les;
  (*as obj. of a prep.*) ellos, ellas
then entonces; luego, después
there allí; **— is (are)** hay; **— was (were)**
  había
therefore por eso; por lo tanto
these (*demonstr. adj.*) estos, estas; (*pron.*)
  éstos, éstas
they ellos, ellas; **— told him** se le dijo
thing cosa
think pensar (ie); creer; **I —** me parece; **I
  — so** creo que sí; **don't you — so?**
  ¿verdad?; **— about** (*have in mind*) pensar
  en; **— of** (*opinion*) pensar de; **what do
  you — of my idea?** ¿qué le parece mi
  idea?
third tercero
this (*demonstr. adj.*) este, esta; (*pron.*) eso;
  — one éste, ésta
those (*demonstr. adj.*) esos, esas; aquellos,
  aquellas; (*pron.*) ésos, ésas; aquéllos,
  aquéllas; **— of** los de; **those that (who)**
  los que
three tres
through por

Thursday jueves *m.*

time (*in general*) tiempo; (*hour*) hora; (*in a series*) vez *f.*; **at the same —** a la vez; **at times** a veces; **for a long —** por mucho tiempo; **have a good —** divertirse (ie, i); **it is — to (end)** es hora de (terminar)

tired cansado

to a; para; *often not expressed with the infinitive;* **in order —** para

today hoy

together juntos

tomorrow mañana

too demasiado; **— much** demasiado

toothache dolor (*m.*) de dientes; **he has a —** le duelen los dientes

top: from the — of desde lo alto; **on — of** encima de

tourist turista *m. and f.*

tower torre *f.*

town población *f.*; ciudad *f.*

train tren *m.*

translate traducir

travel viajar; **traveling companion** compañero de viaje

treat tratar

tribunal tribunal *m.*

trip viaje *m.*; **take a —** hacer un viaje

true: it is — es verdad

truly de veras

trust fiar(se) (de); confiar (en)

truth verdad *f.*

try procurar; intentar; tratar (de); (*sample*) probar (ue)

Tuesday martes *m.*

turn volver (ue); **— back** dar la vuelta; **— to** dirigirse a

twelve doce

twenty veinte

two dos

U

uncle tío; **— and aunt** tíos

under debajo de

understand (*meaning*) comprender; (*sounds*) entender (ie)

unfortunately por desgracia

United States los Estados Unidos

university universidad *f.*

unless a menos que

until (*conj.*) hasta que; (*prep.*) hasta

up: get — levantarse; **go (come) —** subir (a)

up to hasta

upstairs arriba

us (*as dir. or ind. obj.*) nos; (*as obj. of a prep.*) nosotros

use usar

used: — to *expressed by imperfect indicative*

usually en general; por lo común

V

vacation vacaciones *f. pl.*

Valencia Valencia

very muy; mismo; *also expressed by the ending* -ísimo; **— much (interested)** muy (interesado)

visit (*n.*) visita: **pay a —** hacer una visita; (*v.*) visitar

vocabulary vocabulario

voice voz *f.*; **in a loud —** en voz alta

W

wait esperar; **— for** esperar

waiter camarero; mozo

waitress camarera

wake despertar (ie); **— up** despertarse

walk (*n.*) paseo; **take a —** dar un paseo; pasearse; (*v.*) andar (a pie)

want (to) querer, desear

war guerra

warm: be — (*persons*) tener calor; (*weather*) hacer calor

waste (*time*) perder (ie)

watch reloj *m.*

water agua (el)

wave agitar

way manera; **by the —** a propósito; **in this — de esta manera, de este modo**

we nosotros

wear (*clothes*) llevar

weather tiempo; **how is the —?** ¿qué tiempo hace?

Wednesday miércoles *m.*

week semana; **— end** fin (*m.*) de semana

well bien, pues bien; (*health*) bueno

west oeste *m.*

what? ¿qué? ¿cómo? **what a (pleasure)!** ¡qué (placer) (gusto)! **what an (interesting castle)!** ¡qué (castillo tan interesante)!; (*as adj. separated from the noun it modifies*) ¿cuál?; (*that which*) lo que

what (*rel.*) (*that which*) lo que

when? ¿cuándo? ¿a qué hora?

when (*conj.*) cuando; *also expressed by* al *with the infinitive;* **the day —** el día que

where? ¿dónde? ¿a dónde?

wherever a donde

whether si; **it doesn't matter —** no importa que

which? ¿cuál?; *pl.* ¿cuáles?; ¿qué? (*with noun it modifies*)

which (*rel.*) que, el cual, el que; **— (fact)** lo que; **of which** cuyo

while (short time) rato; **be worth —** valer la pena

while (*conj.*) mientras (que)

white blanco

who? ¿quién?

who (*rel.*) que, quien, el cual

whole: the — (city) toda la (ciudad); **my — (body)** todo el (cuerpo)

wholly por completo, del todo

whom? ¿quién? ¿a quién?

whom (*rel.*) que, quien, a quien, el cual

whose? ¿de quién? ¿de quiénes?

whose (*rel.*) cuyo

why? ¿por qué? **that's —** por eso

wide ancho

will querer; *sign of the future*

window ventana

wine vino

winter invierno

wish (to) querer, desear

with con; **the one —** el de; **— me** conmigo

without (*prep.*) sin; (*conj.*) sin que

woman mujer *f.*

wonder: *expressed in questions by future of verb*

word palabra

work (*n.*) trabajo; (*v.*) trabajar

world mundo

worried preocupado

worry about preocuparse por

worse peor; **worst** peor

worth: be — valer; **be — while** valer la pena

would *sign of the conditional;* **I — like** quisiera; me gustaría

write escribir

writer escritor *m.*

Y

year año

yes sí

yesterday ayer

yet todavía; aun, aún

you (*as subject*) usted, ustedes; tú; (*as dir. obj.*) le, lo, la; les, los, las; te; (*as ind. obj.*) le, les; te; (*as obj. of a prep.*) usted, ustedes; ti

young joven; **— lady** señorita; **— man** joven; **— people** jóvenes *m. pl.*

younger, youngest menor

your su (de usted, de ustedes); tu

yours (*adj.*) suyo; tuyo; (*pron.*) el suyo; **of —** suyo

youth juventud *f.*

primavera - spring
otoño - fall
verano - summer
invierno - winter

INDEX

References are to paragraphs

A

a after certain verbs, 72.5b; 79.2; personal, 14; + **el,** 4

absolute construction, 73

absolute superlative, 46

address: forms of, 15

adjectival expressions, 34.7

adjective clauses, 64

adjectives: forms, 31; agreement, 31, 38.2; as nouns or adverbs, 36; comparison, 44, 45; demonstrative, 65; feminine, 32; indefinite and negative, 37; interrogative, 52, 53; of nationality, 32; plural, 33; position, 34, 38; possessive, 38; relative, 71; shortened forms, 35; with **ser** and **estar,** 13.5

adverbial clauses, 59

adverbs: adjectives used as, 36; comparison, 44, 45; formation, 43; indefinite, negative, 37; relative, 71

age: expression of, Chap. II.D

agent: with passive, 26

agreement: of adjectives, 31, 38.2; of verb and compound subject, 15, n.1

al, 4

al + inf., 5

aquél, 'the former,' 65.2

article, definite: forms, 3; as demonstrative, 67; feminine **el,** 3; for possessive, 7.3, 38.4, 39; neuter **lo,** 3; omission, 8; repeated, 6; uses 7

article, indefinite: forms, 3; omission, 8; repeated, 6

augmentatives, 70

B

beber: conjugation, 1

C

cantar: conjugation, 1

-car verbs, *see Chart*

cardinal numerals, 60, 77; to express time of day, 62

causation: infinitive after verbs of, 72.2

-cer verbs, *see Chart*

cien, ciento, 35.2; 60

-cir verbs, *see Chart*

combinations of two object pronouns, 17

commands: familiar, 51.5; formal, 51.1; 55.1; indirect, 51.2–3

comparison, 44; 45

compound subjects, 15, n.1

compound tenses, 11.1

con: conmigo, contigo, consigo, 20

conditional sentences, 48

conditional tense: formation, 1; irregular, 42, n.¹; uses, 42

conjugation: of irregular verbs, *see Chart;* of regular verbs, 1

conjunctive pronouns, *see* Pronouns, personal

conocer: use of, Chap. II.D,n.³

contractions: **a** + **el, de** + **el,** 4

¿cuál? 52; 53.2

cualquiera, 35.2

customary action, 22.1

cuyo, 71.4

D

dates, 60.1; 61

dative: of concern, interest, possession, separation, 19; 29.3–4

day: time of, 62

days of the week, 68

de: contracted with **el,** 4; meaning 'in' after a superlative, 44.2; meaning 'than' before numerals, 44.2; possession, 40; verbs followed by, 72.5b; 79.3; with passive, 26

deber, 11.4, n.¹

debiera, 55.3

definite article, *see* Article, definite

del, 4

demonstrative: adjectives, 65.1; pronouns, 66.2

diminutives, 70

direct object: introduced by **a,** 14

disjunctive pronouns, 20; 75

distributive singular, 7.3

IRREGULAR VERBS (continued)

INFINITIVE	PRESENT IND.	PRESENT SUBJ.	IMPERFECT IND.	PRETERIT IND.	IMPERFECT SUBJ. in-ra	in-se	FUTURE IND.	CONDI-TIONAL	PRESENT PART.	PAST PART.	IMPERA-TIVE
creer to believe	creo etc.	crea etc.	creía etc.	creí crefste creyó creímos crefsteis creyeron	creyera creyeras creyera creyéramos creyerais creyeran	creyese creyeses creyese creyésemos creyeseis creyesen	creeré etc.	creería etc.	creyendo	creído	cree creed
dar to give	doy das da damos dais dan	dé des dé demos deis den	daba etc.	di diste dió dimos disteis dieron	diera dieras diera diéramos dierais dieran	diese dieses diese diésemos dieseis diesen	daré etc.	daría etc.	dando	dado	da dad
decir to say, tell	digo dices dice decimos decís dicen	diga digas diga digamos digáis digan	decía etc.	dije dijiste dijo dijimos dijisteis dijeron	dijera dijeras dijera dijéramos dijerais dijeran	dijese dijeses dijese dijésemos dijeseis dijesen	diré dirás dirá diremos diréis dirán	diría dirías diría diríamos diríais dirían	diciendo	**dicho**	**di** dijo decid
estar to be (See Preliminary Lesson II.)											
haber to have (See Preliminary Lesson II.)											
hacer to make, do	hago haces hace hacemos hacéis hacen	haga hagas haga hagamos hagáis hagan	hacía etc.	**hice hiciste hizo hicimos hicisteis hicieron**	hiciera hicieras hiciera hiciéramos hicierais hicieran	hiciese hicieses hiciese hiciésemos hicieseis hiciesen	**haré harás hará haremos haréis harán**	**haría harías haría haríamos haríais harían**	haciendo	**hecho**	**haz** haced
ir to go	**voy vas va vamos vais van**	**vaya vayas vaya vayamos vayáis vayan**	**iba ibas iba íbamos ibais iban**	**fui fuiste fué fuimos fuisteis fueron**	**fuera fueras fuera fuéramos fuerais fueran**	**fuese fueses fuese fuésemos fueseis fuesen**	iré etc.	iría etc.	yendo	ido	**vé** id
leer to read (Conjugated like creer)											
oír to hear	oigo oyes oye oímos oís oyen	oiga oigas oiga oigamos oigáis oigan	oía etc.	oí oíste oyó oímos oísteis oyeron	oyera oyeras oyera oyéramos oyerais oyeran	oyese oyeses oyese oyésemos oyeseis oyesen	oiré etc.	oiría etc.	oyendo	oído	oye oíd
poder to be able, can	puedo puedes puede podemos podéis pueden	pueda puedas pueda podamos podáis puedan	podía etc.	**pude pudiste pudo pudimos pudisteis pudieron**	pudiera pudieras pudiera pudiéramos pudierais pudieran	pudiese pudieses pudiese pudiésemos pudieseis pudiesen	**podré podrás podrá podremos podréis podrán**	**podría podrías podría podríamos podríais podrían**	pudiendo	podido	
poner to put	pongo pones	ponga pongas	ponía etc.	puse pusiste	pusiera pusieras	pusiese pusieses	pondré pondrás	pondría pondrías			pon